CLASSROOM DISCOURSE ANALYSIS

A Tool for Critical Reflection

Discourse and Social Processes
Lesley A. Rex, series editor

The Rhetoric of Teaching: Understanding the Dynamics of Holocaust
    Narratives in an English Classroom
        Mary M. Juzwik

Discourse of Opportunity: How Talk in Learning Situations
    Creates and Constrains Interactional Ethnographic Studies
    in Teaching and Learning
        Lesley A. Rex (ed.)

Classroom Discourse Analysis: A Tool for Critical Reflection
        Betsy Rymes

Place Stories: Time, Space and Literacy in Two Classrooms
        Margaret Sheehy

Action, Reflection and Social Justice: Integrating Moral Reasoning
    into Professional Development
        Edward P. St. John

forthcoming

Weaving a Tapestry for Daily life in P–16 Classrooms: Ethnographic
    Studies of Peer Cultures and School Cultures
        David E. Fernie, Samara Madrid, and *Rebecca Kanter* (eds.)

Discursive Moves and Agentive Possibilities: Critical Dialogues Across
    Educational Contexts
        Louise Jennings, Pamela Jewett, Tasha Tropp Laman,
        Mariana Souto-Manning, and *Jennifer Wilson* (eds.)

Narrative Analysis for Literacy Teacher Education: Sociolinguistic
    Tools for Understanding Teacher and Learning Interactions/
    Dialogues/Classroom Talk
        Lesley A. Rex and *Mary M. Juzwik* (eds.)

The Spiritual Identities of American College Students: Moral
    Imperatives Around Higher Education's Religious Diversity
        Jenny L. Small

CLASSROOM DISCOURSE ANALYSIS

A Tool for Critical Reflection

Betsy Rymes

University of Pennsylvania

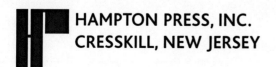

HAMPTON PRESS, INC.
CRESSKILL, NEW JERSEY

Printed in the United States of America

Library of Congress Cataloging-in-Publication Data

Rymes, Betsy.
  Classroom discourse analysis : a tool for critical reflection / Betsy Rymes.
      p. cm. -- (Discourse and social processes)
  Includes bibliographical references and index.
  ISBN 978-1-57273-902-4 (hardbound) -- ISBN 978-1-57273-903-1 (paperbound)
  1. Interaction analysis in education. 2. Discourse analysis. 3.
Communication in education. 4. Sociolinguistics. I. Title.
  LB1034.R965 2009
  371.102'2--dc22
                                    2009009033

Hampton Press, Inc.
23 Broadway
Cresskill, NJ 07626

*Those of us who presume to "teach" must not imagine
that we know how each student begins to learn.*

Vivian Gussin Paley
(*The Boy Who Would Be a Helicopter*,
1990, p. 78)

Contents

Foreword

JoBeth Allen

Dialogue between teachers and students does not place them on the same footing professionally; but it does mark the democratic position between them. . . . Dialogue is meaningful precisely because . . . the agents in the dialogue not only retain their identity, but actively defend it, and thus grow together . . . Dialogue is not a favor done by one for the other, a kind of grace accorded. On the contrary, it implies a sincere, fundamental respect . . .

(Freire, 1994, p. 101)

Reading *Classroom Discourse Analysis* is like sitting down at the kitchen table for a conversation with Betsy, a conversation about teaching and learning, about talking and listening, about reflecting and acting. But be prepared—you won't be idling away the afternoon. Betsy will take you into diverse classrooms, from an urban high school in California to a rural elementary school in Georgia. She will invite herself into your classroom and teach you how to listen—really listen—to your students. She'll ask intriguing questions: How can we learn *how* students think as well as *what* they think? How can we listen not only to our students but with them, studying interactions that are important to them? She'll ask questions you've probably been asking yourself:

> Have you ever asked what you thought was a provocative question and received silence in response?
>
> Have you ever received a response and had no idea how to follow up on it?
>
> Is there a single student whom you never seem to be able to understand, or who never speaks at all?

I have a confession to make. I have not used discourse analysis in my own work, and I haven't always valued it in the work of others. Sometimes I have felt that too much is lost—the big picture, the historical context, the full narrative, the critical lens—when writers focus on a brief moment in a lively, complex classroom. Betsy changed my mind. In each chapter she gave me the big picture by fully explaining the importance of both the interactional context and the larger social context, and showing how to bring those contexts to bear in discourse analysis. She changed my mind by emphasizing how critical classroom discourse analysis becomes a tool for individual (and I would argue collective) agency. She changed my mind by providing powerful examples of many wonderful (and a few not-so-wonderful) interactions among students and teachers that highlight not only the oppression of racial, linguistic, and social class discrimination but also the opportunities we have in classrooms to act as agents of change and to engender and support the agency of our students. She changed my mind by showing me the potential for students and teachers to study language together. What would happen if we inquired with students about the conditions of learning (what is working well, and what not so well, in our classroom) by analyzing classroom discussions? What if together we collected language samples in various contexts (home, school, neighborhood) and analyzed dialects and registers for functions that students identified as important, perhaps for self protection, solidifying friendships, or pleasing teachers? What if we analyzed discourse around entrenched and oppressive practices such as ability grouping, tracking, or gifted and remedial placements?

In inviting language supported by fascinating examples Betsy carefully leads readers through the challenges and possibilities of classroom discourse analysis: recording classroom interactions, viewing those interactions and making observations, transcribing both talk and action, and analyzing transcripts. If you've read the work of teacher researchers like Vivian Paley, Cindy Ballanger, Bob Fecho, and Karen Gallas, you may have wondered—how do they gather such rich, detailed conversations? How do they know what to do with them? In this book, you will learn how. More importantly, you will learn why. Throughout the book Betsy challenges us to think beyond the technical " how to" to the essential "so what" of classroom discourse analysis. She makes the argument that critical classroom discourse analysis is an act of agency, one that leads to dynamic new learning environments, to more democratic teacher-student and student-student interactions. Through such acts of agency we can engage in Freire's vision of dialogue, an all too rare "luxury" in today's stressful, text-driven, test-oriented, gotta-make-AYP schools.

Betsy has spent countless hours in classrooms, first as a teacher and now as a researcher. She respects teachers and students, and values what they say. As she writes in this book, "Schools are filled with stories. Once we start listening to them, our classrooms explode with both the profound differences between individuals and our universal humanity." She has given us a different way to listen—really listen—to the language that comprises classroom stories, to bring more people into the center of the story, even to change the endings of stories of failure and oppression through agency.

Dialogue, as Freire noted, is not a favor the teacher does for the students, say at the end of the period after the real work is done. It is the foundation of a democratic education, a space for students and teachers to create relationships, construct knowledge, interrogate inequities, develop identities, and act on the world to change the world. *Classroom Discourse Analysis* is a powerful tool for building that dialogic foundation. Referring to the work of Vivian Paley, Betsy wrote that "Some books on classroom discourse not only resonate with hope for teachers, but for humanity in general." This book indeed resonates with hope for humanity.

REFERENCE

Freire, P. (1994). *Pedagogy of hope: Reliving Pedagogy of the Oppressed.* New York: Continuum.

Acknowledgments

It is a luxury to finish a book and to allow oneself a moment to think about the people who shaped its current form. It is also daunting: Where to begin? I could never have written this book were it not for the encouragement, guidance, and inspiration of students, teachers, colleagues, schools, communities, and my own family and friends.

From the beginning, Lesley Rex, my editor, encouraged me to go forward with this project and had the patience to stick with it over the years it has taken to complete. I thank her, and three initial reviewers whose comments helped me think carefully about how to represent the material. Gretchen Kreuter read this work from cover to cover, providing well-tempered editorial suggestions, all of which have improved the final version. Many of the ideas in this book developed out of discussion among my colleagues and students in the Athens Discourse Inquiry Group at the University of Georgia: Kate Anderson, Cati Brown, Amy Heaton, Amy Johnson, Paula Mellom, and Csilla Weninger. I owe special thanks to Mariana Souto-Manning, who first insisted I write this book and continued to encourage me and offer feedback and ideas along the way.

Generous discussion with colleagues and friends in Georgia also resulted in ideas that show up in perhaps unlikely places in this book. For these moments of insight, I thank Misha Cahnmann-Taylor, Lisa Caine, Esperanza Mejia, Cindy Molloy, Rachel Pinnow, Don Rubin, and Bettie St. Pierre. JoBeth Allen has been unspeakably generous: She and I were writing books together when I began this project, and as we exchanged chapters I relished her feedback, encouragement, and writerly company.

Sean Hendricks boldly piloted this manuscript while teaching Classroom Discourse Analysis at the University of Georgia, giving me the courage to do so myself, here at he University of Pennsylvania. I am grateful to the students at both institutions who began to analyze classroom discourse with the guidance from various manuscript versions of this book.

At the University of Pennsylvania, the Division of Language and Literacy in Education has provided generous opportunities to present versions of my work and to teach my own course on classroom discourse analysis. Maren Aukerman, Nancy Hornberger, Kathy Howard, Susan Lytle, Kathy Schultz, and Lawrence Sipe have all offered commentary, encouragement and insight on different aspects of this project. These colleagues and the students in my graduate course, Classroom Discourse and Interaction, finally clarified the place and purpose for this work.

Thank you to the generosity, openness, and dedication of teachers at City School and Georgia Elementary School, where I spent countless hours videotaping classroom discourse. I could never have written this book had these teachers not graciously granted me permission to haunt their halls and classrooms, to listen in on talk, and share my analyses with them and with others.

Philadelphia, Pennsylvania
May 2008

1

INTRODUCTION
TO CLASSROOM DISCOURSE ANALYSIS

PREVIEW QUESTION Before you read this chapter, think about what you, as a teacher, can gain from re-examining examples of classroom talk. Think back on interactions in your own classrooms (as either a teacher or student) and recall a moment that made you uncomfortable or indicated some underlying tension. What do you think caused that discomfort and tension?

The purpose of this book is to provide teachers with the tools to analyze talk in their own classrooms. Why take time from already overburdened, underpaid, and chronically busy lives to analyze talk that is over and done with? There are at least four reasons:

1. Insights gained from classroom discourse analysis have enhanced mutual understanding between teachers and students;
2. By analyzing classroom discourse themselves, teachers have been able to understand local differences in classroom talk—going beyond stereotypes or other cultural generalizations;
3. When teachers analyze discourse in their own classrooms, academic achievement improves; and
4. The process of doing classroom discourse analysis can foster an intrinsic and lifelong love for the practice of teaching and its general life-affirming potential.

Let's consider these points. First, insights gained from classroom discourse analysis over the last 20 years have enhanced mutual understanding between teachers and students. This is because looking closely at talk can reveal general patterns of communication differences among different groups of people. Patterns in how teachers and students take turns at talk, introduce topics, use multiple languages and language varieties, or tell stories in different ways can illustrate how misunderstandings between different social groups in classrooms evolve—and how they can be overcome.

These different ways of speaking affect every teacher's daily practice. Take a moment to think about your own classroom. As a teacher, have you ever asked what you thought was a provocative question and received silence in response? Have you ever received a response and had no idea how to follow up on it? Is there a single student whom you never seem able to understand or who never speaks at all? One reason to practice classroom discourse analysis is to be able to understand what causes these inscrutable moments in classroom talk—and, possibly, the exclusion of certain students. By recording, viewing, transcribing, and analyzing instances of talk in classrooms, classroom discourse researchers have shown how differences in communication styles that lead to such lapses are often interpreted by teachers and testing mechanisms as deficits—emblems of lack of intelligence, drive, or ability. However, a closer look at discourse patterns usually reveals communication *difference* rather than *deficit*. Consider the following examples:

- The native Hawaiian "talk story" genre involves multiple participants talking at the same time, but this style had initially been interpreted as disruptive misbehavior by nonnative Hawaiian teachers (Au, 1980).
- African American children's traditional story-telling patterns were interpreted by African American adult raters as sophisticated and well wrought, but by Caucasian adult raters (and teachers) as unfocused (Michaels, 1981; Michaels & Cazden, 1986).
- Appalachian children's responses to workbook problems consistently built on a logic of problem solving from their home-and-family-based work environment, but officially counted as "wrong" on tests, marking these children as low achievers in the classroom (this example discussed in more detail below) (Heath, 1983).

By targeting specific differences in discourse patterns, this research into cross-cultural communication in classroom contexts has been able to enhance teachers' and students' mutual understanding—reconceptualizing *deficits as differences* and *differences as resources* for learning. Instead of interpreting Hawaiian Talk Stories, African-American children's story styles, or Appalachian children's responses as disruptive or signs of low aptitude, teachers began to see these ways of talking and responding to classroom prompts as part of the way these children had been socialized to use language at home and in their nonschool communities. As a result, teachers were then able to use their knowledge of these different language practices as a resource to build mutual, collaborative understandings of the ways stories can be told, questions can be responded to, and problems can be solved.

Katherine Au, Sarah Michaels, and Shirley Brice Heath, who conducted the research mentioned earlier, spent years in their respective contexts, investigating local discourse practices that led to miscommunication in classrooms. Precisely because of the time spent in those contexts, their work is detailed and specific. Any generalizations they make honor the local practices of the children they studied. However, classroom application of their research findings is necessarily restricted to a certain place and time. We would never want to assume that all Hawaiian children these days necessarily partake in the "talk story" genre, that all African-American children tell "topic-associating narratives," or that all children from Appalachia solve workbook problems in the same way.

Therefore, although the first benefit of studying classroom discourse analysis listed earlier is to understand, generally, the communication differences between social groups. The second benefit of learning how *to do* classroom discourse analysis (rather than just reading discourse analyses done by others) is that, once equipped with discourse analysis methods, teachers are best situated to study the *localized* and *ever-changing* discourse patterns specific to their own classrooms. As the sociolinguist Muriel Saville-Troike (1996) has pointed out regarding sociolinguistic research, it may be that, for classroom teachers, the *"methods of analysis* are even more applicable than its *product"* (p. 372; italics added). Applying these methods in your own classrooms may or may not yield results similar to previous studies. But no matter what, the findings will facilitate classroom talk and learning.

This brings us to the third reason that time spent studying classroom discourse pays off: When teachers understand multiple forms of talk in their classroom, school achievement improves.

For example:

- When teachers found that their Native-American students learned primarily from siblings and peers at home, they found that group project work rather than teacher-fronted instruction facilitated school success (Phillips, 1993).

- When non-native Hawaiian teachers learned the native Hawaiian "talk story" discourse pattern, students were able to engage more fully in literacy activities in Hawaiian classrooms (Au, 1980).
- Once teachers in Heath's (1982) studies of rural Appalachia learned about different questioning patterns among certain students, they were able to alter their teaching patterns in a way that encouraged talk among students and improved classroom performance.
- In reviewing multiple studies, Cazden (1972) found that once we consider aspects of the learning interaction such as topic, task, who is asking the questions, and how they are framed, students are better able to contribute to classroom talk.

As these studies all indicate, carefully studying interaction in your classroom and rearranging talk accordingly can lead to more productive and inclusive interactions—interactions likely to contribute to student success.

National Board Teacher Certification, the highest level teachers achieve professionally, is also linked to both understanding discourse patterns in classrooms and the higher student achievement that results. To become nationally board certified, teachers need to be able to "think systematically about their practice and learn from experience" (Core Proposition #4, National Board for Professional Teaching Standards, www.nbpts.org). To illustrate such systematic thinking, a large part of the National Board teaching portfolio used to assess individual teachers includes description, analysis, and reflection on "video recordings of interactions between you and your students"—in other words, classroom discourse analysis. Research on National Board-certified teachers has begun to suggest that developing such habits of discourse inquiry pays off in terms of student achievement. National Board-certified teachers are more likely than non-National Board-certified teachers to significantly affect student achievement (Goldhaber & Anthony, 2004).

Although student achievement is the bottom line in public education, teachers also need to be internally driven to continue the hard work necessary to maintain high levels and equity in student achievement. Teacher burnout is endemic to this profession. This widespread malaise undermines the sense of purpose for both teachers and students. Therefore, a fourth and final reason to learn the techniques of classroom discourse is that practicing classroom discourse in your classroom can enhance the overall experience of teaching and keep you engaged intrinsically in your professional pursuits as a teacher. Although we should not ignore the fact that improved student achievement often results from the careful analysis and reflection involved in discourse analysis, in many cases of teacher research and classroom discourse analysis, the process is a valuable product. Stories and research from teachers who do discourse analysis in their own classrooms suggest that analyzing classroom discourse can foster a lifelong love of teaching.

Teacher/researchers like Vivian Paley and Karen Gallas (whose work I describe in more detail in the chapters to come) habitually analyze classroom discourse, staying constantly attuned to nuances of the talk in their classrooms. Their analyses resonate with their enthusiasm for teaching and, in turn, make their books particularly resonant for teachers. Gathering classroom discourse in the way that Paley and Gallas do also provides teachers with a medium for collaborative, hands-on, professional problem solving. In teacher inquiry groups that center on data gathered in classrooms, a sense of professional community and support can make teaching less isolating and promote teaching habits that are exponentially more rewarding. Inquiry collectives such as the Brookline Teacher Research Seminar (Phillips & Gallas, 2004) illustrate how sharing work through classroom discourse analysis with other teachers in a learning community can help teachers confront seemingly intractable classroom conundrums.

Learning about specific differences between student and teacher discourse patterns, learning the tools to understand those patterns in your own classroom, raising student achievement, and enjoying the personal rewards of re-encountering the intrinsic pleasures of teaching and of problem solving with teaching peers—these reasons may be enough incentive for you to consider embarking on some classroom discourse analysis. But I would also suggest that some of the pleasures of looking at classroom discourse transcend the classroom and the school community. Some books on classroom discourse not only resonate with hope for teachers, but for humanity in general. Vivian Paley's books, for example, which feature her perspectives on transcribed data from her preschool classrooms over the last 30 years, are read and adored by many people who are not teachers. In part, I suspect, because these books are infused with primordial messages of hope for humanity. Despite policy pronouncing lofty goals, there is still a disconcerting achievement gap. Children are being Left Behind. But taking a close look at these children's language, understanding what motivates it and how to connect that language to learning, is a reminder that each day in the classroom is a day spent communing with human beings who love, laugh, think, and grow in unique and fantastic ways. Appreciating and understanding what a child says is the first step toward appreciating and understanding who a child is and, in turn, helping that child learn and grow in a classroom.

As you work through this book, I hope you will see for yourself that analyzing the talk in your own classroom can have positive effects on your classroom environment, your students' learning, your sense of humanity, and your love for your work. You will discover on your own what specific aspects of discourse analysis make it worthwhile for you.

WHAT IS (CRITICAL) CLASSROOM DISCOURSE ANALYSIS?

Before we start working on discourse analyses of our own, however, it would be useful to have a working definition of *classroom discourse analysis*. As discussed next, throughout the book, *discourse* is defined broadly as "language-in-use." *Discourse analysis* is the study of how language in use is affected by the *context* of its use. In the classroom, context can range from the talk within a lesson, to a student's entire lifetime of socialization, to the history of the institution of schooling. Discourse analysis in the classroom becomes *critical* classroom discourse analysis when classroom researchers take the effects of such variable contexts into consideration in their analysis.

Discourse

The simplest definition of *discourse* is "language in use." This may be annoyingly obvious. Language is always in use, so why not just call it language? Because the defining feature of discourse (that it is in use) is a feature that some people believe is not a necessary component of language. Instead, some linguists have argued that the defining feature of language is its ability to be *de*contextualized. For example, the word *tree* doesn't need a tree around to be understood. A student might tell you she saw a tree today, and you would know what she meant. She would not have to point at a tree or draw it for you. In that sense, language is decontextualizable, and this may be a feature that makes language uniquely human.

But would you really know what that student meant or why she was telling you "I saw a tree"? That is a *discourse* question. Understanding what an utterance like "I saw a tree" means involves understanding how that student was *using* the word *tree* in context and her purpose for telling you she saw one. You might have been asking the class whether there were any trees in the desert picture they were just looking at. In that case, she might be talking about a cactus she thinks is a tree (and you might end up correcting her). However, there might be a scrubby Joshua tree in the picture, and she is the only one in the class who knows those are trees and is proving to you that she knows a lot about desert flora. If you were administering a Rorschach blot test, she might be telling you she "saw a tree" in one of the blots that might indicate extreme creativity according to the test guidelines. You could probably think of other contexts in which tree in the sentence "I saw a tree" could mean countless other things. In all of these situations, the meaning of the word tree, and what the phrase "I saw a tree" does, and maybe even what you end up thinking about the student who said it depends on how it is being used. This capacity of language to do infinitely different things when being used in different kinds of situations is the defining feature of discourse.

Context (the Classroom and Beyond)

How a word is being used depends on the context. In this book, most obviously, "The Classroom" is the primary and most obvious context for the discourse we examine. However, the context for classroom discourse analysis also extends beyond the classroom and within different components of classroom talk to include any context that affects what is said and how it is interpreted in the classroom. Context can be bounded by physical borders; for example, appropriate language at home may be different from appropriate language in school. But context can also be bounded not by physical borders, but by discourse borders—appropriate language within a lesson may be different from appropriate language after a lesson ends (even while seated at the same table).

Although we will be looking at talk that takes place in the classroom, everything said in a classroom is also influenced, to varying degrees, by contexts beyond the classroom. Many forms of discourse have different meanings if they occur in a classroom than they would have if they occurred outside the classroom. Classroom research across a range of situations has shown that classroom interaction dramatically constrains what kinds of language and literacy events are encouraged or allowed (McGroarty, 1996), whereas discourse outside the classroom context has a much wider range of acceptable and productive possibilities. In a family or peer group setting, for example, students may be encouraged to talk at length, tell imaginative stories, or skirt the topic initially introduced in favor of an entertaining aside. In school classrooms, such talk can be labeled as an entirely unsuitable excursion off-topic. Curiosity and creativity welcomed and encouraged in other contexts, when brought into the classroom context, may count as disruptive.

Even talk after an official lesson ends occurs within a different kind of context than talk within a lesson; this is not necessarily a difference in physical context, but a difference in discourse context. When a lesson ends, thoughtful teachers may, for example, pick up on stories that students were not allowed to tell during official lesson time. In the excerpt of classroom talk below, while still seated around the table with students but after an official lesson has come to a close, the teacher asks a child about his birthday, acknowledging that it was something the child was "trying to tell us" before the lesson was over (Rymes, 2003a, 2003b):

Ms. Spring: Tell us about your birthday party. *You were trying to tell us earlier and I couldn't listen to you.*

Rene: My birthday party is on Sunday.

Ms. Spring: What are y'all going to do?

As this talk illustrates, this teacher is not opposed to hearing birthday stories, but just not within the official lesson talk context—when she *"couldn't listen."*

Analysis

Discourse analysis, then, involves investigating how *discourse* (language in use) and *context* affect each other. Sometimes understanding why someone said something a particular way involves looking at *previous contexts* of use. Previous contexts can range from the question that came before that utterance to a question from a previous conversation, to the influence of a TV show, to lifelong patterns of language socialization. Shirley Brice Heath (1983) documented how socialization into certain kinds of problem solving at home can adversely affect student achievement in school. This is illustrated clearly in her example of workbook questions in the Piedmont Carolinas. In one class, many students gave the answer to the following workbook question (in which students are to circle the correct number under each illustration) as 2 + 2 = 2 (see Fig. 1.1).

However, the appropriate answer was 2 + 2 = 4. Two plus two equals four, in school. But in practice, two train engines plus two coal cars equal two complete train combinations needed to get a job done. Who misunderstood? Because the teacher has the legitimate authority in a classroom, the students misunderstood the teacher. However, because the teacher is an outsider in the student interactions that preceded this lesson and does not know the work situation of these students, it is also true that

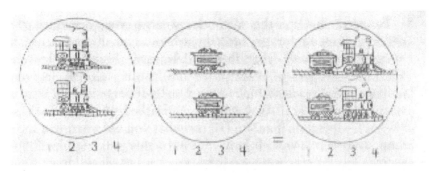

FIGURE 1.1. Example of a first-grade workbook problem (Heath, 1983, p. 291).

she misunderstood the children. By understanding the source of that misunderstanding, the teacher has the opportunity to learn about the children and their sources of knowledge. She also has a basis to explain the "workbook logic" to them without undermining their own reasoning skills.

Although analyzing the relationship between context and discourse always involves looking back to what kinds of talk and reasoning children have used in previous contexts, it also involves looking forward. Sometimes students bring new ways of speaking to the classroom context and change how classroom discourse occurs there. In the classrooms Heath investigated, for example, teachers began to not only investigate students' home reasoning skills (as in the workbook example), but also to incorporate students' ways of using language in the home context (such as how they tell stories or answer questions) into their classroom lessons. This change in classroom context changed students' experience of school, increasing their ability to participate and fostering their classroom success (Heath, 1983).

Classroom Discourse Analysis From a Critical Perspective

Putting these parts together, then, classroom discourse analysis could be paraphrased as "looking at language in use in a classroom context (with the understanding that this context is influenced also by multiple social contexts beyond and within the classroom) to understand how context and talk are influencing each other." I would add, "for the purpose of improving future classroom interactions and positively affecting social outcomes in contexts beyond the classroom." This lofty addition introduces a "critical" component to classroom discourse analysis: Once we are more aware of how context affects discourse, we can work to change those features of talk that may be inhibiting full participation for all students.

ORGANIZATION OF THE BOOK

Summary of Chapters

In this introductory chapter, I have tried to answer two basic questions: Why should anyone do classroom discourse analysis? What is it? I have provided a preliminary rationale and definition for *classroom discourse analysis*.

Chapter 2, "Dimensions of Discourse and Identity," builds on this preliminary understanding of classroom discourse analysis. It provides the overarching theoretical frame for the form of discourse analysis that is undertaken in the remainder of the book. Throughout this discussion, examples illustrate how the process of classroom discourse analysis examines three ever-present dimensions of language in use: (a) social and institutional contexts—the norms that seem to dictate what kinds of things we can do and say in the classroom, including the kinds of identities we project and presume in others; (b) interaction, which can go in unpredictable directions despite normative expectations; and (c) individuals' personal agency, which influences how prepackaged structures are used and taken up in potentially new and creative ways in any given interaction or context.

Chapters 3 and 4 are the most explicit how-to chapters. Chapter 3, "Getting to the Talk I: Recording and Viewing in Three Dimensions," provides an introductory set of guidelines for teachers to immediately begin recording and viewing discourse in their own classrooms. Chapter 4, "Getting to the Talk II: Transcribing and Analyzing in Three Dimensions," introduces transcription conventions and provides an example of how the tools of classroom discourse analysis can be applied to a transcript to understand social context, interactional context, and the role of individual agency.

Chapters 5 through 8 of the book detail more closely the kinds of discourse resources available in any interaction and how they can be analyzed. Chapter 5, "Analyzing Turn-Taking Resources," begins this exploration of discourse resources with a discussion of how built-in constraints of turn-taking and sequence in any interaction control what students say and do not say and who gets to say it.

Chapter 6, "Analyzing Contextualization Resources," illustrates how a range of features from those as subtle as voice quality and intonation, to more salient features like words, phrases, and stock routines, communicate what is going on in a classroom interaction. These resources function differently in different communities. For that reason, this chapter includes examples of cases when contextualization resources cause miscommunication or potentially undermine learning—when, for example, a change in voice quality, or a single word, is interpreted differently across contexts. Throughout, the chapter provides guidelines for analyzing contextualization resources in classroom transcripts.

Chapter 7, "Analyzing Narrative Resources," outlines different ways that narrative analysis has been a part of classroom discourse analysis. It looks at narrative contexts ranging from kindergarten "sharing time" to the stories teenagers tell at recess, to the different kinds of stories students tell around their dinner tables at home. Different kinds of narratives are received differently in different classrooms. The chapter details the possible classroom consequences of particular narrating styles and offers guidelines for the analysis of narratives in classroom transcripts.

Chapter 8, "Analyzing Framing Resources," is the last chapter that examines concrete contextual resources for discourse analysis. This chapter explores how variables from classroom arrangements to routines for interaction shape how students can participate, what language(s) they can use, and how competent they appear.

All these discourse resources—from intonation and tone of voice to narrative and participation frameworks—are resources to do *something*. But what? Why look so carefully at these minute interactional strategies? Chapter 9, "Creating New Learning Environments Through Critical Classroom Discourse Analysis," brings the reader back to the big picture. After reviewing the specific discourse features that teachers gain through classroom discourse analysis, the chapter concludes with suggestions for how teachers can harness the awareness created through discourse inquiry to make lasting, positive change for education.

Terminology

Throughout the text, I have tried to minimize professional jargon. However, certain words that are uniquely useful or likely to come up repeatedly in a teacher's professional life appear in boldface. These words are collected, with short definitions, in the glossary at the end of the book. All boldface words are functionally defined in context, and the reader should be able to continue reading without flipping back to the glossary. Still, if the definition of *discourse analysis* or *anthropological perspective* (see next section) comes up out of context, the glossary should provide a convenient reference.

Source of Examples

In 1995 and 1996, I spent 18 months recording classroom discourse and related talk and interaction in an alternative charter school in Los Angeles (Rymes, 2001). In 1998 and 1999, I spent 2 years recording in a traditional elementary school in rural Georgia (Rymes, 2003a, 2003b, 2004; Rymes & Anderson, 2004; Rymes & Pash, 2001). Many of the detailed examples in the text are drawn from these two field experiences. Other detailed examples are drawn from other published research, and I have credited those sources when appropriate. The remaining examples come from my teaching experiences in a Los Angeles junior high school, in night school classes for English-Language Learning adults, as a university professor, from time I've spent in the schools as a mother and volunteer, and from many discussions with friends, teachers, and students. These examples are generally less detailed and do not come from recorded, transcribed material, but have been passed on and refined through many conversations and discussions. I consider all of these snippets of interaction and their discussion, formal and informal, to exemplify important ways of doing classroom discourse analysis.

CONCLUSION

Nurturing the Anthropological Perspective

Anthropology is the study of different cultural norms and often offers new perspectives on our taken-for-granted assumptions. Although traditional anthropologists have crossed the globe to study remote communities and unique differences, classrooms today are a microcontext for such cross-cultural insights. In classrooms, we come face to face with social differences and a cross-section of communities and cultural practices of the sort anthropologists traditionally have sought out in remote excursions to faraway places. Within such cross-cultural encounters, in order to learn from one another, we have to step outside our own assumptions about what is "normal" and enter into a perspective different from our own. In their classic book on activist pedagogy, which has fueled countless volumes on critical pedagogy, Neil Postman and Charles Weingartner (1969) urge teachers to take this *anthropological perspective*—to not take our common practices for granted, but to question the reasons we do ordinary things. Classroom discourse analysis is one way to take this anthropological perspective because it provides the tools needed to step outside our own position in interactions in classrooms and see multiple sides of any discussion, conversation, lesson, or reprimand. Interactions by definition have at least two perspectives involved. Our goal is to understand those multiple voices and the people behind them.

Maintaining Critical Reflection

When we take the anthropological perspective, we see our classrooms in a new light. We may very well notice parts of the situation that we never had before. This new light might illuminate a critical perspective. Instead of assuming that all of our practices make sense, we can ask, "Why?" Why is it not good to use them in a different way? Consider, for example, this interaction with a first grader, "George," labeled by his previous teachers as a behavior problem (Souto-Manning, 2008):

> Teacher: Today we are going to learn about farm animals
> and zoo animals. Isn't this cool?

> George: Nope!
>   ((*children look around with surprised and fearful faces*))
> Teacher: So . . . what would you like to learn about?
> George: If you ask me, amphibians.

As this interaction continued, George took issue with the time-tested curriculum theme, "Farm and Zoo Animals." After all, he apparently is already familiar with far more sophisticated and discrete categories for animals, like *amphibians*. Fortunately, George's teacher did not simply reassert the need to study farm and zoo animals exclusively. Instead, she talked more with George about his interests, and he explained how he had learned about amphibians on the Discovery Channel. He helped her and the other students think through her "Farm and Zoo Animal's" unit and change it to more broadly address the knowledge and interests students like George brought to the classroom. In keeping with the school's previous assumptions about George as a behavior problem, George's teacher might have punished him for rudely rejecting her unit plans and the school's standard curriculum. Instead, she used this as an opportunity to find out what he would find interesting. By careful listening to George, this teacher was able to resist the negative affects that both curricular assumptions (about the importance of studying zoo and farm animals in first grade) and George's own institutional history (as a problem child) might have had on classroom interactions and learning that year. In this class, George was not only learning more about animals, but he was also learning ways of speaking that afforded his full and productive participation in class.

One of the goals of the approach to discourse analysis detailed here is to illuminate the worldviews and long-standing social and institutional realities that inform talk. Another goal is to use this approach to see that some long-standing practices do not necessarily need to be perpetuated. In the example of the "behavior problem," George, why is it necessary to always study "Farm and Zoo Animals" year after year when students already know about these animals and many more? Why assume he is always a problem child? By gaining familiarity with this kind of critical lens, teachers and students will be able to harness more control over their words, rather than having their words control them. This is what I mean when, throughout the book, I suggest we take a "critical" perspective on the analysis of classroom discourse.

What Schools are For

Sometimes my students flinch at the idea of taking a "critical perspective": Aren't schools for "learning"? Why should we be "critical" of that?

Why is a "critical" perspective necessary? It seems so negative. I agree
that schools are for learning. But I also assume, in this book, that learning
necessitates a critical perspective. Students like George will learn more
because his teacher questioned the standard curriculum after she heard
his perspective on it. When students are also encouraged to question
what they ordinarily take for granted, they will develop important prob-
lem-solving and higher order thinking skills.

To use Postman and Weingartner's earthier phrase, an integral part
of learning and teaching is *crap detecting*. They borrow this term from an
interview with Ernest Hemingway, who claimed that being a good crap
detector was the key to being a good writer. The term is equally important to learning and teaching. To foster learning, you have to move
beyond stereotypical understandings or pre-existing labels of children or
classroom practices. George's teacher took this perspective when she
refused to treat this notorious "trouble maker" as a problem in her classroom. Instead of accepting the labels he had received from society and
from his previous teachers, she cut through those preconceptions and listened to what he was capable of saying and doing in her classroom.
Admittedly, labels exist so students can be served—so that "gifted" children are challenged, so that "autistic" children are not inadvertently
abused, so that "English-Language Learners" are not silenced. However,
labels can also be harmful sorting devices that hamper classroom interaction and learning. A critical awareness of how labels are perpetuated
through institutions can help to prevent their negative effects.

I am not saying that the best teacher should completely ignore labels
or curricular objectives. I am arguing that we all need to be circumspect
and tuned into local discourse, rather than being unreflectively guided by
our social context that produces labels (that can be destructive) and curricular expectations (that can be inappropriate). If being "positive" is to
accept everything we read or are told, and to accept the labels people give
us without thought, then being critical is going to seem "negative."
However, a positive classroom can also be a "critical" one, in which students and teachers are engaged in learning.

What This Book Can Do

In most interactions in most U.S. classrooms, teachers are in a position of
extreme influence and power over many students. In classrooms, teachers are the privileged ones. For the most part, that privilege comes from
traditional kinds of power—socioeconomic status, formal education, and
standard English. Often, however, teachers can feel helpless under the
weight of countless curricular mandates and accountability measures. At
other times, it may seem like students have all the power. They certainly

have power in numbers, and they often have social status, languages, and alternative ways of interacting that can potentially undermine teachers' more obvious and traditional sources of authority. Like teachers at a faculty meeting trying to resolve a compelling issue, for students and their teacher in the classroom, differences in ways of speaking and participating can make conducting a straightforward classroom lesson seem impossible.

I hope this book provides the tools to understand how multiple and diverse ways of speaking and interacting in classrooms can be noticed and fostered through classroom discourse analysis. The liberatory teacher-educator Paulo Freire (1998) urges teachers to talk *with* rather than simply *to* our students. Only by talking with students can teachers learn what is relevant to their students' lives and provide them with the tools they need to be active participants in society. The discussions in this book, as well as the questions, activities, and additional readings I suggest, will give teachers some tools to enter into this dialogue.

QUESTIONS AND ACTIVITIES

Critical Reflection

1. Of the four incentives listed for learning to do classroom discourse analysis, which are most important for you? Why? Do you have additional reasons for studying classroom discourse analysis?
2. Can you think of a classroom interaction you have had that, in hindsight, you recognize as a case of miscommunication? A case in which someone was silenced? What are some ways the interaction could have unfolded differently?
3. One possible strategy that teachers could use to question our own assumptions and take the "anthropological perspective" suggested by anthropologists of education is to make home visits and learn how students learn and interact at home. What are some other possible strategies a teacher could take to understand students' perspectives and value them as different from their own?
4. What might taking a "critical perspective" look like in a classroom you have been in or one in which you are currently teaching?
5. How is the "anthropological perspective" related to taking a "critical perspective"?

Reflective Activities

1. Recall the Heath example given previously, in which some students interpreted two train engines plus two coal cars to equal two engine-

car combinations, resulting in the answer, "2 + 2 = 2." Now look through a workbook or standardized test that is used in your school. Find a question that seems to have multiple possible answers even though only one counts as right. Show it to different people and see whether they interpret the multiple possibilities the same way you do. Ask your students whether they see more than one possible answer. Ask them why one answer counts as right and another as wrong.

2. Use this exercise to investigate how context affects discourse: Ask your students a seemingly open-ended question like, "What do you do after school?" or "What did you do over the summer?" Listen to their answers. What factors do you think are influencing their responses? Make a list. Show your list of factors to the students and see whether they agree with you. Would they have answered differently if, say, a friend has asked them?

3. View the movie *Spanglish* (Sony Pictures, 2004). This movie tells the story of (among other things) a housekeeper in an affluent family whose daughter is offered a chance to attend the same elite private school her employer's daughter attends. Why do you think the girl's mother is opposed to her attending the private school? Did she do the right thing as a mother? Why or why not? Compare your answers with classmates. (This is also a movie teachers could watch with high school students or assign as homework.) What does this discussion tell you about the assumptions you and others have about education and why it is important?

SUGGESTED READINGS

Heath's (1983) classic study, *Ways With Words,* is probably the first example of classroom discourse analysis that examined multiple layers of context informing children's talk in classrooms. She took the anthropological perspective, going into students' homes in the Piedmont region of North Carolina to learn about different ways of speaking in different communities and how that talk reflected on school performance. Vivien Vasquez's (2004) book on critical literacy, *Negotiating Critical Literacies With Young Children,* takes this perspective into practice, documenting the critical curriculum she used in her prekindergarten classroom. Neil Postman and Charles Weingartner's (1969) classic book, *Teaching as a Subversive Activity,* could be considered the original text on critical theory and the inquiry model for educators. As such, it is an excellent introduction to understanding the assumptions behind talk in classrooms. Paulo Freire's (1998) more recent work, his letters to teachers written as columns in a newsletter in Brazil, provides inspiring encouragement to teachers interested in classroom discourse and diversity (*Teachers as Cultural Workers:*

Letters to Those Who Dare to Teach). For a look into current applications of discourse analysis to education, although not strictly in classrooms, see Rebecca Rogers' (2004) edited collection *Critical Discourse Analysis in Education.*

2

DIMENSIONS OF DISCOURSE AND IDENTITY

PREVIEW QUESTION Catha Pollitt (2007) has written that she automatically rejected "men who said 'groovy.'" Do you also have certain words that change the way you think about their speakers?

Now, think about some of the words and phrases used in your classroom (e.g., hey dude, great!, WOW!, ain't, darnit!). Do they mean different things to different people?

Do they have different effects depending on who says them?

Do they affect the way you think about their speaker?

How might such words change how learning proceeds in your classroom?

This chapter builds on the anthropological perspective discussed in chapter 1 to formulate a theory of discourse and identity that will help you analyze discourse in your own classroom. Consistent with current work in linguistic anthropology, I conceptualize a person's "identity" in this chapter as a "quintessentially social phenomenon" (Bucholtz & Hall, 2004, p. 377). That is, the kind of person one appears to be (one's identity) is constructed through discourse (language in use). Whether someone is considered a "good kid" or a "trouble-maker," a "nerd" or a "cool dude" is largely a result of the kinds of social interactions that person has. More specifically, a person's identity is constructed when words that person uses and the context within which they are used interact.

For example, think of the word *dude* I just used. From a one dimensional, a-contextual perspective, it sits there on the page, a line of letters, D-U-D-E, a synonym for *person*. Now think of *using* this word in your classroom. Would you? Would students in your classroom use it? What impressions would you have of a speaker who used *dude* (rather than *person, man, guy, kid*, etc.) during a lesson? Now consider this simple description of a picture offered up by a second grader while the group was discussing a book:

> Teacher: Do men wear a lot of hats now?
>
> Danny: Some don't. *The train dudes—the train people wear*
> they wear these like, big old things that—

Suddenly, the word *dude* gains dimensionality. Danny had an individual choice to make: Perhaps out of habit, he started with the word *dudes*, but he changed to *people*. Why did he make this change? Part of this change probably has to do with his recognition of the context within which he was speaking and the person he was addressing. Clearly, the words *dudes* and *people*, although synonyms at a basic level, have different ramifications in use. This chapter provides a framework for examining how words like *dudes* and other habitual ways of speaking bring meanings with them to the classroom, but also take on new and unpredictable meanings through interaction, and how speakers can potentially create new meanings through the deliberate choice of words.

Building on our preliminary definition of classroom discourse analysis as an investigation into how discourse (language in use) and context affect each other, our framework comprises three ever-present dimensions of language in use: (a) social context—the social factors *outside the immediate interaction* that influence how words function in that interaction (e.g., how does social context influence whether you or your students use the word *dude*? What effects would it have?); (b) interactional context—the sequential or other patterns of talk within an interaction that influence what we can and cannot say and how others interpret it within classroom discourse (e.g., in what sequence of interaction would you use the word *dude*? A greeting? A compliment? What effects would it have on the rest of the interaction?); and (c) individual agency—the influence an individual can have on how words are used and interpreted in an interaction (e.g., When and why would an individual choose to use *dude* and for what purpose? How much can an individual control its effects?).

This multidimensionality—the simultaneous influence of social context, interactional context, and individual agency—is a feature of every classroom interaction. Of course, each of these dimensions is inseparable from the other, and, at times, one or the other is featured more prominently. Teasing them apart through discourse analysis, however, affords greater understanding and control over words in classrooms—so that we will not interpret words one dimensionally, or use or hear language without recognizing its multidimensional power to control how we see ourselves and others.

THE FIRST DIMENSION: SOCIAL CONTEXT

A foundational dimension of classroom discourse analysis is the broad influence of the social context outside the classroom on what gets said inside the classroom. Language in use (discourse) and social context influence each other in a dialectic relationship; not only does what we say function differently depending on the social context, but also what we say changes what might be relevant about the social context (see the following diagram):

Language-in-Use ← affects → Social Context

Discourse Functions Differently Across Different Contexts

Our definition of discourse as language in use builds on ideas from the functional linguist M. A. K. Halliday, who emphasized that different forms have different functions. Some words ask questions and some describe, criticize, problem solve, or make insults. This functionality varies across different social contexts. *How are you?*, for example, takes the form of a question. However, in most contexts in the United States, the phrase *How are you?* functions as a greeting. If you are a teacher in the United States, for example, greeting a student in your classroom will probably go something like this:

Teacher: Hi Jack, how are you?
    Jack: Great, how are you?
Teacher: Great.
           ((*Student proceeds to desk*))

In some contexts, however, the form *How are you?* may be taken as a genuine question, not a simple greeting. Imagine, for example, one of these students paying a visit to the counselor's office, plopping down in the chair in front of her desk. The counselor might start out with the same form, but it might function very differently:

Counselor: How are you today, Jack? ((*concerned expression*))

Jack: Well, not so good actually. ((*bursts into tears*))

As these two hypothetical examples show, two instances of a seemingly identical form function very differently in different contexts:

LANGUAGE FORM	CONTEXT OF USE	FUNCTION
How are you?	a. Teacher addressing a student entering the classroom	a. Greeting
	b. Counselor addressing a student in her office	b. Question

In other words, forms and functions vary across context, so forms take on situated meanings. That is, the meaning of a word varies according to the context in which it is used. *How are you?* means one thing in the counselor's office, something else in the hall, and something else in the classroom. This phenomenon also can be described in terms of types and tokens. Forms are representative types. For example, the word *you* looks the same and has a standardized spelling in every instance of use. Tokens, in contrast, are instances of that type used in a particular situation: Just who *you* refers to depends on the instance of its use.

The fact that word types function differently as tokens in different contexts enables us to use language in new and creative ways every day. Unfortunately, the vast variation in what words mean also provides great potential for misunderstanding, especially for an outsider. Visitors from other countries may have mastered the form of the English language, but have not yet become aware of its varied functionality. International students, for example, who are not familiar with certain situated meanings may think the form *How are you?* is meant as a question and may respond to it as a genuine inquiry about their well-being. When their questioner doesn't seem interested, they may have an impression of native speakers as superficial or uncaring: Why would a person ask such a question and then pay little attention to the answer? An important aspect of becoming a member of a new community is learning local norms for how certain forms function—otherwise, this sort of cross-cultural misunderstanding can result.

Just as visitors from other countries may be unaware of norms for situated meanings of certain forms, visitors from different communities and even generations (e.g., teachers and students, parents and teenagers) may be unaware of the situated meanings of each other's ways of speaking. Adults may find teenage sons and daughters to have developed so many uniquely situated meanings of words that when their teenagers talk among themselves, it is difficult to know what is going on; *bad* can mean good, *sick* can be cool, and a *dog* might be a good (human) friend. (These examples are probably hopelessly outdated right now!)

Discourse Functions Differently in Different Classroom Contexts

Although evanescent teen language may always remain somewhat beyond adult comprehension, teachers can facilitate learning in the classroom by reflecting on the general ways that situated meanings vary across activities in their classroom. Even within the classroom context, the functionality of words varies from activity to activity. Think again about the word *dude*. In the prior example, Danny uses the description *train dudes*, but self-corrects, changing to *train people*. Although only in second grade, he seems to have internalized a sense that the word *dudes* was a less appropriate descriptor than *people* when discussing a picture book. Why? In another activity context, in the same school, the word *dude* is received positively by a teacher. In the following exchange, for example, *dude* receives approval from the teacher:

Rudolfo: ((*Draws a card and reads*)) Dude.
Teacher: Yes.

In this example, Rudolfo is playing the Phonics Game™ with several other students, all English-language learners. In this game, saying the word *dude* indicates he has read it correctly and, perhaps, knows the "magic e" rule for sounding out words like this. The teacher's "yes" has nothing to do with the content of the word *dude,* but rather with his correct reading of the form.

Usually, however, in school and at home, and especially for the new language learners in this group, the meaning of words—not just the ability to pronounce them—counts. In fact, even in the phonics game play, where points are awarded strictly on the ability to say words out loud, students bring meaning to the words through their playful asides:

Rudolfo: ((*Draws a card and reads to the teacher*)) Dude.
Teacher: Yes.
Jose: ((*Turns to classmate and changes to a "cool" tone of voice*)) Hey dude, how you doing?

Jose's aside, "Hey dude, how you doing?" (and many more like it that occurred during this game play), although marginal to the explicit goal of the Phonics Game™, is important because it is a way of testing out possible functions of words. Kids take great pleasure in playing with multiple possible situated meanings and functions. This kind of word play is a developmental necessity. For young students, word play is the basis of nursery rhymes, Dr. Seuss books, and knock-knock jokes. In adult life, this word play develops into an understanding of the multifunctionality of language that makes reading, writing, and thinking a creative pleasure. In schools, however, this kind of interaction is often discouraged. Too many asides can take away from classroom focus. Even at the university level, it can be difficult to negotiate a balance between playful talk and classroom talk without shutting students down. As careful analysis of classroom discourse reveals, however, *more is more:* Paying attention to the multifunctionality of talk is an asset in the classroom and need not subtract from more regimented classroom goals.

For example, despite the potentially decontextualized approach the Phonics Game™ takes to reading, these students loved to play it; their play always included many meaningful asides with words. These students, whom I watched over a semester playing this game, repeatedly found ways to use words in differently functional ways. So, although technically the only object of the game was to sound out words, new situated meanings and functions kept bubbling up. Even the names of the different games within the phonics program (e.g., "Double Trouble" and "Silent Partners") are based on meaningful word play. So, despite the intentions of the game designers, the Phonics Game™ could potentially become a format to experiment with language multifunctionality: to demonstrate and practice not only how to sound out words, but also to enjoy the sheer fun of reading and language.

I do not mean this as an endorsement of the Phonics Game™, but rather as an illustration that, *despite* curricular materials and their implied approach, teachers and students can use these resources and simultaneously use language in creative multifunctional ways. Paying attention to language function and its variation across contexts can be empowering to teachers and students. Take a look at the multiple functions of *dude* we have already encountered.

LANGUAGE FORM	CONTEXT OF USE	FUNCTION
Dude	a. Talking about a picture a book: Train dudes	a. Description in of a picture
	b. Reading a card off while playing the Phonics Game™: *Dude*	b. Display of sounding out ability
	c. Using a word from the phonics game: *Hey dude!*	c. Being funny and/or displaying knowledge of *dude* functionality

Just because differences between home, peer-to-peer, and student-to-teacher language functionality exist, the classroom does not necessarily need to be more homelike or the home more classlike. The classroom (arguably) is a different place and has a different job to do than does dinner conversation or peer-group negotiation on the playground. The key here is to be aware of the different functions that language has in any context. A teacher knows whether her students need to focus more on the rules of phonics or on other functions of language. But doing both is best because both aspects of language are crucial to meaningful language use.

Drawing attention to the multifunctionality of language also helps students make connections among different contexts; classroom learning will make more sense if it can be generalized across encounters. Countless parents and teachers have agonized about a child who reads effortlessly at home, but struggles with reading and writing in the classroom, or a child who calculates and plans an entire garden plot but struggles with geometry in school (Johnston, 2005). These students need to be aware that classroom learning is *supposed* to be relevant in other contexts, although it may sound different there. The word *dude* in the phonics game would be a great word to use in a story or script. Describing train workers as *dudes* could be an excellent descriptive device, but calling out *Hey, dude!* to the school principal might not be such a good idea.

To summarize, we can help students to generalize and use language creatively across contexts and to understand what is not universally appropriate across contexts by encouraging them to explore language multifunctionality. A discourse analysis approach facilitates this exploration for teachers and students because it can make explicit the relationship between language functionality outside and inside the classroom and across multiple classroom contexts.

Contexts Outside the Classroom Also Affect Language Function

So far, the simple examples of *dude* and *How are you?* have illustrated that language functions differently in different contexts—that even within the classroom, language takes on different meanings in different situations. *Dude* has a different meaning in a phonics game than it does during a picture description or when addressing the principal of the school. Now let's turn to the big picture: Language in use is also always affected by social structure outside the classroom. This broader social context includes educational policy and curriculum; socioeconomic, racial, and ethnic backgrounds of teachers and students; and gender norms that develop long before children set foot in a classroom.

Educational Policy and Curriculum

Educational policy and mandated curriculum often tell teachers what
is and is not allowed in the classroom. For example, standardized tests
count a certain form of English as "right" and another as "wrong."
Policies that are based on standardized high-stakes testing potentially
have the effect of silencing those children who do not come to school
already knowing the forms of language that will be deemed acceptable
by tests and standardized curricula. Many teachers have agonized about
how to teach children the English forms needed to succeed on tests without degrading the legitimate languages or language varieties that children speak at home. Think about these two sentences for example:

"I be happy."
"I am happy."

Although a teacher can only count "I am happy" as correct in the context of a test on English grammar, "I be happy" is a correct form within a
system of African-American English. The verb *be* within African-
American English functions as a marker of an ongoing state of happiness—"I am a happy person." However, in school, "I be happy" does not
communicate that sense (Green, 2002). Learning what children's language means for each child, and explaining to children that language
functions differently in different contexts, helps students understand,
without feeling judged, why they need to produce a certain kind of language for tests.

As Freire has written, it is important for teachers to recognize the use-
fulness, rationale, and functionality of "I be" if they are ever to teach students to say, instead, "I am." Freire draws on the simple the contrast
between these two forms (*I be* vs. *I am*) to illustrate the powerful symbol-
ic differences between home language and school language: Without
being recognized as competent speakers of the language they learned
before school, students may not be able to make connections between the
depth of their childhood language socialization and the new language
they are learning in the classroom. Drawing connections between the two
provides openings for deeper learning in the classroom.

By conceiving of learning as an interactive process, through which
learners gain the use of tools necessary to participate in their multiple
social worlds, discourse analysis illuminates the form and functionality
of language inside *and outside* the classroom. Students are not only learning new content, but they are also necessarily and simultaneously learning new ways of speaking and participating—they are learning about the
*multi*functionality of language. With command of multiple ways of
speaking, students who can use both "I be" and "I am" appropriately are

able to function more competently in a range of social situations. In addition, they would be able to distinguish when the use of "I be" is positively functional for them and when it would indicate "incorrect" language use (see the following chart).

LANGUAGE FORM	CONTEXT OF USE	FUNCTION
1. I be "I be happy"	1a. At home	1a. Correct way to express an ongoing state ("I am a happy person")
	1b. On standardized test	1b. Incorrect—indicates lack of standard grammatical knowledge
2. I am "I am a happy person"	2a. On standardized test	2a. Correct—indicates standard grammatical knowledge
	2b. At home	2b. Incorrect—indicates lack of knowledge of home language

As this chart indicates, what counts as functional or correct is dependent on the context of its use. Although in the context of a standardized assessment "I am a happy person" might be considered the grammatically correct way to express an ongoing state of happiness, in the more informal context of a conversation at home, using "I am a happy person," rather than "I be happy" to express an ongoing state of happiness could be "incorrect"—in the sense that it would be interpersonally odd.

But this point is not only about the forms "I be" and "I am," nor is it only about African-American English. Classroom discourse analysis can bring teachers' and students' attention to the different contexts in which words are used and the corresponding functionality of our language. Taking note of different kinds of classroom language and constructing form/context/function charts like the one shown previously (teachers and students can do this together) could be an exercise that accomplishes the Freirian goal alluded to earlier: As teachers and students learn about and document the multifunctionality of language and its dependence on social contexts, they become empowered as capable interlocutors in multiple social worlds.

Background of the Speaker

Characteristics of the speaker are another aspect of context that influences how words function. For example, it often seems to be the case that when the rich and famous use colorful language it is profound, but when the lowly use the same language it is offensive. Sometimes the relevant context for understanding language includes the race, gender, features of the appearance, or the reputation of the person speaking. Unfortunately, sometimes people use these superficial features as a context for understanding what a person is saying. It is unlikely that people would pass negative judgments on a White middle-class professor who knowingly used nonstandard forms like *expecially* for "especially" or *"pacific"* for "specific" or if she jokingly proclaimed "say it *ain't* so!" However, in many situations, cases in which the speaker is non-White, speaks a regional variety of English, is young, is old, has long hair, has short hair, or dresses differently (you name the superficial cue), individuals have far less license with the language. An *ain't* or an *expecially* in these cases may be read as a sign of ignorance or lack of education. Those who pass such judgments are often unaware of the way a person's superficial features are shaping the interpretation of their language.

In a classroom full of children, this kind of misunderstanding may have profound effects on future learning. Remember, for example, the "problem" child, George (Souto-Manning, 2008). He was also an African-American child considered, by many, to be a trouble maker. He had been singled out as a candidate who might be eligible for special education pull-out services. When he claimed that the study of farm and zoo animals was "boring," he could easily have been interpreted as being insubordinate. His teacher could have claimed he did not understand. She could have suggested he be tested for special services or moved to the resource room that day. Fortunately, because his teacher recognized that he, like all students, would have some substantial contributions to make in her classroom, she did not prejudge him based on his looks or reputation. Instead, she continued to talk to George about why he did not want to study farm and zoo animals and what he could learn more from. Rather than letting superficial features influence her interpretation of how his language was functioning, she chose to draw him out and learn what he knew and what he was capable of learning.

Unfortunately, although some interrupting and talkative children are considered bright and curious, others are considered disruptive and less intelligent. So, "this is boring," when uttered by a White child, may be an emblem of giftedness, whereas when it is uttered by an African-American child, it is an emblem of a problem learner (see the following chart). The same sorts of duality of judgment occur when children make reading errors. The linguistic anthropologist James Collins has shown through classroom discourse analysis that children in high reading groups can make small sounding-out errors (reading miscues) while reading aloud and continue reading the story, but children in low reading groups are repeatedly interrupted and corrected by their teachers (Collins, 1996). Similarly, the reading researcher Richard Allington (1980) has shown that children in high reading groups are asked questions about the meaning of a text, whereas students in the low group are asked questions about how to say a word. An important step in refraining from such premature judgment (and avoiding their consequences) is to pay attention to how context is shaping the interpretations we make of students' words. As discourse analysts, teachers can make charts (such as the one that follows) and reflect on whether the same words function differently simply because they were said by someone who looks different or has come into the classroom prejudged as a certain kind of learner.

LANGUAGE FORM	CONTEXT OF USE (who said it)	FUNCTION
1. This is boring	1a. African American 6-year-old	1a. Indicator of a problem child
	1b. White 6-year-old	1b. Indicator of giftedness
2. A reading miscue	2a. Student in the high reading group	2a. Simple error, not needing correction
	2b. Student in the low reading group	2b. Indicator of lack of phonemic awareness or a pronunciation problem, cause for correction

Gender Expectations

Like race, language background, or institutionally endowed categories like "gifted," gender can also impact the way we hear our students; even small differences between how we react to girls and boys can dramatically change their educational trajectories. Recently, I saw some vivid evidence of gender differences in education as I was paging through the Georgia Public Broadcasting program guide. My eye caught a picture of 11 young writers, winners in this year's Reading Rainbow Young Writers and Illustrators Contest. The 11 youngsters ranged in age from kindergarten through third grade and seemed to be a racially diverse group. However, 10 of the 11 winners pictured were girls. Why? There are many possible explanations. Whatever the reason, the fact that only one boy is in the Reading Rainbow awards photo reinforces the idea that this Young Writers and Illustrators Contest is a girlish activity. What boy would want to be in such a contest? Certainly fewer will if they catch sight of this picture! As teachers, through heightened awareness of these gender-based tendencies, we can play a role in countering these limiting definitions of girlish or boyish activity.

However, statistics suggest that this picture represents certain norms in U.S. schools, norms that continue beyond high school. In many universities in the United States, female students outnumber male students—

because more females meet the admissions requirements. Meanwhile, boys are placed in special education classes at a much higher rate than girls. Why these gender differences? How are they related? Why, despite these differences in school achievement, do workforce statistics indicate that grown men are more highly paid than women in the same jobs? Why in most businesses are women, but not men, expected to be the partners who take leave when there is a newborn in the family?

There is evidence that both males and females are privileged differently in different situations. But in terms of classroom discourse, I most want to draw attention to the fact that there are significant differences in the way, in general, females and males proceed through their education and perform in school settings. These general norms of behavior compound themselves in a vicious circle and are reflected in choices later in life. If boys and girls are treated a certain way, they begin to act that way, and so on and so on. In a classroom context, these normative expectations can be limiting for all children.

From the perspective of a classroom discourse analyst, normative gender expectations are often reproduced, if not largely created, through talk. What boys and girls do and say in classrooms is often interpreted against a gender normative backdrop, and there can be substantial consequences in the direction a child's learning takes. For example, in one pre-K classroom that I have observed many times, girls are frequently the only ones at the art center (a table with drawing and painting materials). Boys are spread around, usually busy at many different centers, but rarely putting crayon to paper. Because these art activities are good practice for the writing children will be doing in kindergarten, I mentioned my concern about these differences to the lead teacher. She chuckled, "That's pretty typical. Boys just do not like to draw. They usually come around in kindergarten when they have no choice!"

This teacher's response provides some insight into the "Reading Rainbow" disparity. What boy would voluntarily enter such a contest when all he associates with coloring and writing is being forced to do it? But as a teacher, trying to combat the momentum of this gendered role expectation is difficult. There is even research that further suggests boys' preference not to color has *biological* roots: Developmental research suggests that boys do not develop fine motor skills as early as girls. Girls are much more able to draw at an earlier age (Eaton & Enns, 1986; Martin, Wisenbaker, & Hitunen, 1997). So it makes sense that no boy would want to sit at a table of girls who are drawing much better than he is. In many cases, gross motor activities, like running, might be more desirable for boys and fine motor activities, like drawing, may be more desirable for girls. But need these general differences be compounded in how classroom activities are structured?

Although boys may be minimally represented at the preschool art table, other studies have shown that girls are minimally represented in classroom talk across the school years (Best, 1983). In his study of high school classrooms in England, for example, Ben Rampton found that boys were focal classroom participants as well as the highest achievers. Boys were playful, even exuberant, participants in class discussions. They cracked jokes, made fun of each other, and played with the teacher's language. In this case, these rambunctious boys were also the highest grade earners in the class. Girls didn't participate in this banter and, perhaps as a result, did not identify with school or value classroom participation. Moreover, because of the way boys teased them during class discussions, girls were reluctant to participate, as one student described:

> . . . if I say something, the boys they'll take they'll start saying "oh what're you saying that for" and start on you and laugh at you if you answer this question and it's wrong and like the girls ain't got much confidence I don't think. . . . (Rampton, 2006, p. 64)

Rampton's research echoes a tradition of classroom observation that indicates that girls' voices are silenced in the classroom (e.g., Best 1983). However, such observations—be it boys' exclusion from the art table or girls' exclusion from class discussion—do not necessarily reflect what biologically or socially must be, but rather what developmental psychologists or social scientists have described as being there. This is a chicken–egg situation: If we accept that "boys cannot draw when they are 4" or "girls are excluded from class discussion" as a truth, it will become true. And there will be evidence of it, like the Reading Rainbow awards picture, all over the place. And once again, the truth will be compounded: A child's gender (rather than his or her potential) will become a feature that teachers, parents, and peers will use to judge what they do, how well they do it, and what they are able to do in the future.

The discourse approach provides teachers a way to study children as individuals without interpreting developmental continua as universal or biologically determined and without taking other studies of children's interaction as determinate of what will happen in their own classroom. This is because a discourse approach recognizes the interaction between context and language in use. No speaker is programmed—robotlike—to do gender-normative behaviors at all times. In different contexts, different kinds of behaviors emerge. So, a "shy" girl in the classroom context may be witty and talkative on the playground. A boy who dislikes art at school may be a talented and renowned graffiti muralist in his neighborhood. What's more, once girls and boys and their teachers are aware of how identity is shaped through talk and relative to context, they potentially can make choices about the kinds of identities they want to promote or display in the classroom. A girl can be not only a "girl" or a boy a "boy" in the classroom; instead, an infinite number of identities can be constructed through talk and interaction.

One of the first steps a classroom discourse analyst can take in addressing the number of identities available to girls and boys is to observe students' interactions in multiple contexts. For example, in contrast to psychological research characterizing girls as "relational" rather than "hierarchical" (Gilligan, 1983), the linguistic anthropologist Marjorie Goodwin has shown that girls can be master debaters on the street (1990) and vociferous sticklers for the rules during playground hopscotch games (2002). By recording and reflecting on talk in multiple contexts in this way, teachers can also reflect on gender norms and how they are affecting discourse in their own classroom.

Overdetermination

Just as students evoke teachers' expectations, simply by being boys or girls, so too do words bring vivid histories along with them, making us react to them in ways that sometimes seem beyond our control. Consider this story about language in church: One Sunday morning, a preacher stood up and began his sermon by shouting, "Shit!" Everyone was aghast. Then he explained: "It sure is a sad commentary on our society that good church people would be more upset by a 4 letter word shouted from the pulpit than they are about children dying every day from starvation." Why weren't the good people in front of him enraged by real offenses?

This story illustrates how specific words in our language come with baggage—baggage that can distract us from the human beings behind words. The term *overdetermination*, coined by Louis Althusser (1971), a philosopher of language, is a term for the effects of social histories on what words mean. Swearwords (as illustrated by that preacher) are prime examples of overdetermined words. Over its interactional history, the word *shit* has been subject to the effect of other social structures and practices that change who can use it, what it will mean, and under what circumstances. Some single words are so powerfully overdetermined that they may even be legally designated as "hate speech" that can lead to violence. The *n* word, for example, can be used in a highly degrading way to refer to African Americans in the United States. I would never write that word in this book or use it, even among close friends, because it is layered with social histories that I have little control over and do not fully understand.

But the function of more innocuous words in the classroom also can be overdetermined. For example, why did David think that *dude* was a worse word than *people*? Why is *dude* not a good word for a second grader to use to describe a picture? Like the *n* word, it is possible that the meaning of *dude* is not only situated in its immediate context, but also functionally overdetermined by its own history of use. Unlike swear words, the word *dude* probably will not offend anyone directly, but it may do more indirect damage to the speaker depending on how it is interpreted. The word *dudes* is often more casual sounding than *people* and, therefore, in many school contexts may not be appropriate. Using it on a formal essay exam could give the impression that a student does not know more formal forms of expression.

In summary, single words can cause serious emotional injury to others. Single words can also give lasting impressions about their speakers. Therefore, in classrooms, recognizing and, in some cases, talking explicitly about the overdetermined nature of many words or ways of speaking can be helpful. Children are often not familiar with the same social histories of words that adults are, nor are second language learners. When people cross any social boundary, as most teachers and students do every day when they enter their classrooms, they will meet words and ways of speaking that are overdetermined in ways they may not be familiar with. In practice, any new user of a language (including any new dialect), that is, any student in our classrooms, will likely make some social blunders. Teachers can poll students on which words are painfully overdetermined for them (*stupid*? *fatso*?) and discuss those words. Teachers can talk to students about words or ways of speaking that give poor first impressions academically (*dude*? *homey*?). Even technical language (like the word *gravity* discussed in the next section) may need to be demystified by teachers so that their overdetermined social histories do not skew classroom discourse in favor of a certain minority of students who already know these words. Awareness of how words function in different contexts, again, gives teachers and students more control over how even the most loaded words affect classroom discourse.

THE SECOND DIMENSION: INTERACTIONAL CONTEXT

Language-in-Use ← affects → Interactional Context

Up until now, we have been referring primarily to "social context" and examining how it influences discourse. We have included in social context the world outside the classroom, the history of interactions inside and outside the classroom, the context of the classroom, different activity contexts within the classroom, and broad social categories like race and gender. As discussed earlier, where people say something, what they look like, where they live, and their social history all potentially affect how discourse functions. James Gee, a linguistic and discourse analyst, refers to these aspects influencing language function as "big D Discourse" effects.

In any interaction, however, broad social categories are only as relevant as speakers make them. Therefore, another crucial dimension of classroom discourse is interactional context. Gee refers to the influences of interactional context on language function as "little d discourse" effects. In big D terms, gender has social ramifications; for example, women are still expected to be primary caregivers or responsible for child care as evidenced by the fact that many employers expect women, but not men, to take leave when there is a newborn in the family. Despite big D discourse norms like this, however, in small d discourse terms, individuals potentially renegotiate gender norms in each interaction; for example, a man who talks about his newborn and child-care issues with his colleagues may be refiguring what it means to be male in today's workplace. Similarly, in classroom discourse, the ramifications of being male or female, "gifted" or "special," a "good kid" or the "worst," are determined not only by big D Discourses about these categories, but also by everyday sequences of interaction, or little d discourse. This section is concerned with analyzing classroom discourse at this "little d" level.

Predictable Interactional Context: Adjacency Pairs

Much of what we say every day to students and how students answer back is predictable ("Good morning class!" "Good morning!"). Without this kind of predictability, it would be difficult to conduct class at all—or a simple conversation, for that matter. The field of conversation analysis focuses on the study of this predictability embedded in any interaction. One of the primary tools driving interaction, from this perspective, is the adjacency pair, a two-part interactional sequence in which the first part (e.g., a question) produces the expectation for the second part (e.g., an answer). Admittedly, this is an obvious feature of discourse. But perhaps because of its obviousness, it is easy to ignore how powerful the force of an adjacency pair can be in interaction; if one person says something, another must respond. Even if an addressee does not respond, their silence indicates some kind of response simply because they have been addressed. For example, imagine a teacher greeting a student cheerfully and being met by silence:

> Teacher: Good morning, John!
> John: ((*walks silently to his desk*))

Immediately, the teacher might be wondering what is bothering John. Is he sick? Is he tired? Does he have a hearing problem? Should he be tested? Much early language socialization involves learning to respond appropriately to these sequences; when students do not respond in expected ways, we assume there is a reason.

Because people who share a certain social background have internalized the unspoken rules of adjacency pairs, many responses are very predictable. Some typical adjacency pairs in English in the United States are: Greeting/Greeting, Question/Answer, Invitation/Acceptance, Assessment/Disagreement, Apology/Acceptance, and Summons/Acknowledgment. All of these take place in classrooms day after day in predictable ways (see the following chart).

Typical adjacency pairs in classroom discourse

ADJACENCY PAIR TYPE	EXAMPLE	
Greeting/Greeting	Teacher:	Good morning!
	Students:	Good morning!
Question/Answer	Teacher:	Is today Friday?
	Student:	Yes!
Invitation/Acceptance	Teacher:	Would you like to read next?
	Student:	Sure.
Assessment/Disagreement	Teacher:	This is a beautiful short story.
	Student:	I thought it was creepy, actually.
Apology/Acceptance	Student:	I'm sorry I'm late.
	Teacher:	That's okay—we started late today anyway.
Summons/Acknowledgment	Teacher:	John?
	John:	Yes?

When students' responses counter our expectations, we need to think on our feet—it is not always easy to change the momentum of expectations set up by the first part of an adjacency pair (Do you know what I mean? Are you there? Hello? HELLO?!!).

Unpredictable Interactional Context: Foiled Expectations

Many teachers design and redesign lessons precisely because their expectations for the second part of an adjacency pair sequence have been foiled. One of the most common conundrums teachers face is silence. How teachers interpret these silences and respond to them differs in different classroom environments. In traditional classrooms, for example, silence is often interpreted as an absence of knowledge, as in the following hypothetical sequence:

> Teacher: What's the capital of Portugal?
> Students: ((*silence*))

Here, students' silence suggests they do not know the correct answer. In nontraditional classrooms, however, silence is interpreted as thinking time. Waiting through a silence can give students who ordinarily do not contribute a chance to become participants (Gallas, 1995; Johnstone, 2005). These nontraditional classrooms are founded on an understanding that, although much of interaction is predictable, there is also a great deal that is not predictable—and as teachers, we need to be ready to wait through those silences or unexpected answers to discover what our students know that we could never have predicted.

This approach has been the cornerstone of Karen Gallas' approach to analyzing discourse in her own classroom. As a teacher researcher who routinely analyzes classroom discourse with her primary school students, Gallas has spent years thinking about and changing the way she starts science discussions in her classroom. One method she developed to stimulate students' natural curiosity about science was to have students suggest discussion-initiating questions (Gallas, 1995, 1998). Students originally came up with questions like the following:

> What is gravity?
> How do plants grow?
> Why do leaves change color?
> Where do dreams come from?

These were questions the children all agreed they were interested in exploring during science time. However, Gallas found, in practice, discussions that began with these questions consistently led to silence on the part of a predictable group of students.

When the science questions her students posed weren't generating the kinds of inclusive discussions Gallas had hoped for, she began to look closely at the interactional effects of certain questions. After trial and error—and much recording and discussing of Science Talks—Gallas (1995) found that there were better ways to frame the initiating questions. For example, the question "What is gravity?" worked better as "Why, when you jump, do you come down?" "Where do dreams come from?"

worked better as "How do dreams get into our heads?" (p. 95). What is the difference here? Gallas found that questions that used *overdetermined* science terminology (like *gravity*) invited talk from some students who were already familiar with those terms, but excluded students who did not have this familiarity. Although the question was originally offered up by students, it functioned more like a known-answer question in a traditional classroom:

> Question: What is gravity?
>
> Students: ((*silence*))

When this question was reframed as a question about everyday ordinary experience, rather than one that implied previous knowledge of science terminology, more students participated.

Why then did a question like "Where do dreams come from?" fail? It does not contain any science terminology or presuppose science knowledge. Instead, the problem, Gallas found, was in the abstract nature of the question. When she rephrased it using a personal pronoun ("How do dreams get into OUR heads"), students were able to reference their own experience of dreams in their responses, rather than abstract generalizations about dreaming phenomena. As Gallas (1995) comments, "[I]t seemed as if every child was invited to contribute his or her personal idea" (p. 95).

Creating New Interactional Context:
Interactional Contingency

Gallas' science discussions illustrate that carefully considering the kinds of questions we ask can facilitate learning. In addition, how teachers respond to silences or unexpected answers can change how those answers function as the discourse continues. This ever-present potential for interaction to reshape the meaning of *preceding* individual utterances is called *interactional contingency*. How one person's words function is always contingent on what happens subsequently in talk. In the following interaction, recorded in a second-grade reading group, Danny gives a lengthy response to the teacher's question, but the teacher's subsequent response suggests that what he has said is irrelevant:

> Teacher: Do men wear a lot of hats now?
>
> Danny: Some don't. The train dudes—the train people wear they wear these like, big old things that—and somebody better put on some um things for um there little

thing cause they hurt their ears ((*pointing into his ears*))
because, the noise is come in the air and—

Teacher: But do men, do a lot of men wear hats now?

In this case, the teacher *sequentially deletes* (Ford, 1993) Danny's response.
That is, by reasking her question about hats after Danny has already provided a lengthy answer, she constructs his response as nonexistent. This
tendency to ignore what seem to be digressions can have unfortunate
consequences in classroom discourse. In the case of the "hats" discussion,
it led to Danny's silence for the rest of the session.

Admittedly, it takes careful interactional negotiation to sequentially
construct unexpected or confusing student responses as contributions
that are potentially leading somewhere important. This is where classroom discourse analysis can be helpful. For example, in another science
discussion in Gallas' classroom—about how babies are able to grow in
the womb—one student offers up an initially unexpected answer:

Germaine: It's just like caterpillars.

Teacher: Go ahead.

Germaine: It's just like caterpillars when they grow. They turn
into butterflies. You know how butterflies grow? It
makes more sense if the baby grows like butterflies.

Rather than dismissing Germaine's comparison of babies growing to
caterpillars as inaccurate or off topic, Gallas (1995) reflects on her own
response to Germaine's answer. She writes about it: ". . . I did not completely follow Germaine's thinking, but I had a hunch that it made sense,
and I asked if anyone could help expand the idea" (p. 86). By waiting to
see how Germaine's idea unfolds in discussion, Gallas retroactively constructs his response as important. She also projects a future in which
Germaine will continue contributing to discussion.

Teachers face interactional contingencies like this every day in classroom discourse and struggle with how to treat such departures. In traditional classrooms, more so than in conversation, there is the tendency to
stick to the expected script. In inquiry classrooms, like Gallas', however,
there is interactional space for students to consider and think about
developing interaction and for the teacher to mull over apparent departures. How could this unexpected statement become a tool for thinking
and learning? Gallas developed this ability to use such departures productively over years of recording and reflecting on discourse in her classroom. As Gallas (1995) writes, after having the breakthrough in which she
re-framed the science talk questions,

> After 5 years of watching Science Talks, I was able to see from the development of this class as talkers that even the phrasing of a question, whether asked by an adult or a child, can silence (and thereby exclude) some children. . . . (p. 95)

Although Gallas has also tackled big D issues like Gender in the classroom, in this case, classroom discourse analysis, and in particular analysis of "small d" discourse involving sequences of questions and answers, gradually helped her to open up discussion so that everyone engaged in more productive talk.

THE THIRD DIMENSION: INDIVIDUAL AGENCY

Language in use ← affects → Interactional Context/Social Context

↑ affects ↓

Individual Agency

As the last two sections have emphasized, interactional context and social context play major roles in shaping classroom interaction. Students come to our classrooms with social and interactional histories that shape the way they hear us and the way they interact. On top of that, most U.S. classroom teachers are pressured by federal and state mandates to teach only in certain ways, to use only certain languages, to test only certain skills and ideas—or else. These social and interactional contexts are powerful shaping dimensions of classroom discourse. But how do we change social or interactional contexts we feel are problematic? This section addresses how teachers can use discourse analysis to gain greater control of classroom interaction.

As relationship gurus intone, "You cannot change other people. All you can do is change the way you react to them." This may be good advice for classroom discourse analysts too. In any set of social relations, we need to focus our energies on what we can control instead of battling forces and people we cannot. No matter how frustrated we are by mandated reading curriculum (or science, math, etc.), we are often stuck with those textbooks for an entire year. No matter how much we want someone to answer a question in a particular way, we cannot force them to produce that answer. No matter how much we want to control how our words are interpreted, people may hear them differently from what we intend.

This does not mean we are powerless as individual teachers. Although day to day we may not be able to change the textbooks we use, the social histories of the people in our classroom, or the kinds of expectations people bring to interactions, we can change how we react to these contexts. Understanding the multiple dimensions of classroom talk can be a first step toward gaining personal agency—and beginning to focus more on how we understand and react to administrators or our students, less on changing them. Understanding how powerful our discourse is in creating who we are, how we are understood, and how we understand our students is a lesson we can pass on to students as well.

Do We Have Agency?

By individual agency, I mean personal control, the ability to act in ways that produce desired outcomes or contribute to our own personal goals and projects. Having personal control seems straightforward enough. But, as we have discussed, social and interactional contexts control us far more than we usually notice. When you feel yourself cringing at the word *dude* on an essay or a profane word shouted from the pulpit, how much of your response is your own, how much is dictated by society? In these interactions, social context seems to be in control. When someone asks "How was your day?" at the dinner table and you blurt out "Fine!" even though your day was miserable, how much of your response is actually driven by interactional habit? The interactional context seems to be in control. However, just as social and interactional contexts affect our language in use, our language in use affects social and interactional contexts and how much *we choose* to have them influence classroom talk (see diagram at the beginning of this section). The greater our awareness of these contextual dimensions, the greater force our individual agency can take in shaping the role these contexts play in classroom interaction.

Augmented Agency Through Awareness
of Social Context

As discussed earlier, when people say something, what they look like, where they live, and their social history all affect how discourse functions. Sometimes the ways we read these cues have become so much a part of our interactions that we do not notice how they shape what we say and do. But the more aware we become of how we read features of social context when we listen to our students, the better able we are to *choose* which aspects of social context influence our classroom interactions. Often this is simply a matter of conducting interactions based on our own hopes expectations for students, rather than society's expectations. Think of these three scenarios:

Scenario 1: George (remember him from chap. 1?) came to first grade with a bad reputation, already heading toward special education classes. His teacher faced a choice about how to listen to him—with the ears of the school context, which had already heard him as disruptive, or with the ears of her own perspective that all children have valuable contributions to make in her classroom. She chose to listen to him as a child with potential, and as a child who had the potential to reshape her curriculum. As a result the entire class engaged in an inquiry project about reptiles and amphibians in addition to the rudimentary curricular mandate of "Farm and Zoo" animals (Souto-Manning, 2008).

Scenario 2: Chavo entered AP English his junior year and consistently earned mediocre grades. At first, his teacher used superficial features to explain it away: "He's not a literature person." In many ways, he was not. He spent much more of his time after school practicing for sports than doing schoolwork. However, at the end of the school year, he had the opportunity to infuse his interests into his final humanities project. Each student selected a contemporary thinker, artist, and activist and illustrated through a multimedia presentation how these figures have contributed to culture. Chavo's project illustrated how Jerry Colangelo (an American sports mogul), Michael Jordan (a professional basketball player), and Chris Berman (a sportscaster) have contributed to the U.S. cultural reverence for sport. His project won the contest for best end-of-the-year humanities project. Fortunately, his teacher provided him with an opportunity to be challenged and to illustrate the depth of his thinking, despite her initial impression of him as "not a literature person" (Young, 2004).

Scenario 3: Germaine, a quiet first grader in Karen Gallas' classroom initially struggled to make himself understood and "showed little interest in science work." He also lacked many of the experiences the other children had as resources on which to build scientific understandings. As students gave examples, he continuously ran up against his own limited experience: He had never been to the seashore, he'd never had a pet, he didn't know that homemade bread has holes in it. However, by carefully controlling the format of science talks, initiating them with students' genuine questions, and constructing an interactional environment in which students could voice their own theories—by creating a space for "correct and incorrect thinking"—Gallas bolstered Germaine's interest in science and his influence over scientific thinking in the classroom grew. His curiosity was contagious. Often he contributed outrageous statements, like the following:

[The sun] coulda started in a box, or in a square shape.

[Babies grow] just like caterpillars.

He also began to spontaneously offer up more science questions throughout the school day:

Why is grass green?

How is glass made?

How did the sun get that round shape?

How do butterflies grow when they're in that cocoon thing?

Rather than stifle these comments or questions by offering more correct scientific narratives or approved scientific lines of inquiry, Gallas looked on as Germaine's contributions not only fostered his own natural scientific curiosity, but also brought other quiet children more fully into science talks.

Each of these scenarios exemplifies a teacher acting counter to interactional norms that students brought with them from previous social contexts or histories of classroom interactions. These teachers refused to let normative expectations created by social context exclusively control their classroom discourse. George's teacher heard his negative response to her Animals unit apart from the context of the school, which had begun to label him a problem child. Sam's teacher heard his request to create a literary, sports-based humanities presentation apart from the context of his status as "not a literature person." Germaine's teacher constructed an interactional environment in which his natural curiosities were translated into identification with scientific inquiry. Each of these teachers built on an awareness and deliberate rejection of how social context had been shaping their students' identities. This awareness gave them the tools they needed to exercise personal agency and alter the learning outcomes for students in their classrooms.

Augmented Agency Through Awareness
of Interactional Context

Sometimes those same features of discourse that seem to diminish our agency can, through our awareness, become tools that augment our agency. Because the teachers in the previous three examples were aware of how social context influences talk and interpretation, they were able to choose to use or ignore features of social context. In the same way, although some features of interactional context seem to take away our personal agency—as when the power of an adjacency pair seems to force us to say we are "fine"—when brought to awareness, the force of adjacency pairs (and other predictable features of interaction) can be used as powerful tools in service of our classroom goals. Using adjacency pairs mindfully means training ourselves to be aware of their effects in at least three ways: (a) by being aware of how we craft our first pair parts, (b) by being aware of how our expectations can prevent us from listening carefully to whatever response we get, and (c) by creating an environment in which we, as teachers, are not the only participants starting new classroom conversational sequences.

By carefully choosing a first part of the adjacency pair, teachers have tremendous power to shape what comes next and how students participate in classroom talk. As discussed in the previous section, Karen Gallas illustrated that by using science questions that originate with students and carefully phrasing them, participation in Science Talks grew and scientific curiosity flourished in her classroom. Similarly, in their book on *Kidwatching*, Gretchen Owocki and Yetta Goodman (2002) illustrate how to carefully design first pair parts when responding to students' work: There is an important difference between providing simple evaluative statements and providing questions that lead to more involved accounting. They provide these examples of praise statements that do not probe for more:

> Teacher: I liked your demonstration.

or

> Teacher: You listened well today.

or

> Teacher: Your pictures are great.

Well-placed praise is good, but response to this kind of complement is usually only a perfunctory acknowledgment of some kind—maybe mild acceptance or, out of modesty, shy disagreement. As Owocki and Goodman (2002) point out, alternative forms of praise can turn complements like those above into thought-provoking questions (p. 52):

I liked your demonstration.	. . . could be. . .	What kind of practice did it take to get ready for this demonstration?
You listened well today.	. . . could be. . .	You seemed very interested today. What caught your interest?
Your pictures are great.	. . . could be. . .	Your pictures helped me enjoy your story. How did you think to include the little anchor?

These alternative follow-up questions are an even greater compliment—because they tell students we expect them to keep talking and thinking.

By consistently providing first-pair parts like these, which probe for thoughtful responses, teachers can support students' development far more than through simple statements like "Great picture!" that require only automatic replies like "Thanks."

Asking thought-provoking questions, however, is only the beginning (or, in our new terms, only the first pair part of the adjacency pair). Mindfulness of interactional context also requires awareness of our expectations for certain responses, and being able to get past those expectations so that we can listen to all answers—especially those that do not conform to our expectations.

Listening to the unexpected also means carefully considering what silence means. How, for example, can we learn more about a student who always replies to even our most carefully crafted questions with silence? One way is to listen to that student when we are not asking questions and to take note of the contexts and kind of talk this child feels most comfortable producing. Germaine's teacher, in the prior example, found that listening to Germaine's questions that came up spontaneously throughout the day (not during official "science" time) and later allowing the class to explore these questions provided an entry point to help Germaine notice his own scientific ways of thinking. Once we have found interactional contexts in which students feel comfortable talking, we can also listen for the kind of questions or other first-pair parts that get that student talking, thinking, reading, and writing. For Karen Gallas, this involved using as discussion starter questions that developed from students' own day-to-day curiosities, often voiced outside of science time. For other teachers, bringing students into interaction might start with an oblique comment about current events, a sports score, or a "wondering out loud" stance, rather than a direct question. In any case, by analyzing our own discourse, we can explore the effects of different kinds of first-pair parts, rather than assuming a student is deficient (didn't do homework, is not a good writer, is not a literature person, can't speak English, etc.) for not responding.

Although it is important to provide thought-provoking questions and to listen to unexpected curiosities and unlikely answers, as Gallas' work on Science Talks illustrates, it may be most important, for the life of our classrooms, to ensure that students are also asking the questions. Sometimes expectations for how classes run, for who does the asking, and for who holds the knowledge actually exclude students from the learning process. Helping students learn means helping them think, and this necessitates providing opportunities for students to develop their own curiosities. The only way teachers find a project for the jock who is "not a literature type," inspiration for someone with little scientific experience outside the classroom, or a challenge for the bored "problem student" is by creating an environment in which these students' talk is taken up as important by both the teacher and other students.

Ironically, developing individual agency as a teacher often means letting students do the talking, providing the opportunities for students to ask questions and provide each other with answers. By analyzing classroom discourse, it becomes possible to see which interactional contexts are facilitating student talk and making connections between ideas—and which are not—and to make changes accordingly. With a perspective on productive and unproductive sequences gained through a close look at talk in our classrooms, our *institutional* power as teachers can be harnessed to support our *individual* goals for students' learning.

Agency and Identity

By analyzing discourse, and as a consequence becoming aware of the effects of social and interactional contexts on language function, we can begin to harness agency in shaping classroom learning. This necessarily involves shaping the identities that students have in classrooms. The framework developed in this chapter is based on the assumption that a person's identity is fundamentally a product of social interactions. Consistent with this perspective, James Gee defines *identity* simply as the kind of person someone is in a given situation. This "in a given situation" is an important add-on. Students in school may have different identities in the lunchroom or on the bus than they do in reading groups. Even the "problem child" kind of person may be an "angel" in another class. As teachers, the language we choose and the way we choose to understand the language used by our students significantly shapes what "kinds of people" ("clown," "overachiever," "trouble-maker," "jock") show up in our classroom. In turn, the different identities that students take up in our classrooms can lead to different kinds of learning.

New student identities, then, are *by definition* constructed through talk. Classroom discourse analysis—examining when our students speak, and how we respond to them—provides a tool for considering our role in constructing identities for them: Interpreting a seeming *non sequitur* in the classroom as disruptive begins to construct the identity of that student as a disruptive student. Creating an interactional environment in which students draw connections between each other's questions and theories (as Germaine's teacher did) begins to construct a student's identity as a creative, interesting, and thoughtful learner. As teachers aware of social and interactional contexts and their effects on language, classroom discourse analysts can use and listen to language carefully to collaboratively construct those creative, interesting, and thoughtful learners.

PUTTING IT ALL TOGETHER:
A THREE DIMENSIONAL CLASSROOM PORTRAIT

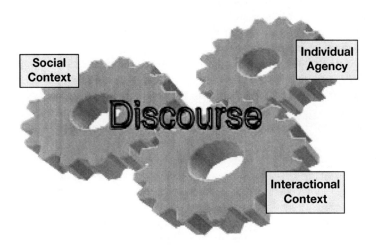

Having agency, running the show, and constructing bright and effective classrooms is all appealing. But here comes the realistic refrain: The meaning and function of classroom discourse is built from social and interactional contexts, as well as individual agency. Imagine each of these dimensions as gears in a classroom discourse machine. Each gear pulls the others along, and no gear can move without affecting the others. Often it is difficult to know which gear is doing the most work. We would hope, in some situations, that our own *individual agency* gear could drive the discourse machine. At times, however, the *social context* gear takes over. We may find ourselves at the mercy of a system that treats our knowledge and accomplishments as meaningless. Sometimes, no matter what we try to say to change the course of an interaction, our conversation moves in an unpleasant or unproductive direction.

This metaphor is rather more mechanistic than actual discourse is in the classroom. However, it illustrates that each of the dimensions of discourse contributes to its functionality. Also, being aware of the machinery of discourse potentially enables some tinkering with it, making adjustments without having to go to an outside authority or presumed expert who might be less familiar with the nuances of our own, particular classroom discourse machine.

This tinkering could also be called reflective practice, a primary goal of classroom discourse analysis. Analyzing the intersecting levels of social context, interactional context, and individual agency aims to improve future classroom interactions and ultimately positively affect social outcomes in contexts beyond the classroom. To see what this tinkering looks like in practice, the next two chapters take readers through the steps to becoming a classroom discourse analyst: recording real classroom interaction, viewing that interaction and making preliminary observations, transcribing the talk and action, and analyzing how social and interaction contexts as well as individual agency affect the direction classroom discourse takes.

QUESTIONS AND ACTIVITIES

Critical Reflection

1. Compare the effects of the words *dude* and *gravity* as discussed in this chapter. How does their functionality reflect social and interactional dimensions of language?
2. Page through a yearbook from a school you have attended or a school in which you teach. In which activities are boys more prevalent? In which activities are girls more prevalent? How do you account for these differences? What kinds of language do you associate with these different activities?
3. Write down examples of these typical adjacency pairs as they occur during a day in the life of your classroom: Greeting/Greeting, Question/Answer, Invitation/Acceptance, Assessment/Disagreement, Apology/Acceptance, and Summons/Acknowledgment. What are some unexpected responses you have heard? What would happen if you or your students responded differently than usual? How could you use your adjacency pairs to change how classroom discourse proceeds?
4. What are your "identities" in the classroom? How are these constructed through your talk? How could this "identity" also be viewed through the biological, institutional, or peer-group lenses?
5. What is an overdetermined word used in your classroom or school? Describe the contexts in which it is okay or not okay to use that word. For example, in many schools, the word *bottom* is used frequently, as in sit on your bottom. However, the word *butt* would be considered offensive. What does this mean? Why is butt so much worse than bottom? Could you try talking about overdetermined words with your students?

Reflective Activities

1. Spend a day or two paying attention to certain repeated or habitual language as it is used around you. Write down your examples in a chart like the following:

LANGUAGE FORM	CONTEXTS OF USE (who said it, where, and when)	FUNCTION
1. Example: "Good morning!"	1a. spoken by teacher, as first student enters classroom	1a. greeting
	1b. spoken by teacher after the bell has rung and students are still talking among themselves, a bit disruptively	1b. a bid for students to stop talking
	1c. spoken by teacher to student who seems to be dozing off in class	1c. an alarm to get student to wake up
2. _____	2a. _____	2a. _____
	2b. _____	2b. _____
	2c. _____	2c. _____
3. _____	3a. _____	3a. _____
	3b. _____	3b. _____
	3c. _____	3c. _____

Use the "a-b-c" sections to record multiple contexts in which the same form is used to different effect. What forms do you hear repeatedly at your school? How does their function change according to context?

2. Between classes or before the school day begins, observe students as they pass your classroom door. Are there certain language forms that you hear repeatedly? What are they? Write them down. Then listen to how they are functioning. Do students use these forms in your classroom? Why or why not?

3. Record one class session of your own teaching in which you are asking students questions and then go back and view it. How do you respond to students' answers? Do you notice that you respond to certain students' answers differently than others? Are you interpreting the function of some students' words differently? How is social context shaping your interpretations? How is interactional context shaping your interpretations?

SUGGESTED READING

Francis Christie's *Language Education in the Primary Years* provides a more detailed description of the distinctions between home and school language (in the primary years), and her *Classroom Discourse Analysis: A Functional Perspective* provides an accounting of the functional approach to classroom talk and writing. Mary Schleppegrell's *The Language of*

Schooling provides another useful introduction to the use of functional grammar to understand classroom talk and text. Peter Johnston, in his book *Choice Words*, makes more specific suggestions for making cross-contextual connections in the classroom so that the differences between home and school are not impediments to learning. James Gee's books and articles on discourse analysis are all lucid and helpful. I recommend, in particular, his review of discourse and identity, which focuses specifically on educational research, in the *Review of Research in Education*. For a more general overview of the discourse analysis method, see the second edition of his textbook, *An Introduction to Discourse Analysis: Theory and Method*. For those interested specifically in interactional context, Paul Seedhouse's *The Interactional Architecture of the Language Classroom: A Conversation Analysis Perspective* provides a detailed and clear introduction to how the insights of the field of conversation analysis can be brought to the classroom.

Gretchen Owocki and Yetta Goodman's *Kidwatching* describes how to pay attention to the ways kids interact as the foundation for early literacy development. For an excellent article laying out a theory of identity as discussed from a linguistic anthropological perspective, see Mary Bucholtz and Kira Hall's chapter "Language and Identity" in Alessandro Duranti's *Companion to Linguistic Anthropology*. If you want to read more about gender identity from a discourse perspective, Penelope Eckert and Sally McConnell-Ginet's textbook, *Language and Gender*, is an excellent starting point.

3

GETTING TO THE TALK I:
Recording and Viewing in Three Dimensions

PREVIEW QUESTIONS Before you start reading this chapter, think about what classroom talk you would like to investigate more closely.

Is there a recurrent event you would like to understand better?

A certain student who influences talk in particularly troublesome or favorable ways?

Topics that are difficult to discuss?

A certain event you would like to share with a colleague or administrator?

What might you discover by recording and viewing these forms of classroom interaction?

In this chapter, I describe foundational steps for doing discourse analysis in any classroom, from where to set up a camera to what to make of a recording later as you view it. Four basic steps—recording real classroom interaction, viewing that interaction and making preliminary observations, transcribing the talk and action, and, finally, analyzing those transcripts—lay the foundation for the work of classroom discourse analysis. This chapter begins by detailing the first two steps: recording and viewing. In what follows, I provide guidelines for how to record and view video in ways that can account for the social, interactional, and agentive dimensions of classroom discourse analysis discussed in chapter 2.

RECORDING IN THREE DIMENSIONS

Unavoidably, a recording of anything subtracts from the multidimensionality of lived experience. A camera literally takes three dimensions and transforms them to two. An audio recorder turns us into blind observers. Still, in all recorded life events, something of value is preserved; we continue to take pictures and videos and to go back to our vacation snap shots or videos again and again. Sometimes it even seems like these recordings are not merely preserving memories but also reconstructing our lives for us. At times, we may feel at the mercy of these old one-dimensional, selective portraits of ourselves. The unidimensionality of these recorded memories can sometimes represent us in ways that do not feel accurate to the breadth of our identities. Do I enjoy seeing a home movie of myself falling off a bicycle and yelling at my brother over and over again? I much prefer to think of (and see) myself as a competent, cooperative child. Why don't we have any movies of that?

This kind of one-dimensional accounting can be damaging to classroom identities too. Do I really want to see the one clip of myself ignoring a student question? It may be important to become aware of that behavior. However, to understand it fully and make necessary and effective changes, I also want to represent the social context of that ignoring, the interactional context that led up to it, and whether that ignoring was a deliberate, agentive choice. Accounting for these dimensions of discourse is important the moment an investigation begins, when we set up that camera in the classroom. The following two sections on recording address how to set up the camera to document aspects of both the social dimension (through "establishing shots") and the interactional dimension (through recording of "speech events") of classroom discourse. A third section on recording then illustrates how the deliberate choices we make in recording can be an act of agency because these are simultaneously choices about what we want to change in our classrooms, how we make those changes, and how we justify them to outsiders. Carefully gathered discourse data provide evidence that our changes are based in empirical inquiry, not whim, fad, or random desire.

Recording for Social Context:
  ### Establishing Shots

Accounting for a bicycle tumble in a home movie could have simply involved backing the camera up enough to show the neighborhood bully giving me a big push! Similarly, contextualizing a recording inside the classroom involves getting a bigger picture—understanding how the activity under focus is connected to other activities that take place in that classroom, the school, and in the world at large. Although this may sound daunting, this is something filmmakers accomplish in rudimentary and efficient ways. Some of the same basic techniques filmmakers use to paint a picture of a social context for a scene can help portray the social context of your classroom interactions.

Outside the Classroom and School

Like a filmmaker, as discourse recorders, we have the opportunity to focus on a single interaction while representing the school context within which that interaction takes place. Before a pivotal office scene, for example, a filmmaker might situate that talk by showing a tall building from outside, then zooming in, right up to the window of the office where, presumably, the important interaction is taking place. Seeing that this office is on a high floor, in the corner, high above the bustling streets of New York City, can affect how we view the interaction that follows. Similarly, recording the context outside of a school can raise our awareness of its effects on classroom discourse. Different situations outside the school will make for different kinds of interactions inside the school. Picture the differences in these three settings:

- Outside a Los Angeles alternative high school, there are no playgrounds and no sports fields—only buses and cars whizzing by, students still ambling in, past graffiti-strewn walls, at 11 a.m. Just inside the door, security guards watch as students pass through a metal detector. On the other side, friends are clustered in groups buzzing with talk.
- The front door of a rural Georgia primary school waits in complete silence at 11 a.m. Children have been settled in their classrooms for hours, and parents and school buses have long since dropped off children and moved on. An expanse of green lawn sprawls to the side of the building, dotted with playscapes awaiting recess climbers. Inside the vacant entrance hall, soft music plays and a goldfish aquarium bubbles.
- A view of the parking lot before evening courses at the university shows cars pouring into the parking lot at 5 p.m. Teachers, having commuted from all over the city's metro area, finished with a long day of teaching, cross the lot into the university building. Inside, they become adult students, greeting each other and quickly catching up as they fan into university classrooms.

Each of these contexts outside of schools will influence the interaction that goes on inside. At the Los Angeles alternative school, students do not have designated school time for outdoor recreation, sports, or camaraderie. They come to school at different times, often focused on meeting up with friends; for many, school is the one place they have to make these connections. This is different at the primary school described—these students will be funneled in an orderly way into classrooms, and later into recess, where they can yell, run, play, and socialize at full throttle for exactly 45 minutes. As students file into my university courses, I know they have not been studying in the library all day and may have countless classroom concerns still buzzing in their heads as they settle into their seats.

Capturing this context in your recording can be invaluable. It is also simple to do: Set up your camera *on a tripod* (do not try to hold your camera by hand) outside school one morning. Pan slowly across the school grounds and back. Slowly zoom in to the front door and then back out, providing a broad visual impression of the context of your school day and classroom. Understanding the social context of your interactions will take more than a simple recording, of course, but these establishing shots, or recordings that capture the broader social context of an interaction, will prime you for these considerations when you get to the next steps of viewing, transcribing, and analyzing.

Inside the Classroom

Within the classroom, you can also record context that shapes interaction, but might otherwise be overlooked, by taking some establishing shots. Pan slowly around the room to capture the classroom context, what is going on around the students, what is on the walls, hanging from the ceiling, and sitting on the desks. Any and all of these contextual features might influence subsequent talk, where participants sit, and how they interact.[1] Laura Sterponi (2007), for example, has illustrated how "clandestine interactive reading" is facilitated by a layout that includes isolated nooks and crannies throughout a classroom, each with just enough space for a pair of peer readers to cozy up with their books, out of the teacher's direct field of view.

---

[1] In classroom discourse analysis, just as in film analysis, the explanations we provide for what establishing shots mean and how we understand the layout and objects in a classroom are of course dependent on knowledge of the social milieu. For this reason, constructing an analysis may also require long-term residence in a classroom—not only as a teacher, but also as one who mingles with students and empathizes with their perspectives, taking in multiple sources of data. In this sense, discourse analysis also requires the development of what Carolyn Frank (1999) has called "Ethnographic Eyes." Talking over transcripts with students is another way to include multiple perspectives. This is discussed later in this chapter.

Recording for Interactional Context:
Speech Events

In chapter 2, we distinguished between social and interactional dimensions of classroom discourse. The social dimension comprises social demographics like class, race, and gender and speaker characteristics that can be accounted for by circumstances outside the immediacy of a single interaction. As discussed previously, "establishing shots" can begin to provide documentation for some aspects of this social dimension of discourse. In contrast to the social dimension, the interactional dimension of classroom discourse comprises those interactional expectations for turn-taking, storytelling, or problem solving that can be witnessed in face-to-face classroom talk. In this section, I address how careful recording can help document this interactional dimension of classroom discourse.

To do justice to the multiple features of the interactional context, have your camera situated so that it can capture an entire discrete speech event within the classroom. This speech event can be any typical classroom activity with discernable borders. Every classroom day includes multiple speech events, formal and informal. For example, in many primary school classrooms, "Calendar Time" is a common speech event—beginning when children sit down in front of the calendar and concluding when students return to their desks. An equivalent in high school might be a time for "Current Events," beginning, perhaps, when the teacher makes an announcement and pulls out the day's newspaper, concluding when the teacher announces a transition to another activity.

Although I have defined a speech event largely in terms of what one might see on a classroom agenda, recording a speech event needs to account for all the possible kinds of interactions that are going on during and around a speech event—not only those that directly connect to formal learning goals or a teacher's lesson plan. From a discourse perspective, learning is an interactive process embedded in a larger social context, through which learners gain the use of tools necessary to participate in multiple social worlds. Each speech event comes with its own conventional ways of speaking and interacting, and children learn these conventions in school (e.g., raising one's hand to answer questions in a traditional classroom). But students also learn ways of speaking creatively outside the conventions of any event (e.g., learning how to sneak in a response without raising one's hand or learning how to raise one's hand so as *not* to be called on). This process is part of student learning, too, and this chapter addresses both the conventional and creative aspects of interactions. Making recordings that capture the socially and interactionally layered nature of classroom learning will require techniques that can account for the multiple voices involved—both within an event and on the borders of discrete classroom events.

Within an Event

Recording by video and/or audio is often the best way to capture the complexity of interaction within a learning event. For example, in her book *Talking Their Way Into Science* (discussed in chap. 2), Karen Gallas (1995) remarks that her classroom Science Talks often seemed chaotic, but recording that apparent chaos provided her a closer look at how children develop their thinking through talk. She never witnessed a child's fully developed thought appear within a single explanatory turn. Instead, her students' thinking developed across many turns, overlaps, and interruptions. For Gallas, noticing collaborative and pivotal learning events—and being able to build on them—often involved going back to seemingly chaotic interactions she had recorded.

In the following excerpt, for example, students are exploring the question "How do babies grow inside the mother?" Each of the brackets in this excerpt represents an overlapping utterance:

Mike: It starts like, sort of like a small little ball, like an egg.
[Charles: A seed]
Mike: not exactly a seed, but
[Charles: Yeah, a little]
[Maurice: Yeah.]
Mike: A little ballish thing that looks kind of
[Charles: tiny thing.]
Mike: like a seed and then it kind of like gets little bumps on it
[Charles: It gets, and then]
Mike: and then it grows,
[Charles: It shapes, it shapes]
Mike: it grows and then the bumps grow and then it shapes and
[Charles: Our shapes come out.]
[Maurice: and that's the way it starts] (p. 109)

As the brackets indicate, virtually every turn of talk in this discussion overlaps with another. The participants in this event, Michael, Charles, and Maurice, developed into what Gallas called the "big talkers." As their overlapping voices indicate here, there is no space between turns for any other students to enter the discussion. Returning to this talk, however, Gallas was able to unravel patterns in the Science Talks she wanted to promote—and patterns she wanted to avoid. She was able to see, vividly, how ideas were developing, who was having voice (the big talkers), and who was being silenced (all the other students prevented from getting a word in by the constant big-talker repartee).

By recording carefully, Gallas was also able, later, to talk to the group about their variable participation in developing Science Talk. I show this example here to illustrate just how layered talk can become in this kind of exploratory classroom (where there are no explicit rules like "One person talks at a time") and to emphasize that recording quality and comprehensiveness are necessary to capture the nuances of learning in interaction.

So, before you start recording, ensure that you will have data that are worth going back to. The camera should be trained on the entire group. To ensure you have everyone, you may need to get a wide-angle lens. You may also want to start recording by focusing on a small group at work. This way you can be assured of including all participants in the camera and of capturing their voices on the audio. Once you set up the camera and are certain you can capture all the participants, do not move it. Put it on a tripod and leave it. Watching a jostling video later, repeatedly, is not a pleasant experience.

Situate your camera, as much as possible, to catch significant eye gaze and gesture. This is especially important if you will be participating in the interaction during the recording and will not be able to take notes. Eye gaze often can help you recognize student knowledge that will never be verbalized. Gallas describes, for example, the significant looks exchanged by students in her second-grade class as she replayed a tape of their Science Talk for the whole class: "The following day we listened to the tape of that Science Talk with the whole class. Looks were exchanged as the dominant talkers heard themselves" (p. 91).

Rather than recording with a camera, Gallas was witnessing these looks and recording them in her notes. As "looks were exchanged," she registered that the dominant talkers recognized, in some way, that they were having significant affects on the Science Talks. Gallas was able to follow up on this recognition in a discussion with the students and, later, with a suggestion that none of the dominant talkers speaks until the quieter students had contributed. Eye gaze, then, potentially provides us, as teachers, with important cues to how students are processing information and when the time is right to make new suggestions. Gallas was able to capture those looks, in this case, without a camera. While we are talking or bustling about the room, however, students exchange significant looks that we never see. A good recording can capture those and possibly provide a new view on students' awareness level in interactions.

A good recording also captures gesture and body position. Single gestures can lead interactions in new directions. A bowed head can suggest noninvolvement and lead to a student's exclusion. (I have recorded reading groups in which one student had her head down on her desk the entire time.) A stretching, stretching, stretching arm can indicate a desperate need for involvement and bring a student into an interaction. Bodies suddenly crunching up together over a problem or a book can indicate sudden attention to a particular topic or interesting word (I have seen faces suddenly light up and bodies cluster in together when the name of a Pokemon character came up during a reading lesson), leading to more involvement in the subsequent reading tasks. Again, although a camera is ideal for picking up these nonverbal features of interaction (and helping us to notice them after a lesson is long over), if only audio recording is feasible, supplement that with careful note taking to record gesture and body language.

You will also need to be sure that the camera's audio recorder can pick up everyone's talk. If the camera recording quality is low, supplement that recording with a simple audio recorder. If possible, attach an external microphone to your audio recorder and place that in the middle of the table or group. Later, it will be helpful to have audio distinct from the video to pick up talk that is not clear in the video recording. Creating a sound and transcribable audio recording will depend a great deal on the individual acoustics of your room and the configuration of the group you are recording and, as such, will probably be a matter of trial and error. Experiment with different sound configurations and talk to a specialist to hone in on the right combination of equipment. Alter the setting for your focal interaction (would a corner in the back of the room be better?). Do not be discouraged if your first recordings are nearly indecipherable. Gradually, as your ears become more adept at picking out voices and you find the most ideal recording device, and perhaps even change the place you hold the focal interaction, your recordings will become more effective.

These recording suggestions underline important considerations in capturing interaction in classrooms: Record in a way that can account for nonverbal interaction like eye gaze, for the quiet asides by students, for overlapping, and for utterances that may at first seem to be sidetracking. Often learning how to make use of those sidetracks necessitates first understanding their relationship to an entire context. Beginning to understand all the voices that comprise classroom learning necessitates a clear recording of all of them, as well as who is addressing whom.

On the Borders of Events

Just as important as accounting for overlap and apparent side tracking during an event is accounting for interaction that leads up to and follows an event. Within each discrete speech event, there are sets of social and interactional rules that, to varying degrees, guide how language can be used within that event. From event to event, the rules change quickly.

7. Is there a certain event that works well and you would like to know why (so that more activities can work as well)? (Record that event.)
8. Is there a certain event you would like to record to show to students to raise their awareness of social and interactional context? (Record that event.)
8. Is there a certain event you would like to show to a colleague or friend so that you can work together to brainstorm solutions or possible changes? (Record that event.)

Whatever event you choose to focus your camera on will become your object of analysis and possible change. Thus, in selecting an event to record, choose an interaction you will want to view repeatedly—and that you will be able to redo and record again later, making changes. This way, your viewing and analysis can be focused on future classroom learning. For example, you may choose to record a common everyday occurrence like Calendar Time. Calendar Time will then become a focal area of classroom social action for you. By choosing an event that recurs, you need not choose such a traditional classroom feature. Karen Gallas (1995) turned her analytic lens on Science Talks initiated by students' own questions about the natural world, a recurrent event in her inquiry-based second-grade classroom. Instead of a recurrent event, you may choose to focus on a recurrent topic. For example, in a Los Angeles alternative high school, I recorded talk on recurring troublesome topics, including going to jail, writing graffiti, and getting out of gangs. Sometimes these discussions were led by teachers, sometimes by students.

If all aspects of the recording situation are carefully attended to, if the event you record has been thoughtfully chosen, you will have a recording that is high quality and relevant. Not only will this recording allow you to reflect as an individual on how social and interactional dimensions are affecting your teaching practice, but this will also be a recording that you can share with other teachers and possibly administrators. Having high-quality recordings that are sharable and decipherable by many people also increases your agency because it allows you to show others a rationale for the discourse changes you are making in your classroom. Many teachers, for example, wonder how they could introduce events like Gallas' Science Talks when their school administrators judge classroom success on how quiet the room is when they visit. What if these teachers could show how classroom involvement changed with the introduction of this new event? How previously silent students were now involved? Seeing is believing: Good recordings allow others to see your good work and believe in the changes you have made.

VIEWING IN THREE DIMENSIONS

Choosing what to record is a decision that necessitates critical reflection. Viewing those recordings, because watching ourselves teaching sparks more critical reflection, allows us to take an anthropological perspective into our own classrooms. Suddenly we are outsiders looking in. Instead of seeing everything from our own perspective as teachers, we can see many sides of any discussion, conversation, lesson, or sequence. Viewing videos made in our own classrooms, then, allows us to reflect not only on our own actions, but also on the multiple perspectives involved in any interaction. Our goal is to understand those diverse voices and the people behind them. We begin to see how several contexts are layered in our classrooms. We see that these contexts affect how language functions there. By viewing with the social, interactional, and agentive dimensions of discourse in mind, we can judge a *situation* of language use, *rather than individual people*, as effective or ineffective, and plan for realistic changes. A viewing log (see the following chart) can help focus attention on the dimensions that affect classroom discourse while we view each classroom scene.

Viewing Guide: Elements of Context and Individual Agency

DISCOURSE EVENT	DATE/ TIME	ELEMENTS OF SOCIAL CONTEXT	ELEMENTS OF INTERACTIONAL CONTEXT	EVIDENCE OF THE ROLE OF INDIVIDUAL AGENCY
1. *Calendar Time*	2/6/03 Start: 9:03 End: 9:25			
2.				
3.				

Focus your viewing on whatever events you chose to record in the previous section. For example, you should now have recordings of a certain common everyday occurrence like Calendar Time. You would enter Calendar Time and the Date and Time (enter start time and end time) for the initial session in your log under the Event Column. If you, like Karen Gallas, recorded Science Talks, you would put that in the Event Column. If, instead of a recurring event, you choose to record talk on a certain topic, like Graffiti, record Graffiti Talk in the Event Column. Then fill in the Date Column and you are ready to view. No need to transcribe (yet)! But you will need to watch actively, preferably with peers, and take notes. You will probably notice elements of social context, interactional context, and individual agency simultaneously as you view. In the sections that follow, I break out these three dimensions to highlight the kinds of observations you might enter in each column.

Viewing Social Context

Viewing social context requires backing away from the focal event to view the broader concerns that are shaping situations in a classroom or school setting. You can think about it as attaching a wide-angle lens to your own perspective—suddenly you are seeing more than what is in your ordinary viewing lens. Two ways to start this mental wide-angle lens functioning are to (a) view your establishing shots, and (b) share your views with peers, classmates, or your students.

Viewing Social Context
Through Establishing Shots

No matter what your focal event is, begin by viewing the establishing shots and considering how this context affects classroom discourse. While viewing the outside establishing shots, you may use these questions to start your observations:

1. How are students arriving at school?
2. How do they greet each other?
3. What kinds of interactions are students having outside the classroom before they enter?
4. What kinds of interactions are students having as they enter? With faculty or staff? With other students?
5. What kinds of opportunities for socializing will students have during school or after school?

These external social contexts affect how students use language in the classroom. Students who arrive without breakfast may be more silent in class. Students who have not had a chance to talk with each other on the way to class may want to interact with each other in the classroom. Students who know they will have recess at the end of the lesson may be more able to withhold their social talk in class than those who see class as their only opportunity to make connections with their friends.

These contextual features will also affect how students' language functions in the classroom. Often in my night classes at the university, for example, students preface their remarks, even in more abstract discussions, with statements about themselves and their concerns. Their remarks may be functioning in more than one way. Students may be responding in an appropriate way to a discussion about class reading while also raising concerns they faced that day in their classrooms as teachers. Their responses may function to assert their identity not only as students in my class, but also as teachers of their own classes. These statements about their own teaching may also establish common ground with their peers in the university classroom or with me as a fellow teacher. Broad establishing shots potentially foreground context that informs how students in any classroom contribute and how their responses can be heard.

Interior establishing shots can provide additional perspectives on how language functions in the classroom. While viewing interior establishing shots, these questions can get your observations started:

1. How is the classroom arranged?
2. What kind of work is the classroom set up for?
3. Where do the kids sit?
4. What can they look at?
5. What are they wearing?

These elements of classroom context also affect how we understand language in use. If students are wearing shirts that say "LA County Jail," for example, we may hear them differently than if they were wearing Khaki's and blue oxford cloth shirts. If chairs are arranged in a circle that does not include the teacher, students' statements may function as much to accomplish school tasks as to make an impression on each other as peers. If a teacher is included in the circle, language may change its form to accomplish more strictly academic functions. In a classroom with both native English and native Spanish speakers, for example, I noticed Spanish and English as languages of learning when the teacher was out of earshot, but exclusively English as the teacher approached.

Viewing Social Context With Peers, Classmates, and Students

Of course, there is a great deal of relevant social context that your establishing shots will not capture. So, if at all possible, watch these with a peer, a classmate, or your students. Another perspective can always add another layer of context. Compare notes after viewing—see what other viewers know or notice that you may not. If you cannot watch the video with someone else, try to talk with a peer or with classmates or students about what you have seen. At the University of Georgia, for example, several colleagues and I were puzzled by a new development we had noticed in our interactions with students after class. Students were lining up after the first day of class to introduce themselves and shake our hands—even after large lecture classes of 300 undergraduates. Some were making appointments to talk with us during the first week of classes—then simply chatting and leaving after a few minutes, saying, "Well, I just wanted to introduce myself personally." What was going on? Why were students suddenly so excited about shaking hands with professors?

After a little discussion among peers, we came to the bottom of this new interactional mystery. We found out that institutional context was playing a role in shaping these interactions: At the Fall Convocation, the president of the university had urged students to take time to meet their professors personally. He had literally told them it would be a good idea to go up after the first day of class, introduce themselves, and shake their professor's hand. Little did he know this would lead to long lines of students waiting for this "personal" encounter.

To understand why students were so eager to shake their professors' hands, we needed more than simple establishing shots—we needed to back all the way up to Fall Convocation. Similarly, understanding how students interact in our classes or why their behavior changes unexpectedly will require more than a simple view of their arrival to school. Students come from a much wider social sphere that is filled with interactions of which we are completely unaware. It would be a full-time endeavor to keep backing the camera up farther and farther until our view encompassed the entire neighborhood, each home interior, and ultimately the global system affecting each interaction. But hearing multiple perspectives can function like another kind of wide-angle lens. So, if possible, view your establishing shots or talk about the context of your situation with others. Ask the viewing questions and answer them together.

Peers can provide an added perspective on relevant context—and they can also talk through possible solutions. For example, once my peers and I understood how the administration was guiding students to shake professors' hands, we could begin to think about alternatives. Getting to know professors is a good idea—but lining up to shake their hands is not necessarily accomplishing this. Instead, organizing a social event with students at the beginning of the semester, when everyone has a chance to meet and talk, might be a better way to humanize professors and establish relationships between professors and students.

When students take part in the viewing, they are often much more efficient at coming up with answers and solutions. Students might have been able to clarify the handshake line long before the mystery was unraveled by peer professors. In a different school context, after viewing interior establishing shots from the alternative school in Los Angeles, students could talk at length about graffiti—where it came from, who drew it, and what it meant. Teachers drew on this contextual knowledge to find solutions with students, and because students knew who drew which graffiti signs, students were the best monitors of each other. The leaders then, within school, became not the writers of graffiti, but the students who prevented others from writing on school interiors. They also came up with a better plan for graffiti use within the school. Graffiti did not necessarily do damage to other people or property, so drawing was not banned. Students could freely write their signs on paper and post them on bulletin boards. However, when people wrote on bathroom walls, whoever wrote it could be easily identified by their peers, and the responsible party would be required to clean it up. Eventually, then, this same group, in collaboration with the art and drama teachers, created decorative murals on the interior and exterior of the school.

In the graffiti scenario, viewing establishing shots with peers and students, even apart from classroom interaction, could help to build solutions. But even without this kind of concrete problem solving, establishing shots can set the stage for viewing interactional context by keeping social context in mind. Shared viewing of these scenes will build understandings of the many possible worlds that shape how words function in your classroom.

Viewing Interactional Context

If viewing social context involves widening our lens and backing farther away from our focal event, viewing interactional context involves zooming our lens in more tightly on that focal event, to look at how it is patterned, and the sequences within it.

Unlike many features of the broader social context, the machinery of interactional context that can drive talk is not as readily apparent when simply viewing an interaction. To focus your viewing, it may help to take three steps, asking three questions:

1. What are the (usually unspoken) interactional rules governing this speech event (e.g., the teacher asks the questions)?
2. What are the typical sequences within this speech event (e.g., teacher question followed by student answer)?
3. How are they functioning? (They may be functioning in a variety of ways; e.g., student evaluation, peer group affiliation.)

Viewing Interactional Rules in a Speech Event

Although a classroom as a whole usually has explicit rules that govern behavior (e.g., "I will always do my best," "I will respect my property and the property of others"), a class day is comprised of numerous speech events, each with its own set of unspoken interactional rules. As you watch your focal event, you should be able to discern a general framework for your event—what kinds of questions occur where and what kind of responses are appropriate in each miniature interactional context. In a speech event I call "introducing a new book," for example, a typical outline for the event might be as follows:

1. Announce that the class will be reading a new book together (e.g., *Charlotte's Web*). Show the book and describe the cover. (Question: What do you see here?)
2. Ask children about their experiences with this topic (spiders, pigs, farms) or whether they know something about this particular book (read it before, seen the movie). (Question: Have you ever . . . ?)
3. Speculate about what this book might be about using clues from the title and cover. (Question: What could that mean, *Charlotte's Web*?)
4. Start reading. (Question: Are you ready to start reading?)

Within this "introducing a new book" activity, expectations for different kinds of talk are built into each step. Children experienced with this kind of book talk will take part in expected ways. Children who are not might want to start reading immediately, talk about pigs during the "Reading" step, tell everyone the entire story (if they have already heard it or seen the movie), tell about their plans for the weekend, and so on. The possibilities are endless. All children have had experience participating in speech events, but some will not be familiar with the rules of this particular one. Building a classroom culture includes building expectations for these unspoken rules—taking the anthropological perspective as you view makes it possible to see these rules that usually go unnoticed.

Although the "introducing a new book" event is traditionally a teacher-centered modeling of a reading practice, patterns and expectations for patterns are part of even the most (seemingly) loosely structured speech event comprised of predominantly student talk. In her inquiry-based classroom, for example, Gallas discerned a cyclical pattern in the Science Talk speech event:

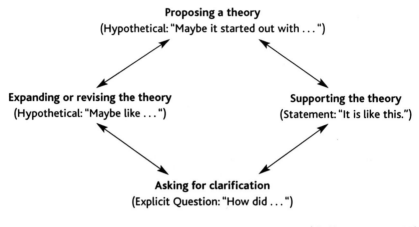

Proposing a theory
(Hypothetical: "Maybe it started out with . . . ")

Expanding or revising the theory
(Hypothetical: "Maybe like . . . ")

Supporting the theory
(Statement: "It is like this.")

Asking for clarification
(Explicit Question: "How did . . . ")

(Gallas, 1995, p. 39)

As you can see, even in this loosely structured exploratory Science Talk, each step includes expectations for a certain kind of contribution. When students start making contributions that do not match the expectations for this kind of talk, the process does not function the same way. So accounting for these patterns is an important first step to understanding certain expectations for speech events. These patterns also govern more specific expectations for sequences within that event, and they help us to understand why sequences function in certain ways. Your next step in viewing, then, will begin to account for these unspoken expectations within sequences.

Viewing Sequences Within a Speech Event

Recall the range of adjacency pairs that occur, without fail, every day in interactions in and out of classrooms: Greeting/Greeting, Question/ Answer, Invitation/Acceptance, Assessment/Disagreement, and Apology/Acceptance. A good way to focus your viewing is to zero in on one of these kinds of adjacency pairs within your focal event. However, interaction is much more than one adjacency pair after another. Instead, the first part of an adjacency pair, perhaps a question, sets up expectations for a second part. Those expectations may not be met or some side questions may be asked and addressed in the middle, as in this example:

Teacher: Taylor, do you know where Jackson is?

Taylor: Jeremiah, did you see Jackson at soccer yesterday?

Jeremiah: No, I think he was feeling sick. His mom said he might go to the doctor and get checked out.

> Taylor: I guess he might be going to the doctor today.

As this exchange illustrates, even a seemingly simple question can quickly turn into more than just two parts—but the intervening talk between Taylor and Jeremiah relates to the teacher's initial question. Technically, Taylor and Jeremiah's sequence is an "insertion sequence" that functions in service of the teacher's initial question about Jackson:

Teacher:	Taylor, do you know where Jackson is?		
Taylor:	Jeremiah, did you see Jackson at soccer yesterday?		Q/A Sequence
Jeremiah:	No, I think he was feeling sick. His mom said he might go to the doctor and get checked out.	Insertion Sequence	
Taylor:	I guess he might be going to the doctor today.		

We call the interaction that attends to an initiating first-pair part—including the related insertion sequences like side questions, misunderstandings, and any other possibly related contributions—a *sequence*.

The question/answer sequence is a traditional focus of classroom discourse analysis. Studies in traditional classrooms have repeatedly shown that questions are almost exclusively asked by teachers. In inquiry classrooms, however, students ask many of the questions and do much of the exploratory talk. Because this kind of nontraditional questioning event is less predictable than a traditional interaction, it is a rich area for investigation. Also, as discussed earlier in the section on recording and agency, recordings of nontraditional events provide both a resource for reflection and evidence in support of teaching methods that are new in your school context (and may be objected to by administrators).

Viewing How Sequences Are Functioning

Questions are also notoriously multifunctional—especially in classroom discourse. Because a simple form like "What's that?" can have so many potential meanings, questions are ripe for misunderstanding. After identifying a questioning sequence, the next step, as a viewer, is to ask how that sequence is functioning in your event. Consider, for example, this question asked during a first-grade field trip to the zoo. The class had just approached the black bear habitat, and they were lucky—one of the bears was out for a stroll.

> Teacher: Oh look! What's that?

How is this token of *What's that* functioning? It takes the form of a question, but this teacher may simply be calling students' attention to the bear. However, she could be asking a quiz question, and because she is a teacher, the chances are good that students will interpret it this way. Remember: How a single form functions is interactionally contingent—its function depends on how people respond to it in interaction. Jack's answer, in this case, effectively turned the teacher's remark into a quiz question:

> Teacher: Oh look! What's that?
> Jack: It's a mammal!

Whatever the teacher's initial intentions, Jack turned the sequence into a chance to display his knowledge. The teacher was impressed, but also a bit surprised by a response that did not match her expectations, so she flashed him a quizzical look. Again, he transformed her look into an opportunity to display some more knowledge:

> Teacher: Oh look! What's that?
> Jack: It's a mammal!
> Teacher: ((*flashes Jack a quizzical look*))
> Jack: Well, can't you see, it has hair?

Although the teacher may have been intent on simply drawing students' attention to the animals (a real live bear!), Jack was creating a classroom lesson. This viewing might lead to a closer look at Jack's knowledge: His enthusiasm for learning and for piping up with extra tidbits of information could become an asset for everyone not only on the fieldtrip, but also back in the classroom.

Questions can be a ripe area of noticing as you view and review. Do not jump to conclusions about how questions (or any other part of a sequence) are functioning. Although some questions may at first seem open ended to us as teachers (remember, "What do you do after school?"), students may perceive teachers as having certain kinds of answers in mind ("Homework!"). Or, as illustrated by Jack and the bear, what initially appears to be a rhetorical question—"What's that?"—can be perceived as a quiz question, especially when asked by a teacher (even in the context of a field trip). Additionally, responses usually accomplish more than one possible function within any sequence of talk. A student may be displaying knowledge for a teacher, practicing new vocabulary, or trying out a new identity. All these might be occurring in a single cry of "It's a mammal!"

As you notice sequences, watch carefully and think about how responses within those sequences are functioning. After transcribing those sequences in detail, you may be able to see the mechanisms that perpetuate certain patterns. For example, after transcribing instances of troublesome talk in her classroom, Gallas was able to see that the way certain "big talkers" worded their responses—as self-evident truths, rather than possibilities—functioned not only to answer the question, but also to block out other students' possible responses. So, as you view, take note of the kinds of sequence that you would like to focus on and that will be worthy of later transcription and analysis.

Viewing Interactional Context With Peers and Students

While you are viewing and thinking about interactional context, you will find that viewing with peers, classmates, and students can help you see sequences and how they are functioning—because peers, classmates, and students all bring different perspectives to bear on what they see. Try to watch your video closely, with a peer, zooming your lens in on a sequence. Then zoom your lens out again to ask how both interactional context and social context are shaping what words can mean.

Viewing for Individual Agency

By viewing a video, we can watch as we interact within a web of social and interactional forces. We can see how our own and our students' words are guided by social and interactional context—perhaps more than by our image of the kind of teachers or learners we want to be. By gaining this awareness of how context controls much of what we say and how we are interpreted, we can begin to gain individual agency over subsequent interactions. Just as we are able to exercise agency (and take responsibility) by making careful choices about what to record in our classrooms, we also exercise agency (and take responsibility) when we view those events by zeroing in on those sequences that can be changed in the future.

However, our own changes are only one side of every interaction. To make changes in our classrooms, we may need to make not only ourselves, but all participants aware of social and interactional contexts. Viewing tapes with students can also increase their agency as learners. Like teachers, students will gain more control over their own classroom roles by the awareness they gain of social and interactional constraints. For example, when troubled by the dominant speakers in her second-grade class, Karen Gallas had them listen to themselves—with the explicit goal of changing patterns of participation in this group. After viewing how the "big talkers" dominated Science Talks, the class was able to brainstorm new discussion instructions that would lead to fuller participation for all students. After listening to the problematic Science Talks as a class, students shared the following suggestions for subsequent talks:

- Classmates should say "I think" when giving an idea.
- Dominant talkers should talk "a little less loud."
- Dominant talkers should wait after saying one idea and not talk again until someone else contributed.
- Dominant talkers should wait 10 minutes before speaking again even if no one else had contributed. (p. 91)

The class took up these suggestions in their next Science Talk and, with some tinkering, brought many new talkers into the discussion. As Gallas writes, these second graders' "explicit work on talk behaviors" had permeated not only the Science Talks, but other areas of the class' work as well. Meanwhile, as the school year continued, she "watched girls who had been terrified of speaking in Science Talks become active and vociferous theory builders," and boys who had previously been the big talkers, "giving up the floor graciously and attentively to other, less extroverted talkers" (p. 94).

By analyzing discourse in her own classroom and then sharing her recordings with students, Gallas was able to turn those second graders into discourse analysts too. The result was heightened awareness of habitual roles—and increased agency for everyone to resist automatically taking up those roles.

This example begins to touch on another way that viewing classroom discourse can begin to provide agency to those viewers. In viewing how language functions in our classrooms, we also witness how identities are shaped there. In Gallas' classroom, certain boys were developing routinized identities as "big talkers" and certain girls as "shy and silent girls." Some of these "shy" girls were also new English speakers, who are often constructed as shy people in English medium classrooms (although they may be extroverts in their home language). As Gallas' work illustrates, however, these identities were neither biological destiny nor necessary because of varied English ability, but largely constructed by the interactional patterns that had developed in Science Talks.

By viewing videotapes with an eye toward how language is controlled by interactional and social contexts, and contemplating what interactional changes could be made to resist those social and interactional forces, individual agency gains more clout as a driving gear of classroom discourse. In other words, because viewing helps you to take the anthropological perspective, to see the unspoken rules that usually go unnoticed, viewing also sharpens your "crap detector" (see chap. 1). You are now able to view patterns that might not be necessary or worth reinforcing. Viewing tapes with students multiplies the power to resist this "crap"—unproductive interactional patterns and the identities associated with them. Remember the classroom discourse gears? When students and peers jump on the individual agency gear with us, everyone has a better chance of resisting unwanted interactional patterns and social identities—and a better chance of learning new ways of interacting in and out of the classroom.

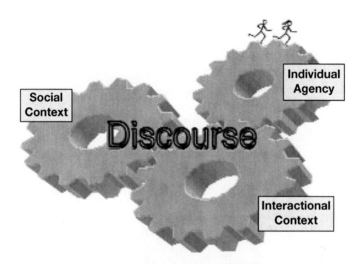

PUTTING IT ALL TOGETHER: RECORDING AND VIEWING IN THREE DIMENSIONS

You are now ready to embark on the journey as an analyst of classroom discourse. Camera and tape recorder in hand, and with an eye for the multiple dimensions of any interaction, key considerations inform your work as you set up a camera and record life at school. As you record, consider the *social context* by videotaping the social spaces inside and outside the classroom, viewing with peers, and considering the potential effects these broader contexts might have on interaction inside the classroom. Also, consider the *interactional context* by setting up a camera in a way that captures all participants within an event, as well as the interactional context that borders that event. Most important, as you take on the responsibility of *individual agency*, ask: What is a relevant event to record? What event will stand up to repeated viewing and yield an analysis that will inform positive change within my classroom?

With a recording that ideally includes establishing shots and with a carefully selected classroom event, you are ready to view those scenes in their multidimensionality. As you sit and actively view with a peer or a classmate, and perhaps later with students, consider the social context:

1. How do the establishing shots contextualize how language functions in my classroom?
2. What other social contexts might be in play?

Consider the interactional context:

1. What are the (usually unspoken) interactional rules governing this speech event? (Make a map or outline.)
2. What are the typical sequences within the focal event and what are the possible normative expectations that accompany them?
3. How are the parts of these sequences functioning? Are they accomplishing multiple functions?

Consider the role of individual agency:

1. How is language use controlled by interactional and social contexts?
2. How can or should this be modified next time?

The viewing guide we began this chapter with is now filled with questions for you to consider through your own recording and viewing.

Viewing Guide: Elements of Context and Individual Agency

EVENT	DATE	ELEMENTS OF SOCIAL CONTEXT	ELEMENTS OF INTERACTIONAL CONTEXT	EVIDENCE OF THE ROLE OF INDIVIDUAL AGENCY
Identify a relevant and recurrent classroom event	Date of the recording/ time start and finish	How do the establishing shots contextualize how language functions in the classroom? What other social contexts might by in play?	Identify a typical pattern for this speech event Identify typical sequences and possible normative expectations that accompany them. How are the parts of these sequences functioning? Are they multi-functional?	How is language use controlled by interactional and social contexts? How can this be modified next time?

As you view your own video, use this guide to help you jot down ideas and compare notes with a peer. These are important but initial considerations. After recording and viewing, you may already have ideas about how you will arrange your classroom context for new ways of interacting. You now are also ready to take a closer look. The next chapter introduces you to the third and fourth steps in classroom discourse analysis, guiding you through the transcription and analysis of a set of data recorded in your own classroom.

QUESTIONS AND ACTIVITIES

Critical Reflection

1. Describe the scene surrounding your school, inside the front door, and down the halls. How do you think this context affects interaction in your classroom?
2. List additional features of the broad social context that may affect interactions in your classroom. Which of these do you think are most important in relation to interaction in your classroom? Why?
3. What are some daily speech events in your classroom? How would you outline or diagram the overarching pattern for that event? What are some of the unspoken conventions that guide participation in this event? Are you detecting any unnecessary conventions that are counterproductive?
4. Think about one speech event in your classroom. What is a typical sequence that occurs within that event? For example, what kinds of questions are usually asked and what kinds of expectations are built into those questions? Do you think these sequences are indicative of patterns of interaction outside the classroom?
5. What are some speech events that take place outside of your classroom? How do you think these are patterned? Do you think these patterns affect talk inside your classroom?

Reflective Activities

1. Watch a movie or TV show of your choice. What techniques does the director use to illustrate layers of context surrounding an interaction? For example, do you view the outside of a building before you view the interaction inside that building? What effects do these layers have on your viewing of the interaction? (In the case of a TV show, you may want to think about the introductory scenes repeated, during the theme music, before each weekly episode.)

2. After recording establishing shots and a focal interaction in your classroom, watch your video and fill out a viewing guide with a peer. Use the focusing questions listed in the chapter's conclusion. After you've recorded and viewed, consider any changes you might make in how you arrange for interaction in your classroom.

Viewing Guide: Elements of Context and Individual Agency

DISCOURSE EVENT	DATE/ TIME	ELEMENTS OF SOCIAL CONTEXT	ELEMENTS OF INTERACTIONAL CONTEXT	EVIDENCE OF THE ROLE OF INDIVIDUAL AGENCY
1.				
2.				
3.				

3. Explore speech events that take place outside your classroom, in your students' homes, neighborhood parks, church, or other likely setting. You might do this by having students record a speech event in their out-of-school life and share it with you and the class. Work with the students to identify a pattern for this speech event and the sequences within it.

SUGGESTED READING

Books and articles by Karen Gallas provide excellent examples of the use of classroom discourse analysis to inform inquiry-based teaching methods. I have drawn heavily on her study written up in *Talking Their Way into Science: Hearing Children's Questions and Theories, Responding With Curriculum*. Paul Seedhouse's *The Interactional Architecture of the Language Classroom: A Conversation Analysis Perspective* provides step-by-step detailed suggestions for looking carefully at interactional context. Shirley Brice Heath's linguistic anthropological look at language inside and outside of school, *Ways With Words: Language, Life and Work in Schools, Communities and Classrooms*, discusses different speech events inside and outside classrooms and includes many examples of oral and literate traditions not only in schools, but also in students' homes and community settings like the church. These examples provide good models for someone considering exploring speech events outside the classroom. The linguistic anthropologist, Dell Hymes, is responsible for the original definition and elaborated discussion of speech events and the kinds of cultural expectations that accompany them. His model for careful analysis of speech events can be found in his book *Foundations of Sociolinguistics: An Ethnographic Approach*. For those who would like to pursue the theoretical foundations for taking a layered, discourse-based approach to viewing classroom talk, Mikhail Bakhtin's *The Dialogic Imagination* discusses how broad historical and social context are part of any dialogue—and how dialogue is embedded in any singular utterance. This discussion is taken up in Jan Blommaert's lucid theoretical discussion in chap. 3, "Text and Discourse," in his book *Discourse.*.

4

GETTING TO THE TALK II
Transcribing and Analyzing
in Three Dimensions

PREVIEW QUESTION Before reading this chapter, think of students in your class who have distinctive (to you) ways of speaking. How could you represent that distinction in a transcript?

Think of the different voices that you, as a teacher, use in your classroom. How could you represent these distinct voices in a transcript?

How do these different ways of speaking accomplish different functions for you and your students?

I transcribe each day's play and stories and conversations and then make up my own stories about what is happening. The next morning, my reality will be measured alongside the children's.

—Vivian Gussin Paley (1990, p. 18)

In chap. 3, we walked through the first two steps of classroom discourse analysis: *recording* and *viewing*. This chapter continues through the third and fourth steps of the process: *transcribing* the talk and action and, finally, *analyzing* those transcripts. Again, with each step, I provide guidelines for how to account for the multidimensionality of discourse—social and interactional context as well as individual agency. By the end of this chapter, you will be ready to begin transcribing and analyzing a set of data recorded in your own classroom. This will be the start of a new kind of journey through your school—as classroom discourse analysts.

TRANSCRIBING IN THREE DIMENSIONS

By now you have recorded a focal event in your classroom as well as the context around the school and classroom that may inform talk in that event; you have viewed those scenes, identifying broad interactional patterns within the focal event, and sequences within it. You have made hypotheses about how they are functioning. You may have even started to make changes in how you conduct that event when it occurs again.

At this point, transcribing—writing down what everyone said—may sound like a time-consuming and trivial activity. But transcripts can become powerful documents that shape perspectives on classroom interaction, future interactions, and the course of learning in our classrooms. For those reasons, transcribing is anything but trivial. Also, because transcribing, like recording, removes us another degree from the lived experience of interaction, critical considerations must inform just how we represent talk as we write it down. Just as we make selections while recording about how far we back the camera up, how much we zoom in, and which kinds of contexts we consider critical, while transcribing we are constantly making decisions about what level of detail to include. We are always trimming away contexts and potential considerations while focusing on certain elements. Transcribing involves continually—mindfully—weighing the importance of social and interactional context, creating ways to represent that context, and using this powerful form of documentation as a source of agency in schools. As the teacher/researcher Vivian Paley put it, transcripts became a way for her to measure her own reality alongside the realities of her students.

Transcribing for Social Context

How can social context be represented in a transcript? At first it seems, as a record of words spoken, that a transcript is only involved with the interactional and individual dimensions of discourse. But transcripts will represent social context regardless of whether we intend them to. Like dialogue in a novel, a transcript invites readers to visualize a scene, imagine how each speaker sounds, and make judgments about those speakers and that situation based on their imagined view of the scene. As you share your transcript with peers or students, you may be giving it to them without the video or audio accompaniment. So as you transcribe, you need to consider how readers will view the interaction and how they will hear the distinct voices. These are features you can control, to a degree, in how you transcribe.

Establishing the Scene

As you introduce an excerpt, you will have to devise ways to re-create relevant aspects of the experience of the event without the images and sounds from a video. You can efficiently identify the players in the scene and where they are with a list of participants and a simple diagram. For example, if four children are sitting with a teacher at a round table for a reading group, you could introduce the transcript with a diagram like this:

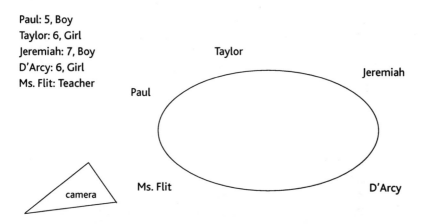

Paul: 5, Boy
Taylor: 6, Girl
Jeremiah: 7, Boy
D'Arcy: 6, Girl
Ms. Flit: Teacher

This picture instantly and easily places people in the interaction. Include the camera in your diagram so you will be able to orient your diagram to the video. This quick view of the scene will also be helpful later as a quick reference to the situation. As you make your diagram you can vary the level of detail—including books or computers on the table, a bookcase, whiteboard, or parent conference center, for example. You might also choose to make a diagram from a still shot of a video by writing the names of the participants across that image. If, in contrast, you have audio recording only, you should take careful notes about nonaudible features of the interaction being recorded. A diagram should be the first thing you include in these notes. Then as you go back to transcribe, you will be able to place the participants and the voices.

You may also want to briefly introduce the excerpt before you start the word-for-word transcription. A simple setting of the scene might be: "The students are seated at an oval table, facing Ms. Flit, who is holding up a copy of the book they will be reading that day." Then the transcription begins.

Recognizing Unique Ways of Speaking
and Communicating

Once you begin transcribing, you face many more decisions about
how to represent the textures of classroom interaction in the flattened
medium of written language. Although writing by its nature flattens the
character of our speech, you need to be able to show, in a written transcript, that there are unique ways of speaking and communicating non-
verbally. People have significantly different ways of talking, and much of
what we mean comes across in *how* we say something, not only in *what*
we are saying. Moreover, much of what we ascribe to a student's or a
teacher's "personality" (shy, outgoing, lazy, ambitious, spacey) comes
from how that person speaks.

For example, consider these two possible transcriptions of the same
statement, part of a seventh grade language arts lesson (adapted from
Bloome et al., 2005):

A) Teacher: We are talking about 1865.
                     And we are talking about a period of
                     time when slavery was still instituted.

versus

B) Teacher: We're talkin' about 1865.
                     And we're talkin' about a period of
                     time when slavery was still instituted.

Transcripts A and B are different representations of the same teacher
uttering the same sentences; representing her talk differently creates a
different portrait of who she is. Although A may be a more standardized
representation of her talk, it does not capture the nuance that the contractions and elisions represented in B do. As this example illustrates, you do
not want your transcript to make everyone sound the same, and transcribing distinct features of an individual's talk can help represent distinct ways of speaking.

Ways of speaking do not vary only among individuals; they also vary
according to context and purpose. The different ways of speaking illustrated by Transcripts A and B might accomplish very different goals with
their different forms of talk. A teacher going over the directions to a standardized test will have different diction than that same teacher engaged
in a lively discussion with her students during review for that test—and
those different ways of speaking, used in different contexts, accomplish
distinct functions. As teachers, we have many different voices for many
different purposes of classroom talk. These are distinctions you do not
want to lose in your transcript.

Avoiding Stigmatized Transcription

While you do want to capture distinctive personal speech styles as well as functional differences in ways of speaking, you want to avoid stigmatizing certain individuals by the way you transcribe their voices. In particular, you do not want to end up overly marking speech that is different from your own. For example, compare the representations of teacher and student in this hypothetical example:

Teacher: Are you **going to** finish your book tonight?

Student: **Yeah**, I'm **gonna** try.

Do you detect the bias in this example? The teacher and student are represented differently here—and that difference is encoded in how *going to* is transcribed. In the United States, few people say "going to" in spoken English; nearly everyone says "gonna" (try listening for this one day). But the teacher here is represented as using English formally, and the student—with the combination of "yeah" and "gonna"—as using English informally. Were this taken from a real recording, I would suggest listening again. Probably the teacher said "gonna" too. But because the student's talk is transcribed differently, this student is represented as distinctly more slack than this formal teacher. This kind of stigma can carry consequences. One might begin to doubt whether this student really will finish that book.

Furthermore, these distinctions in transcription can fall along race or class lines. For example, transcribing all the vernacular features of African-American children's speech in painstaking detail, while the European-American children's speech is represented in strictly standard written orthography, will result in a wildly skewed transcript of classroom interaction. *Nobody speaks in standard written English.* So, as a transcriber, you need to make carefully considered decisions about which features of vernacular speech you want to include. The following observation from a lawyer looking at transcripts in a court trial (excerpted from a Forensic Linguistics listserv) illustrates the problems inherent in transcription that can become "editorializing."

I am engaged in a criminal case in a United States District Court. One item of evidence is a tape recording of my client and others. Over my objection the judge has allowed the jury to read a transcript prepared by the other side, the prosecution. The transcript is an aid to the jury, though I believe the recording is quite audible/understandable without the transcript.

The several voices heard on the tape are those of black adult males and females. Most of them speak quite casually. The concern I had was with the spelling of the use of a number of words. For example, instead of "What's up", the transcript reads "Wassup." Other examples: "nuttin'" (for nothing), as well as sayin', dealin', nothin', gonna, soundin'.

My concern involves spelling. . . . I get the sense that the spelling in this transcript conveys a mocking quality.

Additionally, where a person speaks emphatically, the transcriber included exclamation points. I objected to this as "editorializing."

I should also point out that the sound as written appears to be largely correct. Yet when it comes to transcripts from court proceedings, I do not see this. I speak a fairly standard American English, and probably drop my ending g's and say prob'ly rather than probably. Thankfully, no court reporter who has transcribed my speech has ever put it close to how I really sound.

This courtroom example draws our attention to just those features of transcription that we need to carefully consider as we transcribe—and how powerful representations in transcripts can be. Nearly all spoken English involves contractions and dropped gs. Why represent these selectively? In this case, they could lead to a prison sentence. In a classroom, they could lead to misjudgments about students' abilities and future learning.

As these examples suggest, there is a fine line between making everyone sound the same and stigmatizing the voices of those who strike you as different. Through reflection and shared viewing, that is the fine line you want to walk while creating your transcription. Avoiding homogenizing voices or stigmatizing voices is not simply a matter of transcribing "accurately." Rather, it is a matter of weighing social context (our own social histories and the social histories of the voices we are transcribing) and how it informs the way we transcribe different ways of speaking. Each decision made in transcribing a voice is a decision about what kinds of social context are affecting this talk and how you want to represent that social context. Transcribing for social context involves thinking about the social history of each speaker (including habitual ways of speaking and interacting), the social history of the transcriber (including habitual ways of speaking and interacting), and the social context of transcription as we create a representation of that speaker's voice.

Transcribing for Interactional Context

As shown earlier, transcribing for social context involves attending to context outside the interaction. In contrast, transcribing for interactional context involves capturing how a speaker's talk is oriented to the immediate talk (or silence) within a speech event. Although representing social context involves making decisions about how to represent voices in relation to their social histories outside that interaction, representing interactional context involves making decisions about how to represent voices with respect to one another within a single interaction. The act of transcribing itself often reveals previously hidden sequences and nuances of interaction that lend an understanding to talk in classrooms. Silences, nonverbal contributions like eye gaze, pauses, overlap, and variation in volume and pitch all contribute to discourse functionality. It is important, then, while transcribing to listen to and watch for these nuances and to represent them in your transcript.

Representing Silences and Nonverbal Contributions

Sometimes the most dramatic feature of an interaction is silence. Imagine waiting through 5 minutes of silence during a class discussion. This takes guts! But silence is not only dramatic, it is also thinking time. Consider, for example, the significance of this teacher's silence in a traditional first-grade classroom I observed:

Austin: ((*reading aloud*)) "Please turn in your form to the secret airy."

Teacher: ((*silence*))

Austin: ((*continues reading*)) "secretary! between the hours of…"

During these silences, I can almost hear a student's brain clicking (and the teacher biting her tongue). Here, during that silence, *secret airy* is magically transformed into a word that makes more sense—*secretary*. Through multiple interactions like this one, students are learning that they can read new words on their own. Both sociocultural theory and research on classroom interaction confirm that waiting, allowing students to think through reading miscues like this or questions asked by a teacher or peer, raise the level of learning in a classroom (Owocki & Goodman, 2002; Rowe, 1986). Because this waiting is so important to student learning, because for many teachers it does not come naturally, and because we know there are interactional pressures not to wait, keeping track of silences like this could be a crucial component of a transcript and an analysis.

If silences become a significant feature of your transcript, you will need to decide the level of detail necessary; if you are investigating your own patterns of wait time within question sequences, it may be important to time those pauses. Research has shown that the difference between waiting 1 second after a question and 3 seconds after a question can be critical to change the pace of student interaction. It can invite more participation as well as more thoughtful questions and answers. Monitoring the time of pauses in your classroom could have significant benefits (Rowe, 1986). Timing pauses may help you notice and compare how they function. This need not involve fancy instruments.

You can time pauses the same way you count seconds when you do not have a watch with you. Count like this, "no – one – thou – sand – one, one – one – thou – sand, two – one- thou – sand, etc." Each syllable can be counted as two tenths of a second, with the pause in between each "thousand" marking an entire second:

no – one – thou – sand – uh
.02 - .04 - . 06 - 08 – 1.0
one – one – thou – sand – uh
1.2 – 1.4 – 1.6 - 1.8 - 2.0

If you wait in silence for "no- one- thou-sand-uh- one-one- thou," while listening to a transcript, that is a 1.6 second pause. You can note that in the transcript like this:

Austin: ((reading)) "Please turn in your form to the secret airy."
Teacher: (1.6) ((silence))
Austin: "secretary ((continues reading)) between the hours of…"

Although your approximate counting may not match precisely the ticking of a stopwatch, it will be close, and, most important, it will be consistent for you. This will allow you to make relative comparisons.

As you start to notice pauses, you may also see that within those silences usually other forms of communication are occurring. If the nonverbal behaviors seem significant, transcribing them is a way to ensure they remain visible and analyzable. Double parentheses are one possible tool for transcribing the nonverbal. For example, while one student is thinking about a reading miscue, the teacher may not be the only one waiting in silence. You might want to record the nonverbal behaviors of the other students:

Austin: ((*reading*)) "Please turn in your form to the secret airy."
Teacher: (1.6) ((*silence*))
Students: ((*looking at paper*))
Abby: ((*looks from paper to teacher to Austin*))
Austin: secretary ((*continues reading*)) between the hours of…"

When transcripts include these descriptions of nonverbal behavior, they offer an initial interpretation of this sequence. In this case, including the nonverbal behavior of Abby and the other students indicates the pressure this teacher may be under, interactionally, to correct Austin, rather than wait for him to re-read the word in context. Abby seems to be wondering what the teacher will do—but the other students seem unconcerned with the reading of "secret airy." All of these observations and many more potentially enter into transcription. You are making decisions, again, about how much of the interactional context you need to include. If, on consideration, nonverbal interactions seem significant in your classroom, another option is to give them an entire column:

SPEAKER	NONVERBAL	VERBAL
Austin:	Reading from a handout	Please turn in your form to the secret airy.
Teacher:	(1.6) Silently waiting, looking at Austin.	
Students:	Looking at the same paper Austin is reading from	
Abby:	Looks from paper to teacher, then back to Austin	
Austin:	Self-corrects then continues reading from the handout.	secretary between the hours of

This kind of table may give nonverbal interaction a higher priority (visually) than it usually gets in a transcript. In her essay, "Transcription as Theory," Elinor Ochs (1979) points out that because transcription traditionally features talk, it privileges verbal over nonverbal communication. If you want to change this bias, you need to change how you transcribe. To prioritize nonverbal or some other aspect of interaction, you can give that feature its own column and move that column to the center or the far left (left is a privileged position in a left–right reading system). Once you start experimenting with columns, double parentheses, and other possibilities, you will see there are infinite options for representing interaction—including silences—in a transcript.

Representing Overlap and Near Overlap

Just as dramatic in a classroom as silence is total lack of silence. Sometimes overlapping voices can be a prominent feature of classroom talk. Often as teachers we can fear that this overlap is preventing learning. By representing overlap in a transcript, however, we can begin to examine more closely just how it is functioning and who is saying what.

In the following interaction, for example, square brackets indicate overlap and clarify who is answering first:

> Teacher: What do all the men have on their heads?
> Tiffany: Ha[ts
> Rene: [Hats

Tiffany answers the teacher's question, and Rene, a new English speaker, answers swiftly on her heels. But once the transcript is printed this way, it raises a question: Is Rene answering the teacher's questions or closely monitoring his peers? It is impossible to answer that question on the basis of this single sequence. However, if Rene always waits for a hint from peers before providing his own answer, his teacher may want to think more carefully about Rene's form of participation. She might consider asking different kinds of questions or mandating wait time before students respond. In contrast, this pattern of overlap may suggest that Rene is learning a lot from his peers. Working in collaborative peer groups might be an effective approach for him. In any case, noticing this pattern of overlap could lead Rene's teacher to try orchestrating interactions differently. Initially overlap may be difficult to hear and transcribe, but attending to it could indicate how interactional patterns develop in your classroom. Using square brackets at the point of initial overlap (as shown above) is a simple convention for noting this.

There are also many cases of near overlap—in which someone talks between another participant's words. When the first speaker continues a sentence after the intervening talk, transcribe this continuation using latching marks as follows:

> Teacher: The train people that=
> Tiffany: Like this ((*Pointing to the picture emphatically*))
> Teacher: =that drive the train.

In this case, the latching marks (equals sign) indicate that the teacher's sentence continues across Tiffany's interjection.

Representing Different Ways of Speaking

As discussed earlier, a large part of representing different ways of speaking, including degrees of formality or variation in dialect, involves considerations of how social contexts outside the immediate interaction affect how language functions within that interaction. But many different ways of speaking are also tuned carefully to the immediate interactional context: Loud talking, whispering, dramatic changes in pitch or volume—all of these different voice effects can have functional differences in interaction, and there are standardized ways of transcribing them. The following are standard transcription conventions originally formulated by Gail Jefferson (1984):

Exaggerated volume: ALL CAPITALS
Elongated single sounds: Elo::ngated S::ingle So::unds
Whispering or other feature: ((*whispering*))
Raised pitch: You're ↑kidding
Lowered pitch: No, I'm ↓ not
Quiet voice: *something said in a quiet voice*

Although these are typical and recognizable within the field of discourse analysis, you may find other ways you prefer to represent pitch, overlap, or other voice characteristics. You do not need to use these particular conventions, but you do need to be clear about what your transcript means and how it should be read.

Representing Different Addressees and Speakers

Paying attention to who is speaking to whom is another crucial component of transcription, especially in classrooms, where interactions usually include more than two speakers. Often representing an addressee is as simple as indicating this as a stage direction in double parentheses, as in this example:

Cory: ((*to Darius*)) Is today the magic show?
Darius: ((*looks from Cory to the teacher*))
Teacher: No, the magic show is on Friday. How many days away is that? ((*to Darius*))

Representing Different Conversations and/or Multiple Topics

Often interaction does more than break off into simple side comments here and there. Instead, it can schism, resulting in multiple simultaneous conversations. This kind of splintering can be represented in a transcript with columns. For example, during a current events speech event in a Los Angeles high school classroom, what was initiated as a discussion about the anniversary of the *Brown v. the Board of Education* Supreme Court ruling schismed, through word play, into another conversation, filled with bantering about James Brown and Al Green. When we analyzed this event, my colleagues and I decided it could best be represented in two columns: one for the "Teacher Script" and one for the "Student Script."

TEACHER SCRIPT	STUDENT SCRIPT
T: What did the Supreme Court decision in *Brown v. the Board of Education* have to do with?	
	S: James Brown?
	S: Richard Brown?
	S: Shut-up
	S: You shut up
	S: James Brown?
	S: Al Green

Columns can also be useful in representing an interaction that schisms into two different topics. In this case, for example, when kids were playing the Phonics Game™ and one of the cards contained the name of a Pokémon character, I called one column the "Teacher Zone" and the other the "Student Zone."

TEACHER ZONE	STUDENT ZONE
Teacher: -C- -H- says?	
David: Can	
Rene: an- chan-	
Teacher: Chan- -C- -Y-(2.0)	
Rene: Chances.	
Teacher: Cha:n:c:y	
	Rene: Chancy.
	Rene: Ohp ((looking at David and smiling)) Pokémon.
	David: It's a Pokémon.
Teacher: And you have to tell me why the –a- is short.	
	David: Chancy! I got it.

Note that sometimes students participate in the teacher zone. In teacher-directed classrooms, this is where they are expected to be. But only students are in the student zone. Language functions differently, and identities are different in the interactional context of one column from the interaction context of another—although these interactions may be occurring in the same place, embedded in one another. Friends talking about Pokémon use language differently than students sounding out words. Students answering a teacher's question about current events may talk differently than students who are bantering about pop culture personalities. Irving Goffman (1961) calls the interaction that develops alongside more sanctioned institutional talk *underlife*. Underlife flourishes in class-rooms—and can be a source of deeper and more relevant classroom learning if pulled into the curriculum. That is, it *can be* if we as teachers have the courage to cross over into that column. Transcribing underlife can be a first step toward noticing these interactions and changing the way they function in the classroom.

As these examples have shown, however, interactional pressures can control our behavior as teachers. In some cases, students' nonverbal behavior pressures us to answer questions too quickly or not wait for a reader to self-correct a miscue. In other cases, expectations built into our event model of, for example, playing-the-Phonics-game or conducting-current-events, will pressure us into ignoring student comments that stray from that predictable pattern. Transcribing, however, involves noticing and noting interactional context in ways that reveal new possi-bilities for action in the classroom—and possibilities for augmented agency.

Transcribing for Individual Agency

Paradoxically, by understanding our lack of agency, we have more agency. Because we know about the potential for colloquial features of talk to be transcribed unequally, we can struggle to be fair about how we represent colloquial features of talk in a transcript. Because we are aware that, following a question or a reading miscue, interactional pressure builds to provide an answer or a correction, we can transcribe the evi-dence of those interactional pressures that make teachers impatient or cause students to blurt out answers without thinking. By using our understandings of the ways social and interactional contexts influence how and what we transcribe, we are better able to weigh exactly how we want to represent those contexts. This means taking responsibility for the purpose of our transcript. Resisting being unwittingly socially and inter-actionally contextualized through transcription necessitates taking up individual agency in the transcription process. The following considera-tions about transcription conventions and representation can enhance this mindfulness.

First, although transcription conventions are needed, they can be lim-iting. The lawyer who, in the prior excerpts, observed transcript bias in court, concluded with a question: "Are there any standards on how speech should be transcribed?" I have indicated some standard tools for representing talk and options for using them, yet taking responsibility for representations in your transcript means you need to consider far more than a simple set of transcription conventions. We need to consider social context in selecting these tools. We may also need to create new ways of representing talk and interaction.

To present voices fairly, we also need to resist the illusion that there is even a possibility of re-creating speech perfectly in a written transcript—to focus, instead, on how that speech is functioning and how transcription can illustrate that function. For example, because I have been doing research in Georgia, and because I am not a native of this region, elongated vowels are obvious to me. Because they are so noticeable, I could easily find myself unthinkingly transcribing all the elongated vowels, using the conventional colon, as in "Have a great Da::y." Instead, however, I have chosen not to transcribe elements that strike me only because they are part of a speech variety that is not my own. During the phonics game, however, transcribing certain elongated vowels (and other sounds) is important because the teacher exaggerates these sounds in an attempt to make them explicit for her students. Transcribing the elongated vowel in "cha::n" when the teacher is trying to tell her something about "short *a*" is important because it is intended to serve a particular function in the interaction. In summary, although conventions will be helpful, as teachers we need to jettison the illusory goal of accuracy and instead transcribe with the goal of relevance.

Next, to avoid unwittingly contextualizing yourself or your students, bring multiple perspectives to bear on any transcript. This is another paradox: As teachers, the more we are aware of the perspective of others, the more possibility for individual agency we have. As you begin to write down what you hear on your tape, you may notice that at times you do not understand what you are transcribing. Noticing this is important. Questions that come up in the transcription process provide you with an excellent opportunity to draw on the perspectives of others. Sharing your transcript with peers, classmates, and students can add layers of awareness to a transcript and may dramatically change how you represent and understand voices within a transcript—and your classroom. For example, while working in an alternative high school in Los Angeles, I asked many students to explain why they had been kicked out of previous schools. When Federico replied with this story about the last school he had attended, I could not figure out how, exactly, it connected:

> Federico: Our neighborhood started having shit with that
> neighborhood down there? So I went over there to
> the bus so they came and hit me up I said my neigh-
> borhood and they said fuck that so they socked me?
> ↑Everybody rushed me. hn. Then the next day we,
> we and the homeboys went down (0.6) and they got
> me. So that's it.

How was this story an explanation of being kicked out of school? It just sounded like a fight story to me. But after spending some time in the break room with Federico and his friends, wearing earphones, listening to tapes, and reading along on transcripts, I understood. After listening to Federico talk about this transcript, I knew this was a story not only about a fight, but also about Federico's lack of agency. He could not even take the bus to his last school (he only lasted a week there) because the bus stop was in a rival gang's territory. Here is an annotated version of the story, reflecting this new perspective:

Federico: Our **neighborhood** [gang] started having shit with
           that **neighborhood** [gang] down there?
           So I went over there to the bus so they came and **hit
           me up** [asked me what gang I was from]
           I said my neighborhood [remained loyal to my gang
           by claiming my allegiance, even in front of these
           threatening rivals, in their territory].
           and they said fuck that so they socked me?
           ↑ **Everybody rushed me**. hn. [He was one person,
           attacked by a big group of people]
           Then the next day we, **we and the homeboys went
           down** (0.6) [His gang retaliated the next day, as a
           group]
           and **they got me**. [The school authorities caught
           Federico fighting, so they kicked him out of school]
           So that's it.

Federico stood up for his gang by claiming his allegiance to them. But that loyalty inevitably led to a fight—and to Federico getting kicked out of school. As framed by Federico, he had no choice in the matter. He was not necessarily against school or actively belligerent toward anyone. He did what he had to do. By talking to Federico, I was able to recognize the dilemma his story contained (and how this story functioned as an explanation for why he left school): He had to go to the bus stop to get to school. The bus stop is in a rival gang's territory. He had to claim his loyalty to a different gang, so they beat him up. The next day, his gang had to retaliate to protect their name and self-respect. This led to a big gang fight. The fight indicated to the principal that Federico better not go to that school.

I am not endorsing gang violence. However, understanding its source and how it keeps kids away from school may be the first step toward bringing those kids back to school. Developing an understanding of talk collaboratively with students like this has the potential to enhance our agency—and theirs. Only after we understand a student's story from that student's perspective can we start to problem solve. Questions rise to the surface: "Why do you 'have to' do these things?" "Who is telling you this?" At the time, I was not teaching at the school: I was observing and recording. But I was also talking with teachers about what I recorded and saw. At this school, the atmosphere was such that Federico's teachers could sit down with him and say, "Okay, we know this situation about your gang involvement and rivalries. So: How are we going to keep you in this school? How can we help you resist the sense that you 'have to' claim your gang, get in fights, etc.?" Having Federico's perspective articulated in a way his teachers could understand was an important step toward getting his story across—and to moving on to problem solving. In fact, rival gangs were able to attend this alternative school, and they did not fight each other. Sharing backgrounds in this way, teachers and students did not need to feel they were being controlled by antagonisms brought on and fostered by social contexts and interactional misunderstandings. Transcribing together gave Federico and me a document that could be understood by both of us—and enable us to present a situation from our different perspectives.

We can also discover different facets of our own perspective in transcription by going back to our tapes and re-reading a transcript after some time has elapsed. As teachers, even within ourselves, from day to day, our perspective potentially changes, and we can see ourselves and our students differently. Karen Gallas (2003) articulates this changing perspective within herself when she describes her initial attempts to understand Denzel, a child she struggled to reach in her first- and second-grade classroom. Through her struggle, she recognized that her framing expectations for him, shaped by her own identity and ways of imagining, diminished her ability to see his progress:

> I realize now that my sense of failure with Denzel was, in part, due to my inability to see the steps he was making. I was expecting the form and content of his imaginative work to mimic or mirror mine. In fact, it was because we were so different that I perceived our interactions as being without real gains. (p. 40)

She was able to review her interactions with Denzel by looking back at field notes she had taken from multiple interactions and classroom talk she had recorded and transcribed. This going back adds new perspectives—simply the distance elapsed between the recording and the transcribing of an interaction can provide us with new ways of seeing and hearing what we write down. This is another important way of giving ourselves multiple perspectives when we transcribe: Transcribe once, then wait. Go back to your transcript a week later and read it while you watch the video. What do you need to change? What did you hear wrong? What did you represent in a way that seems inaccurate now? Your transcript will be powerful as long as it is a living document, so transcribe with action in mind. Your transcript will be most powerful when it is informed by multiple considered perspectives.

I repeat: Transcripts can be powerful documents. A transcript is something you can show people not only to gain their feedback, but also to promote change. Showing Federico a transcript helped us clarify his story—but it also helped him and his teachers consider his actions and the best strategies to keep him in school. Reviewing her transcripts helped Karen Gallas clarify her interactions with Denzel—but it also helped her rethink the role of imagination—and various ways of imagining—in her classroom. In our classrooms, recording and transcribing are powerful ways of documenting our actions—and augmenting our potential to make classroom interaction more productive.

DOING THREE DIMENSIONAL ANALYSIS: AN EXAMPLE— IGNORING A STUDENT'S CONTRIBUTION

At this point, "doing analysis" might seem a bit anticlimactic. Much of the analytic work is already done in selecting events to record, focusing on sequences within those events, viewing that interaction, and then transcribing. Now, however, you have a distinct analytic object to focus on. As you reflect on how social context, interactional context, and individual agency are in play within it, your analysis will bring it back to life. Having recorded, viewed, and transcribed with these dimensions in mind, you are well prepared for a rich analysis. Remember, the heart of discourse analysis is an examination of the relationship between context and language in use. To illustrate, this section walks through a possible analysis of a single transcript, beginning with a look at how social context affects discourse in the following interaction.

Social Context

After viewing the establishing shots, you should be able to decide on which elements within those you want to focus on. The excerpt we are about to analyze is taken from 2 years of research I conducted at an elementary school in the rural southeastern United States. My drive there took me past farmland and pastures—but also by rapidly rising subdivisions with middle-class homes. The school, surrounded by green grass and trees, is located on a picturesque winding road and sits atop a small rise. There is plenty of room to run and equipment to play on during recess. However, there are also several portable classrooms out back. Like the rising subdivisions, these portables represent rapid growth in this area, which is quickly changing from a rural small town to a third-tier suburb of a large metropolitan area.

I include these details when contextualizing this example because this rapid growth means the schools in this area have many more students and different kinds of students than they did only a few years ago. Because of this school's earlier history of slow growth in a small community, it went for many years with minimal change. Still, at the time of this recording, the teaching was traditional, built on expectations that students there would be from backgrounds familiar to the teachers. There were initially no programs or curricular innovations in place, for example, which addressed the growing multilingual population at the school. During my second year of research there, this school began a program for English-language learners, but during my first year, these new English speakers were simply distributed between mainstream classes. These primarily Latino students who were recent immigrants had joined a school population of predominately White students and a substantial minority of Black students.

This excerpt is taken from an event within a reading group that includes one of these new English speakers (Rene), two African-American children (Tiffany and Danny), two Euro-American children (Sara and Jenny), and their Euro-American teacher. All of these students have been identified for different reasons as struggling readers. For this reading group, they have been pulled out to meet in a separate classroom and are sitting at a small table. In the following sequence, five second graders are reading through a picture book with their teacher, and she has paused to ask them questions about one of the pictures.

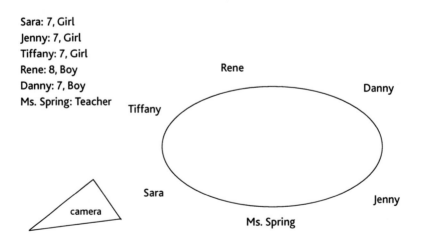

Sara: 7, Girl
Jenny: 7, Girl
Tiffany: 7, Girl
Rene: 8, Boy
Danny: 7, Boy
Ms. Spring: Teacher

Train Hats

Teacher:	What do all the men have on their heads?
Tiffany:	Ha[ts
Rene:	[Hats
Teacher:	Hats. Do men wear a lot of hats now?
Danny:	Some don't. The train dudes- the train people wear they wear these like, big ol [things that
Teacher:	[The train people, that=
Tiffany:	Like this ((*Pointing to the picture emphatically*))
Teacher:	=that drive the train (0.2) wear hats.
Danny:	And somebody better put on some um things for um there little thing cause they hurt their ears. ((*pointing into his ears*))
Teacher:	Ah,
Danny:	Because, the noise is come in the air and (0.4)
Teacher:	But do men, do a lot of men wear hats now?

After broadly contextualizing and presenting your example this way, the next step in the analysis of social context is to look at the text. You want to think about how the text is related to social context, including social histories that precede this interaction. To do so, begin by asking yourself these questions:

- Which particular words and/or grammatical forms and/or ways of speaking stand out for you?
- How are they functioning?
- Is discourse being informed by contexts outside this interaction?
- If so, how can you tell?

What strikes you? At this point, all you are doing is noticing certain features of this interaction that might be informed by social contexts that precede this event. Some of these have already been noted in the discussion leading up to this analysis. In this excerpt, for example, the word *dude* stands out for me. It seems to be functioning for Danny in multiple ways. On the one hand he is using it to tell a story, to describe the men who work on trains. On the other hand, when he self-corrects, he suggests that he knows, at some level, that this word is not the right word for this context. This makes him seem self-conscious about his language, and it suggests to me that he has been corrected before for language that may have seemed functional to him, but was deemed inappropriate for the classroom. He may have internalized a sense that language he speaks freely in another context is not appropriate in school.

Next, I am struck by the fact that Danny's relatively lengthy contribution about the hats train people wear is ignored by the teacher. How do Danny's description and the fact that it is ignored relate to social contexts outside this interaction? His talk about the train people seems to be informed by language patterns outside this reading group and by context outside the school. There are train tracks running through this small town. Maybe he has seen the hats those men wear. He may be more interested in describing those hats than the kind of hats his teacher is thinking of. In any case, his contribution is ignored. As soon as he finishes his discussion of trains, the teacher simply repeats her question, "But do men, do a lot of men wear hats now?"

The teacher's action—ignoring Danny—may also be informed by circumstances outside this interaction. This teacher has a history of interacting with Danny, a buildup of expectations for how those interactions will go. Danny has a history of misbehavior. He has an unruly family situation. He has been diagnosed as having ADHD. However, like George (whose rejection of the teacher's curriculum was translated into an inquiry project for the entire class—see the discussion in chap. 1), he also has something to contribute. As his attempt at talking about train dudes shows, he wants to contribute.

All students are ignored at one point or another. But some students, we know, are ignored more than others. I, as a teacher, am likely to see the eager look in the eye of a student I know has the right answer and to ignore the one who (I think) did not do the reading. Many teachers are likely to call on more boys and ignore more girls. Some teachers may ignore new English-language learners so they can focus on the native speakers (Santa Ana, 2004; Vasquez, 2004). Unfortunately, but inevitably, we may occasionally ignore people whom we find hard to understand. We may find ourselves ignoring quiet students, students with accented speech, or students who explain things in ways that seem inscrutable or off topic. This kind of ignoring can, functionally, translate into racism, sexism, and classism. All of these -isms may have their foundations in such misunderstanding.

In the case of this excerpt, it is important to know that Danny is Black, his teacher is White, and that Danny has a history of behavior problems and underachievement. However, that does not mean it is necessary to reinforce these social conditions in the analysis. Instead, by examining how this discourse is also interactionally contextualized, we can begin to unravel ways to change this pattern—at least in the classroom, if not society at large.

Interactional Context

Being ignored—although it may be generated through a long history of misunderstandings between people of different races, classes, or genders—is always an interactional problem too. Remember the gears of classroom discourse? The social context gear and the classroom interaction gear are pushing each other. Likewise, our analyses of the social and interactional contributions to classroom discourse are always interconnected. However, figuring out why something is not working interactionally involves temporarily putting aside our socially contextualized analysis involving categories of race, class, gender, a changing community, or a students' individual history of unruly behavior—and zooming our lens in on how that talk is contextualized in sequences of interaction within classroom events. Although Danny has a history of unruly behavior, in this case, it is also clear that his response about train hats is not an unruly one. It is an attempt at legitimate participation. However, it does not conform to his teacher's expectations.

We can become more aware of this buildup of expectations by breaking down the event and the sequences within it. For example, when analyzing why, Danny seems to be getting ignored, we have to consider these kinds of questions:

- What event is this sequence a part of?
- What sequence is this within that event?
- How are interactional expectations guiding what gets said?
- How are interactional expectations guiding how words function?

This particular sequence about hats is part of a larger event—reading a story as a group. Within this event, at each page, the teacher questions the students about the pictures. On this particular page, the teacher has a distinct event structure in mind. She wants the students to look at the picture and use visual clues to determine when this book took place. Therefore, as she asks students questions, she wants them to talk about how aspects of the picture are different from features of contemporary life. This particular event has a distinct structure that could be represented this way:

1. Ask a question that will prompt students to describe the picture.
   (*What do all the men have on their heads?*—Ideal answer: *Hats*)
2. Ask a question that will indicate this is different from how we live today. (*Do a lot of men where hats today?*—Ideal answer: *No*)

3. Ask students, then, to deduce whether this story took place in the past or the present. (*So, do you think this story took place in the present or the past?*—Ideal answer: *The past*)

This event structure illustrates the teacher's effort to address curricular objectives while reading literature. However, the nonfunctionality of this structure becomes clear when we zoom our analytic lens in on a single adjacency pair. What was meant as a quick and contextualized display of the concepts of past and present story settings gets side railed at the question in Step 2, "Ask a question that will indicate this is different from how we live today":

Teacher: Do men wear a lot of hats now?

Although the question was intended as a rhetorical question, with an obvious "no" answer, Danny provided, instead, a lengthy description of a kind of hat that people *do* wear today. Meanwhile, the students, who were not aware of the teacher's agenda at this point, struggled (e.g., pointing emphatically at the book) to make Danny's point clear for her.

This interactional analysis suggests that, in this case, Danny was ignored because his response was not one of the ideal responses needed to contribute to the event structure she was expecting. On the level of interaction, then, this sequence reproduced the effects that broader social context was having on Danny's education. Although Danny was not being unruly here, even though he was not speaking out of turn, his response was treated as irrelevant. To use the term introduced in chapter 3, when the teacher re-asks her question after Danny's lengthy turn, his response is "sequentially deleted" (Ford, 1993), as illustrated next:

Train Hats (excerpt)

Teacher: ... **Do men wear a lot of hats now?**   ← initiating question

Danny: Some don't. The train dudes- the train
people wear they wear these like,
big ol [things that

Teacher: [The train people, that=

Tiffany: Like this ((*Pointing to the picture
emphatically*))

Teacher: =that drive the train (0.2) wear hats.   Danny's
Danny's response   response

Danny: And somebody better put on some um
things for um there little thing cause
they hurt their ears. ((*pointing into his ears*))

Teacher: Ah,

Danny: Because, the noise is come in the air
and (0.4)

Teacher: But do men, **do a lot of men wear**   ← same question
hats now?

After Danny's response was ignored in this sequence, he stopped volunteering answers that day. The way Danny's contributions unfold interactionally, and the reputation he carries as an ADHD child and an underachiever from a problem home, seem to be compounding each other.

However, as we saw in the example of George in chapter 1, it is possible, at the level of classroom interaction, with the help of the gear of individual agency, to change the direction those discourse gears turn. Within the teacher's room, changes are possible.

Individual Agency

Untangling these interactional and social conditions that produce an "ignored" child is crucial to finding solutions that will facilitate this child's learning in this context. Remember the paradox of agency: The more we are aware of the conditions that control our behavior, the more we are able to overcome those conditions. Questions that can facilitate analysis directed at renewed agency are:

- What social conditions (context outside the interaction) are shaping this interaction? Is this necessary?
- What interactional conditions (immediate context within the speech event) are shaping this interaction? Is this necessary?

- What changes could I make that will counteract negative social or interactional effects on a child's participation?

In the case of this interaction, it is likely that social conditions are shaping how Danny's contribution is taken up. He speaks in an African-American English variety, and his self-correction suggests that he is aware that his language may be marked. He may have been corrected by others in previous interactions. He has also developed a reputation as a difficult child, and perhaps this calls for some differential treatment. However, in the case presented, his response does not seem to be inappropriate, antisocial, unruly, or even far off topic. There is no clear reason for him to be ignored.

Interactional conditions are also shaping this ignoring, however. Danny's question is not one of the "ideal answers" needed to propel this sequence in a way that will conform to the event structure—and the lesson about past and present settings. However, any event structure that has "ideal answers" built into it is likely to exclude any child who does not think like the teacher. When most teachers come from backgrounds that are different from their students (an increasingly common scenario), this kind of misunderstanding will happen frequently (Ladson-Billings, 2001). Fortunately, this sort of interactional constraint is not necessary. In each of our classrooms, we are not bound to repeat conditions that lead to misunderstanding. I know that I am not a racist for simply not understanding students who are racially different from me—but I become racist if I never examine and change the conditions that lead to my misunderstanding.

An important element of any discourse analysis is recognizing that words always have meaning *for their speakers* (Blommaert, 2005). In this case, recognizing Danny's contribution and its potential relevance to him (not relevance to our social categories, his reputation at school, or the event structure guiding the teacher's questions) is the first step to creating the conditions, in this classroom, in which more of his answers will be relevant. So, the next step to agency, in this analysis, is rethinking the event structure of book reading so that it might include Danny, and then acting on these new plans.

PUTTING IT ALL TOGETHER:
MULTIDIMENSIONAL CLASSROOM DISCOURSE ANALYSIS

As this example analysis begins to illustrate, becoming a classroom discourse analyst can be empowering precisely because it raises the possibility of resisting those unpleasant conditions that often seem to control us. You may disagree with some of the analytic claims I have made. In fact, I would hope you are prepared to challenge them. One analysis of one excerpt is only a starting point. Discourse analysis is a recursive process. You will be viewing many events, with many sequences within them, and each time you will be noticing new configurations of the layers of social and interactional context and the potential for individual agency. The following chart summarizes the analytic questions to which you will keep returning. As you begin to look back at your transcripts, use these questions to trigger further discussion, analysis, and change. Your analysis will become more relevant the more you think through the social and interactional layers that inform it and how you can use that awareness in future actions.

Overview of Multidimensional Classroom Discourse Analysis

SOCIAL CONTEXT	INTERACTIONAL CONTEXT	INDIVIDUAL AGENCY
Which particular words and/or grammatical forms and/or ways of speaking stand out for you? How are they functioning?	What event is this sequence a part of? What sequence is this within that event?	What social conditions are shaping this interaction? Is this necessary?
Is discourse being informed by contexts outside this interaction? If so, how can you tell?	How are interactional expectations guiding what gets said? How are interactional expectations guiding how words function?	What interactional conditions are shaping this interaction? Is this necessary? What are possible changes I could make that will counteract negative social or interactional effects on a child's participation?

Your analysis will also become more relevant the more you talk it through with other people. Try to find a way to discuss your analysis with a peer, classmate, or student. These analytic questions should help you work together to focus your observations and compare notes.

In the next four chapters, I introduce further characteristics of talk and interaction and their relationship to social context and agency. Chapter 5, "Analyzing Turn-Taking Resources," zooms our analytic lens in on typical—and nontraditional—turn-taking patterns in the classroom.

QUESTIONS AND ACTIVITIES

Critical Reflection

1. Go back to the preview question at the beginning of this chapter: Think of students in your class who have distinctive (to you) ways of speaking. How could you represent that distinction in a transcript?
2. Go back to the preview question at the beginning of this chapter: Think of the different "voices" you use in your classroom. How do you change your way of speaking to accomplish different functions?
3. Vivian Paley says her transcripts (transcribed nightly after school!) help her to measure her own reality alongside the reality of her students. What does she mean by this?
4. How can you envision transcripts enhancing your agency as a teacher? Within interactions in your classroom? As an individual in your institution? Changing educational policy?
5. How would you answer the analytical questions about the Train Hats excerpt? Do you have different interpretations of this excerpt? Compare your analysis with a peer.

Reflective Activities

1. Create a diagram for the classroom event you have recorded, including the cast of characters and where they are all sitting.
2. Create an event structure diagram for a classroom event you have recorded (see the science talk and book-talk models given in this chapter).
3. Take one day and pay attention to your students and/or your wait time in interactions, considering the following questions: When you address a question to the class, how long do you wait for an answer? When you address a question to an individual, how long do you wait for an answer? Does wait time vary depending on whom you are asking? Does it vary depending on the event within which you are asking a question? When students ask each other questions, do they wait long enough to get an answer from their peers?
4. Transcribe a recorded classroom sequence once; then wait. Go back to your transcription a week later and read it while you watch the video. What do you need to change? What did you hear wrong? What did you represent in a way that seems inaccurate now? How do you explain these differences the second time around?
5. Analyze that transcribed sequence using the analytic questions (considerations of social context, interactional context and individual

agency) presented in this chapter. On the basis of your analysis, are there any changes you would like to consider making in your classroom?

Suggestions for Further Reading

Examples of classroom discourse analysis are the best reading materials to enhance your own analyses. As you page through journals, look for articles that include transcripts and discussions about them. Again, all of Karen Gallas' books are stellar in this regard. Vivian Gussin Paley is another brilliant teacher/researcher who examines classroom discourse in her preschool classrooms. As you scan the literature, take note of alternative transcription formats and consider those that might be useful for you.

Laura Sterponi's (2007) article, "Clandestine Interactional Reading," illustrates some useful ways of diagramming a classroom, organizing a transcript, and integrating video stills in a classroom discourse analysis. Elinor Ochs' (1979) classic essay, "Transcription as Theory," provides both a theoretical argument about the importance of weighing transcription decisions carefully and a number of useful transcription formats. David Bloome and his colleagues (2005) have written a book, *Discourse Analysis and the Study of Classroom Language and Literacy Events: A Microethnographic Perspective*, which is full of examples of classroom interactions and their microlevel analysis.

5

ANALYZING TURN TAKING RESOURCES

PREVIEW QUESTIONS Before you begin reading this chapter, think about turn taking patterns in a class you teach, a class you are taking, a class in which you once participated. Who does most of the talking? Who takes most of the "question asking" turns? Who takes most of the "answer" turns? Who holds the answers? How do these factors change across different classroom speech events?

How students think—indeed the extent to which they really need to think in school—and consequently what they can learn depend a lot on how their teachers respond to their students' responses.

Martin Nystrand (1997, p. 29)

This chapter is about analyzing turn taking in classroom talk—those responses to responses that Nystrand describes as critical to thinking in classrooms. Taking turns, asking and answering questions, providing feedback, and encouraging more thinking are the discourse elements that build a classroom's intellectual life. Questions asked in classrooms can spark dramatic outbursts and cacophony, deathly silences, or discussions bursting with multiple perspectives, problem solving, and growing curiosity. As students and teachers learn to take turns in classroom talk, the patterns they construct together regulate what teachers and students are able to say and what they do not say. When patterns develop that inhibit a variety of understandings from being voiced, classroom learning can stagnate.

Classroom discourse analysis is our tool to investigate these turn taking patterns and their effects on learning. This analysis involves looking at how turn taking machinery drives interaction in the classroom, how social context outside the classroom is relevant to these interactions, and how social context can play a different role in less traditionally organized classroom events. Throughout, the goal of our analysis of turn taking is to raise our awareness that turn taking is controlled by both interactional context of the classroom and the different patterns of interaction students bring to the classroom from home and community contexts. This awareness (of how both small-scale interactional and large-scale social features of context inform turn taking) has the potential to lead to changed patterns—to augment our individual agency as teachers as well as our students' individual agency, and to build a discourse climate that fosters learning opportunities for everyone.

ANALYZING TRADITIONAL CLASSROOM TURN TAKING PATTERNS

Turn taking—and the associated opportunities for learning—unfold differently in different classrooms and for different activities within the same classroom. Compare, for example, these two descriptions of classroom talk. The first is an excerpt from Karen Gallas' (1994) field notes taken about her own first- and second-grade class discussions:

> The question under consideration for our first science talk is: How did animals begin? The children sit in a circle, and I am *silent as usual*. (p. 62; italics added)

Karen Gallas, the teacher in this classroom, describes herself being "silent as usual." Does this strike you as atypical? Gallas' inquiry approach is not built on traditional teacher-centered instruction. In traditional classrooms, the teacher rarely remains silent. Compare Gallas' field note with a typical university classroom in Europe, as described by Jan Blommaert (2005), a university professor and discourse analyst:

> [The] senior faculty member will be the one who designs and offers the course, who will do most of the talking during the course during the class hours, who will give assignments to the students, and who will grade the exams. (p. 132)

These different descriptions of classroom procedure highlight differences in how turn taking is organized, what kinds of questions are asked, and who will do the talking. For Gallas, interaction during Science Talks is organized around questions generated by students, and the students do most of the talking. In Blommaert's description of a typical university class, turn taking is organized by the teacher, who will also do most of the talking and ask most of the questions. As Blommaert (2005) says, "this general pattern of authority goes back centuries" (p. 132). To this day, turn taking still unfolds in most classrooms, most of the time, in traditional, teacher-centered sequences. (You might take time to observe in classes around your school or the university and see whether this is true in your context.) Classroom discourse analysis affords a closer look at how this centuries-old pattern permeates traditional classroom interaction.

The Interactional Dimension of Traditional Classroom Turn Taking Patterns

Typically, you begin your classroom discourse analysis by isolating a recorded event, say test review or poetry discussion, and examining sequences within those events. Two critical questions to ask about turn taking within this event are, "Who asks the questions?" and "What kind of sequences develop from those questions?" Chances are, in a traditional classroom, within a traditional event like test review, the teacher will be asking the questions. Although you may find some of the typical two-part adjacency pairs discussed in chapter 2, you will probably also find a new three-part sequence called IRE, which is described next.

Initiation, Response, and Evaluation

Interactionally, the centuries-old "pattern of authority" in classrooms described by Blommaert is driven in large part by the Initiation, Response, and Evaluation (IRE) pattern of classroom discourse, initially discussed by Hugh Mehan (1985) and epitomized by this kind of sequence:

Initiation: Teacher: What time is it?

Response: Jackson: One Thirty.

Evaluation: Teacher: Very good, Jackson!

Although this exchange serves an obvious purpose in a traditional lesson, evaluation like this during a conversation with a peer would be unlikely.

Imagine if you asked a friend the time and then evaluated her response with hearty praise after she said it was half past one ("Very good!"). Clearly, the IRE sequence differs from question sequences outside the classroom. Instead of the typical two-part formula of most adjacency pairs (question–answer, summons–response), it includes that odd third appendage: *evaluation*. In most conversations, we do not explicitly evaluate other's statements. Instead, we respond in functional ways:

Request for information:	Teacher 1:	What time is it?
Supplying information:	Teacher 2:	1:30.
Preclosing:	Teacher 1:	Oh! I have to go!
Closing:	Teacher 2:	Okay, see you tomorrow!

Obviously, Teacher 2 is competent at telling time here. But more important, she supplied information that Teacher 1 needed. What if that teacher's watch actually read "1:32"? This slight inaccuracy—in this context—would not matter. Her answer was not right or wrong (although we could evaluate it to be either). It was functional.

The Function of IRE in Multiple Contexts

As the prior examples suggest, unfortunate fallout from an abundance of IRE sequences is that language in classrooms can start to be constructed as *correct* or *incorrect* exclusively (and according to the teacher's standards), rather than *functional* or *nonfunctional* in a larger world of communication in which all our students are learning to participate.

Still, as we read through our transcripts, we encounter IRE sequences. This is not necessarily a sign of a hopelessly decontextualized teaching style. However, being able to analyze how these sequences function can raise our awareness of exactly what we are teaching and why. At the most rudimentary level, IRE sequences are a quick way of gauging students' knowledge on a topic. Like flashcards, IRE serves a purpose, but a rudimentary one. This sequence can reinforce basic skills and information. However, when strictly evaluative sequences like this come to dominate the classroom, a teacher becomes nothing more than a human deck of flashcards.

Classroom talk accomplishes many more functions than simply evaluation and so, potentially, does the IRE sequence. You may find it used in multiple contexts, and many examples already discussed in this book contain IRE sequences. In talking through the pictures in a storybook, for example, the IRE sequence can also serve to focus students' attention on the same details:

Initiation: Teacher: What do all the men have on their heads?
Response: Tiffany: Ha[ts
                Rene: [Hats
Evaluation: Teacher: Hats.

When reading, an Initiation turn can nudge a student into problem solving:

Initiation: Teacher: What other word does that word look like?

When talking about current events (specifically the 30th anniversary of the *Brown v. Board of Education* Supreme Court decision), an Initiation turn can gauge how much students know about a new topic:

Initiation: Teacher: What was *Brown v. Board of Education* about?

In a conversation class for new English speakers, the Initiation turn can ask about popular culture:

Initiation: Teacher: What's your favorite movie?

All of these initiating turns potentially begin IRE sequences and potentially lead into much longer sequences and important classroom learning.

IRE sequences are always multifunctional. Although they are initiating turns that probe for responses, they may also be bringing new students into a discussion, changing topics, closing down an activity, or leading students incrementally on to a larger thematic point. This was illustrated in the analysis of the "train hats" sequence in chapter 4. Recall that the teacher had intended her initiation question "Do men wear hats today?" to lead students incrementally to a point about the temporal context of the picture book. Instead, it prompted Danny to tell a long story about "train hats." (We return to this example at the end of this chapter.) When analyzing discourse in our own classrooms, IRE sequences can be a useful entry point for a sequential analysis, but do not assume they are functioning in one particular way. A closer look reveals their multifunctionality.

Kinds of Questions Within IRE

A certain kind of question anchors the IRE sequence. Two broad categories can be helpful in making initial distinctions between question types: known-answer questions and open-ended questions. *Known-answer questions* (also called test questions, display questions, or convergent questions) are the prototypical IRE sequence initiators. Their primary function is to prompt students to display information already known to the asker. The response to "What do all the men have on their heads?" when looking at a picture in a storybook in which all the men are wearing hats, for example, has got to be "hats." A prototypical known-answer question has one and only one right answer—usually one the teacher has in mind. (The answer "hair," although correct, might be considered supremely smart-alecky in this context.) For this reason, Postman and Weingartner (1969), in a pithy critique, call them "guess what I'm thinking" questions. In contrast, *open-ended questions* (also called genuine, authentic, information-seeking, or divergent questions) do not seek one right answer, and the asker may not have any predetermined answer in mind. The questioner may genuinely want to know the answer to questions like, "What's your favorite movie?", "Where are the crayons?", or "How are you going to continue this story?" As a result, open-ended or genuine questions are more likely to lead to discussion between teachers and students than to the teacher-directed IRE pattern (Nystrand, 1997).

Look for and compare these question types within your focal classroom event. You will probably find both kinds of questions. However, you may also find that these distinctions break down easily in real classroom discourse. **Interactional contingency** (the ever present potential for interaction to change our intended or normatively expected meaning) can dramatically reshape how questions function. What begins as a known-answer question designed to get students to display their fluency with telling time, for example, might be constructed by the response to it as part of a different two-part sequence. Here, an accusation and denial:

> Teacher: What time does school start?
> Student: ((*walking through the classroom door*)) I'm not tardy!

Known-answer questions might also be constructed as their opposite—open-ended questions:

> Teacher: What color is my shirt?
> Student: I would call it "tangerine."

Open-ended questions can also become part of an accusation-denial sequence:

> Teacher: Where are the crayons?
> Student: I didn't do anything with them!

Open-ended questions may be interpreted as their opposite—known-answer questions, with one right answer, and one right way of saying it:

Teacher: How are you going to continue this paper?
Student: ((*tentatively*)) With the conclusion?

Unfortunately, students who are habituated to typical known-answer questions embedded in the IRE sequence might come to see all questions as teacher-centered "Guess what I'm thinking" questions—and not questions about students' own thoughts and experiences. When a new teacher or a new kind of lesson or curriculum encourages students to respond in new ways, and provides unanticipated answers, children who are not used to this interactional format may not realize initially that they are being asked to think critically—to do more than simply decipher what the teacher thinks they should say. Recording and analyzing discourse in our classrooms can begin to raise our awareness about how habits of responses are generated initially through interaction in classrooms. As the following examples begin to illustrate, it may be possible to make significant changes in our classrooms simply by changing a question here or there.

*Variations Within Tradition — From IRE to IRF
to Mr. Wonderful*

As simply a vehicle for known-answer questions, the IRE sequence can stagnate classroom learning. Although the abbreviation IRE stands simply for Initiation, Response, and Evaluation, the word spelled by these letters, *ire*, is defined by my Microsoft dictionary as "a feeling or display of deep anger or fury." Some possible synonyms offered are *anger, rage, fury, indignation,* or *bile.* Coincidence? You might feel bilious if you spent every day in classrooms subjected exclusively to the IRE questioning pattern. Certainly, IRE is problematic. However, this basic three-part sequence can function productively in classroom discourse. Gordon Wells (1986) tweaked the format a little, changing the evaluative "E" to a more generative feedback turn, in what he called the Initiation, Response, Feedback (IRF) sequence. In this formulation, the third turn does not conclude the sequence, but provides feedback for ongoing interaction, building another sequence into it. Through the use of this slightly augmented third turn, a teacher does not simply supply a closed-ended evaluation, but a scaffold for students' ongoing participation. This kind of feedback turn can change simple praise (evaluation) into an opportunity for more involved talk, as in the following example, adapted from Owocki and Goodman (2002).

EVALUATION . . .		. . . FEEDBACK
Your pictures are great.	. . . *could instead be* *formulated as* . . .	Your pictures helped me to enjoy your story. How did you think to include the little anchor?

Even in a math lesson, evaluation can be transformed into more productive feedback,

EVALUATION . . .		. . . FEEDBACK
That's correct..	. . . *could instead be* *formulated as* . . .	That's correct. How did you get that answer?

In these reformulations, the feedback turn, although still evaluative, is not oriented to closure. Instead, it becomes an invitation to students to draw on their own experiences, reflect on their process, and think critically.

This kind of feedback can happen in any classroom setting. In her research on a favorite ESOL class, for example, Laurie Verplaetse (2002) describes how a middle-school biology teacher she calls "Mr. Wonderful" infused wonder into both his initiation and feedback turns during traditional class discussions. He transformed a typical IRE-style event into an interactional context that promoted ongoing problem solving. Instead of posing questions to the class as if they sprang from a wellspring of knowledge within his own head or a published textbook, he posed them as instances of student curiosity. For example, in a unit on genetics, he raised an important question not by orienting his question to the book or a test they would take soon, but by attributing it to a student from another class:

Teacher: Somebody from the other class brought up a question. . . .
And that is, what determines whether your zygote is
going to turn into a male or a female?

Students in Mr. Wonderful's class discussed this at length, and he refrained from evaluating their responses. Eventually, as he gave the class homework to continue working on this problem, he had so effectively decentered himself as the source of knowledge that students asked whether he knew the answer to this specific question:

Teacher: . . . you're going to draw a picture explaining how you
get boys and girls. Now we know that it has something

> to do with fertilization. We know that it has something
> to do with X and Y chromosomes.
>
> Lina: Do you know?

Mr. Wonderful did, reluctantly, admit that he did know, but because he had refrained throughout the talk from directly evaluating any student hypothesis, students were not sure he actually did have the answer. Because Mr. Wonderful only provides feedback—but not direct evaluation—his initiating questions function as prompts for students to think on their own and to develop possible solutions, rather than to unthinkingly call out answers the teacher will anoint as "correct."

Karen Johnson (1995) also illustrates how the third feedback turn can be used not as a direct evaluation of student talk, but as a scaffold for further discussion in L2 classrooms:

Initiation:	Teacher:	Vin, have you ever been to the movies? What's your favorite movie?
Response:	Vin:	*Big.*
Feedback/ Initiation:	Teacher:	*Big,* OK, that's a good movie, that was about a little boy inside a big man, wasn't it?
Response:	Vin:	Yeah, boy get surprise all the time.
Feedback:	Teacher:	Yes, he was surprised, wasn't he? Usually little boys don't do the things that men do, do they?

This student is a new English speaker, and his teacher's questions function to pull him into a conversation about a movie. Her third turns do not exclusively evaluate whether Vin's contributions are right or wrong. More importantly, that third turn provides feedback that illustrates the potential function of Vin's comments within an ordinary conversation in English. The classroom researcher Martin Nystrand (1997) calls these productive third turns "high-level evaluation" and defines this quality of evaluation as including two parts—"certification of the response" (e.g., "Okay, that's a good movie) and "incorporation of the response into the discourse of the class" (e.g., "That was about a little boy inside a big man wasn't it?").

So as you read through your transcript and identify three-part IRE-type sequences, ask yourself, how is that third turn functioning? Is it a closed-ended evaluative comment? Or is it generative feedback (Wells, 1986) or "high-level evaluation" (Nystrand, 1997) that will support further thinking and interaction?

The Social Context Dimension
of Traditional Turn Taking

Although turn taking is largely interactionally driven, turn taking patterns also powerfully draw social context into every interaction because these patterns have long interactional histories. More accurately, some turn taking patterns have long interactional histories for some people. For other people, traditional, school-based, turn taking patterns are new and unusual—and can inhibit rather than foster participation in learning events. These differences illustrate that turn taking patterns, although a feature of interactional context, are also critically affected by social contexts and individual histories that precede a classroom interaction.

Differences in Language Socialization

In the previous sections, I briefly described the IRE sequence and the kinds of question types that keep kicking those IRE sequences along. I provided minimal context for those examples because I suspect the readers of this book are primarily people who are familiar with this form of classroom talk (either as teachers or students) and will quickly recognize the pattern and the expectations associated with it. Most people in the United States, having grown up with IRE-type ways of using language in schools and possibly even within interactions at home (cf. Heath, 1982), are communicatively competent in traditional school discourse patterns. However, this discourse knowledge, although interactionally driven, is also deeply contextualized cultural knowledge that is not universally shared. Students who are socialized into different forms of talk may have difficulty recognizing and functioning within the norms of IRE described previously.

Wait Time

One feature of the IRE sequence that can limit opportunities for some students is the limited wait time between the initiating question and the student response. Typical TV game shows make it painfully obvious that answering trivial questions quickly (even impulsively and without thinking) is behavior that is rewarded in popular U.S. culture. In classrooms, too, teachers may face a swath of raised hands eagerly thrusting for recognition—even before the teacher has fully formulated her question. Fred Erickson (1996) has conducted a detailed classroom discourse analysis illustrating how, within the IRE pattern in one classroom, those students who can read the most intricate details of the interaction were able to dominate the talk. These were not necessarily the students who had the best answers, but those who were best at reading the patterns of inter-action and inserting their voices at the most opportune moments. While one more soft-spoken student formulated her responses to the teacher's questions, IRE-adept "turn sharks," as Erickson calls them, had already finished off the sequence. Not all students are experts at inserting them-selves into the IRE sequence.

The time students may take to formulate an answer varies across communities, and the patterns of interaction socialized within them. For example, Ronald and Suzanne Scollon's (1983) research has shown that the typical wait time between speakers among Athabaskan Indians is "just enough longer [than English speaker norms] that by the time the Athabaskan is ready to speak, the English speaker is already speaking again" (p. 26). Gallas, as noted in chapter 2, recorded how, even in her nontraditional Science Talks, certain boys more readily inserted them-selves into the dialogue, eliminating openings for other students, includ-ing new English speakers. When Gallas and her students instituted new turn taking norms, the formerly quiet students, including the new English speakers, were able to participate more fully with their previous-ly dominant classmates.

Although the IRE sequence does not mandate these kinds of imbal-ances in turn taking, without close attention to wait time between initiat-ing and responding, responding and evaluating, students who do not immediately accommodate the established pattern can be left out of learning. Moreover, they can be evaluated as not knowing simply because they were not participating in this particular socioculturally informed discourse pattern.

Known-Answer Questions

The prevalence of known-answer questions within the IRE sequence can also silence students who are not familiar with this way of asking questions or who give answers that teachers do not understand. A num-ber of researchers have discussed how the known-answer questions typ-ical of the IRE sequence are not culturally familiar to certain children. Consistent with Heath (1982), Lisa Delpit (1996) has pointed out that some children are confused by teachers who ask questions they already know the answer to. From these children's perspective, known-answer questions are odd precisely because they have no practical function. Students may think, "Why are you asking me if you already know? What's the point?" Other discourse analytic classroom research has shown that known-answer questions, as discussed in chapter 1, usually have more than one right answer—although only one may be right in the mind of the teacher or the educational system. When students give seemingly odd answers to known-answer questions, the problem is often not with what the student does not know, but with what the teacher does not know about the student's life.

Praise for an Individual

The evaluation turn in the IRE sequence is also unfamiliar within certain cultural contexts. In their comparison of language socialization in homes and Sunday school lessons in Western Samoa, for example, Sandro Duranti and Elinor Ochs (1988) found that the IRE patterns practiced in the Sunday school ran counter to the values socialized within Samoan homes. In Samoan society, praise for one individual is unheard of. Instead, any suggestion of individual accomplishment is met with recognition that the group made it possible, in a pervasive conversational sequence called *maaloo*.

When a driver, for example, narrowly avoids another careening vehicle, the *maaloo* interaction proceeds like this:

Passengers: Well done the steering!

Driver: Well done the support!

This *maaloo* sequence is antithetical to the kind of individual praise embedded in IRE sequences and this difference in interactional sequence represents deep differences in Western values of individual achievement and the indigenous values of collective Samoan society.

I am not suggesting that we simply start waiting longer, eliminate known-answer questions, and refrain from praising students in our classrooms. Differences in how students perceive wait time, known-answer questions, and individual evaluation illustrate just a few of the different kinds of expectations students may bring to classroom interaction. Through the analysis of classroom turn taking, it becomes possible to detect when, and to begin to reflect on why, certain students participate variably in what are habitual classroom sequences for most U.S. teachers.

Procedural Display

Habituated classroom sequences like IRE may limit learning not only for students who are unfamiliar with them, but also for those students who are so familiar with them that they can participate in such sequences appropriately, but unthinkingly. In some cases, the IRE structure can serve as a scaffold not necessarily to classroom learning, but to superficial participation rather than substantive engagement in classroom events. *Procedural display* (the opposite of substantive engagement) is a term coined by Shirley Brice Heath (1978) and elaborated by David Bloome and his colleagues (Bloome, Puro, & Theodorou, 1989) for the condition in which a teacher and her students work collaboratively to appear successful while minimal learning may be going on. Imagine a teacher confidently strolling the aisles, questioning a class on information they already know, students providing instant responses. A visiting accreditation team might be impressed by this display, but the students and teacher may be primarily *performing* a learning event, rather than actively learning. The IRE sequence is an ideal vehicle for procedural display. Because, in many cases, students can participate in IRE sequences superficially, this form of interaction can mask the lack of any deeper participation and understanding while, to an outsider, the class may appear to be slick and effective.

Agency and Traditional Turn Taking

As the discussion of procedural display suggests, traditional turn taking sequences, although often familiar and comfortable, may provide only an illusion of control over the learning in our classrooms. Paradoxically, a turn taking pattern that seems to provide structure and control can be limiting as a resource to engage both teachers and students as learners. Instead, learning is being controlled by those "centuries-old" discourse patterns that habituate certain questions and student responses. These entrenched turn taking patterns can inhibit classroom learning for everyone.

Inviting more perspectives into classroom interaction and including critical voices does not necessarily mean eliminating traditional turn taking resources completely. However, to exert agency as teachers who control those resources and use them effectively requires a fine-tuned awareness of what these tools do in our classrooms. Analyzing turn taking effects helps us evaluate when and how traditional turn taking patterns are necessary and when they are inhibiting critical thinking and multiple perspectives.

After developing a picture of turn taking patterns within an event, ask yourself these questions about the patterns you are noticing:

1. Do turn taking patterns ensure that learning is challenging and inclusive?
2. If so, what precisely makes them work? Could I use this type of turn organization in more classroom events?
3. If not, what changes in the organization of turn taking could I make?

Because you have a transcript and an event, and because your event is presumably one you can return to as a teacher, you can reflect on these questions and return to the classroom event with enhanced agency. If your current patterns are inclusive and promote full participation, see what about them produces this positive interactional climate. If not, you can consider what interactional changes are needed to ensure that turn taking resources are a tool available for all participants and make those changes. As you study turn taking and modify classroom discourse patterns, you may become aware of how students draw on different turn taking resources when they participate in nontraditional learning events, discussed next.

NONTRADITIONAL TURN TAKING PATTERNS

As discussed, some turn taking patterns have long interactional histories for some people. The implications of this statement can be damaging for the learning of both those who are familiar with those patterns and for those who are not. As the discussion of "procedural display" suggests, although some people may be habituated to certain turn taking patterns, this does not necessarily mean they will be learning much more in classrooms. Socially entrenched, unquestioned classroom patterns inhibit everyone's learning. Postman and Weingartner lamented this condition nearly 40 years ago:

> Have you ever heard of a student suggesting a more useful definition of something that the teacher has already defined? Or of a student who asked, "Whose facts are those?" Or of a student who asked, "What is a fact?" Or of a student who asked, "Why are we doing this work?" (p. 23)

Even decades after Postman and Weingartner penned this complaint, classrooms are still largely organized through predictable interactional routines that can help us avoid these messy questions. However, in the previous chapters, I have included classroom examples in which students do question the curriculum (remember George) and in which teachers are not the only ones who ask the questions or define the terms (remember Gallas' Science Talks).

In nontraditional interactional contexts, different kinds of students—those who are neither accustomed to nor comfortable with more canonical classroom discourse patterns—may be more able to participate. You will likely see qualitatively different kinds of sequences: more of the two-part sorts of initiators we read about in chapter 2, more genuine questions, more wait time, and less praise without feedback.

These are also contexts in which the discourse will be less predictable than in traditional lessons. Discourse analysis provides a tool to see alternative turn taking resources at play within these changed formats for learning.

Accounting for Different Social Contexts by Changing Interaction

Nontraditional learning events are not teacher centered. Talk within nontraditional learning events often builds on the multiple social contexts within which students live. This more inclusive kind of learning event can emerge through basic changes in the turn taking patterns—changes in who asks the questions, whose experiences are included, and whose languages are heard.

Many teachers have avoided the pitfalls of entrenched traditional turn taking patterns by building their classroom interactions on significant problems for investigation; in these inquiry-based classrooms, students are driven to think critically and to draw on a variety of resources to investigate problems. Teachers are not asking all the questions. Students' experiences are included as relevant to learning. Students' multiple ways of speaking are heard. The emergence of these characteristics of classroom talk, just like the emergence of more traditional turn taking patterns, can also be studied in a classroom discourse analysis.

Who Asks the Questions? What Kind of Questions Are They?

Two critical questions to ask about classroom turn taking are: "Who asks the questions?" and "What kind of sequences develop from those questions?" As already discussed, in traditional formats, the teacher will ask most of the questions and some version of IRE will follow. But in nontraditional, inquiry-oriented classrooms, teachers design events in which students' questions can dominate. Karen Gallas (1994), for example, generates the topics for her Science Talks by soliciting questions from the students. To illustrate for students, Gallas starts the first Science Talk by modeling a possible inquiry question:

Why do the leaves change color?

What kind of question is this? It is completely open ended. It is a question that most first and second graders do not know the answer to. Although the teacher probably does know an officially sanctioned answer to this question—one that will earn points on a science test—the students are directed to listen and respond to each other as they discuss possible answers, so that their discussion is not a right answer search, but an exploratory science-like investigation of meaning.

In these talks, three-part IRE sequences do not exist. There is no "evaluation" turn. Gallas explicitly instructs her students not to raise their hands—she does not want to be the moderator of the discussion. As students discuss, Gallas is silent. Eventually, students seek out additional resources to find answers to their questions—there are documented scientific explanations for why leaves change color—but their investigation starts from their own curiosity.

Following this initial model of an inquiry talk, students generate dozens of science questions they want to consider as the year progresses. The only criteria that guides the student-posed questions is that they be open ended, and that they are generated out of their own experiences and often from experiences they have shared in the classroom. For example, after months of feeding the class bird, one boy proposed the question, "Why don't birds have teeth?" Other questions generated by students included:

How did the moon begin?
Why is the center of the Earth hot?
Why do the seasons change?
How do people age?
How do our bones stay together?
Why do people die?
What color were the dinosaurs?
Are dragons real?
What makes the wind?

These are questions that students want to talk about because they want to know the answers—not because they need to provide the answer for the teacher, for a worksheet, or for a test. Nevertheless, in these talks, students nearly always contribute in ways the teacher wants to hear—not because she is supposed to hear this or because they are coming up with "right" answers, but because their answers are functional in the children's world. When students talk about science on their terms, they bring their own knowledge to bear, they hear each other's possible theories, and they develop a curriculum together—one that is attuned to their desire to learn and that builds on a set of experiences they already have.

These sorts of inquiry questions and the emergent curriculum they can generate need not be limited to Science Talks or to primary school. All ages can participate in inquiry lessons on all subjects. Vivian Vasquez (2004) developed critical literacies among 3- to 5-year-olds by building a curriculum from their own questions about everyday life. Often these were deep cultural questions—and investigating them included cracking into some entrenched cultural assumptions about what boys and girls can do, about the environment, about fast food, and about vegetarianism. In the process, the class constructed a visual trail across the walls of their room, posting artifacts (like storybooks, advertisements, pictures, stories made by students, school flyers, and photos), the questions those materials generated, and the trail of subsequent questions and answers the children followed.

Whose Experiences Are Included?

In the previous section, we asked, "Who asks the questions?" and "What kinds of sequences develop from these questions?" Another fundamental question that follows is "Whose experiences are included?" In traditional turn taking formats, student responses are often measured against a standardized curriculum and the experiences they are expected to have within it (Nystrand, 1997). However, when students ask the questions and explore multiple possible answers, classroom talk can overflow with new knowledge impossible to contain within a set curriculum. Remember George? The formal curriculum in his first-grade class included the study of farm and zoo animals. When he questioned this curriculum and suggested the class study amphibians instead (something he knew a little about from watching the Discovery Channel), the entire class (which already knew plenty about farm and zoo animals) participated in learning more about reptiles and amphibians.

Similarly, teacher/researcher and author Vivian Paley lets children's play drive their stories, which in turn drive much of the learning in her classroom. Instead of trying to push students' stories into preordained formats, she watches children's play to see how the roles there have meaning within the children's worlds. On hearing students' stories, Paley does not simply offer praise or direct them to standardized formats; rather, she asks questions that come from within those student stories— questions she could not possibly know the answer to. Consider this story, told by the kindergartner, Simon:

> Simon: Once there was a little squirrel. And his mother said, "Go sleep in a waterbed." So he did. And he drownded inside. And he got not-drownded because it leaked out and he leaked out. The mother told him to swim home. But he couldn't swim. (Paley, 1990, p. 21)

There are infinite possible teacher responses to this story, told by a 5-year-old. Probably the most traditional would be an evaluative: "Good!" or "Oh dear, the poor squirrel!" Paley, attending carefully to the context of this particular story, responded instead with the following:

> Teacher: How does the little squirrel get home, Simon? Since he can't swim?
>
> Simon: It wasn't a ocean. It was just a stream. So he walked home.

Instead of offering a sequence-closing evaluation, Paley, because she has been watching his play and listening carefully to his story, can ask a question that draws out his thinking a little further. As she says, she sees it all in there, "this original intellectual and emotional energy—a garden waiting to bloom" (p. 21).

But that garden is not the exclusive realm of kindergartners. This kind of energy is waiting to bloom in any classroom interaction. The examples of George and Simon and the students in Vivian Vasquez's classroom illustrate that tapping into that energy necessitates tapping into forms of experience and expertise that extend beyond the standard turn taking patterns or the curriculum they help to enforce. Literature discussions like the one Vivian Paley had with Simon are possible at all age levels. When these literature discussions in a middle-school or high school context take an exploratory form, they can turn IRE into what Ralph Peterson and Maryann Eeds (1990) call *grand conversations*. From their perspective, turning IRE into a grand conversation involves following two simple rules:

1. Respect the interpretations of others.
2. Never enter a discussion with a plot in mind.

Taken together, these rules suggest that we have to do a lot of listening during literature discussions, and none of it involves traditional known-answer questions or evaluating student responses. Within these literature discussions, students are also more likely to make relevant connections between literature and their own lives—helping them to clarify their own experiences, as in this example of a fifth-grade discussion of Betsy Byars' *After the Goat Man* (Peterson & Eeds, 1990, p. 57). In the story, Harold had been feeling guilty about his friend Figgy's bicycle accident, worried that it might be his fault. In the book discussion, the student, Tom, talks about similar feelings he has had:

Tom: I felt like that one time because my brother—he was allergic to strawberries and chocolate and stuff like that and I fed him Froot Loops and he ended up in the hospital.

Joyce: ((to Tom)) What happened?

Tom: Well, my brother's allergic to strawberries—strawberries and chocolate. My little brother, he's allergic to like tall grass, dust, mold, chocolate, strawberries . . .

Joyce: ((impatient)) Okay.

Tom: Well, I fed him Froot Loops and the next thing I knew he ended up in the hospital.

Bobby: You knew that it had something in it that he was allergic to, so, yeah . . .

Tom: Yeah, that's why we had to move out here [to Arizona] because if he had went into the hospital one more time . . .

Do you see any IRE in this discussion? Who is asking the questions?

This discussion contains neither IRE sequences nor a teacher's questions. As Tom shares the connections he made with the book, he also shares his own experiences with the rest of the group. The teacher is not evaluating his interpretation ("Good!"). Instead, this discussion has involved several students. They are the ones drawn in, asking questions about Tom's experiences and helping Tom to clarify his own anecdote. Like Simon's peers (and through close observation, Simon's teacher, Vivian Paley), Tom's peers provide probing, functional responses because they are the ones who are closest to his perspective.

Although it may seem to math teachers that literature lends itself more easily to incorporating student experiences, all subject areas are ripe for this transformation from the traditional format to more inclusive inquiry. Math problems can be solved in more than one way. Word problems can be generated from the circumstances of students' lives. Current events can be selected from the students' interests. Connections to mandated curriculum can build on students' worlds, rather than subtract from them. Even high school math curriculum can be "covered" by building first on students' logic. Each innovation will require careful negotiation of, in the words of the discourse analyst Courtney Cazden (2001), "the dilemma of honoring child logic and teaching conventional knowledge" (p. 54). Recording and analyzing the discourse in your classroom, however, provides you with a powerful tool to investigate both "child logic" and "conventional knowledge" and to begin to negotiate this dilemma.

Which Ways of Speaking Are Heard?

Once your classroom discourse analysis begins to explore and compare the traditional and the nontraditional, new forms of participation will emerge. Within these new forms of participation, which ways of speaking are heard? In a traditional classroom, answers that are formulated in a certain kind of English using a certain register will be recognized. In a less traditional classroom, turn taking patterns open up to include different registers. *Registers* are ways of speaking that vary according to activity. For example, most students will use a "casual" register (less concerned with standard grammar or pronunciation, sprinkled with youthful vocabulary and idioms) when talking with friends on the playground and a "formal" register (marked by standard grammar, pronunciation, and vocabulary) when greeting the principal or delivering a graduation speech. In any classroom, discourse analysis can reveal that varying registers will produce different effects.

As discussed in chapter 2, in Gallas' Science Talks, for instance, while the teacher remained silent, a limited number of students came to dominate Science Talks. So, she began to trouble-shoot using discourse analysis. She looked back at the discussions and analyzed why certain students were being shut out and how the talks changed once those voices were reincorporated. She, along with her teaching intern and students, discovered that certain ways of asking questions automatically closed out certain other contributions.

Inclusive wording invited more students to participate.

INCLUSIVE WORDING . . .		. . . ABSTRACT WORDING
How do dreams get into our heads?	. . . *worked better than* . . .	Where do dreams come from?

Eliminating technical language and terminology also invited fuller participation:

COLLOQUIAL WORDING . . .		. . . TECHNICAL WORDING
Why, when you jump up, do you come back down?	. . . *worked better than* . . .	What is gravity?

Words like *gravity* kept students who were unfamiliar with those terms from jumping into the conversation. It also permitted the students who used those words to use them in unthinking, superficial ways.

Gallas also found that changing the way more confident students introduced their theory was closing down the inquiry stance. So, quiet talkers suggested these big talkers say "I think" or "maybe" before their statements. Like the performed curiosity of Mr. Wonderful, these markers of tentativeness (Johnston [2004] calls these "linguistic lubricants") helped open up discussions and enable more thoughtful experiences for all participants.

This added transparency of norms changed who could participate in Science Talks. Initially, certain students who habitually expressed ideas more directly or had been exposed to vocabulary (like *gravity*) outside of the classroom were able to dominate. After analyzing what kinds of turns shut down other students, the class—together and explicitly—developed new norms to create more egalitarian turn taking within science talks.

As the example of the subtle shifts in Science Talks illustrate, even slight differences in ways of speaking or vocabulary choice that originate outside the classroom context can affect who is able to participate fully. When colloquial wording is not permitted in the classroom, only those students who come to class *already knowing* classroom-based vocabulary like *gravity* will be able to participate fully. When students' languages vary more dramatically, exclusion looms. This is precisely when we can use discourse analysis as teachers to investigate: Who asks the questions? Who holds the answers? Whose experiences are included? Whose voices are systematically silenced?

Agency and Nontraditional Turn Taking

As individual agents in our own classroom, discourse analysis provides us the tool to understand how our turn taking patterns—and dominant turn taking patterns of certain students—can silence certain voices. Discourse analysis also provides us the tools to identify discourse modifications that could make classroom participation a possibility for everyone.

Every day in my teaching, I fall again into the familiar IRE pattern. I may use it to check what students know, to kick along a tired discussion, or to set up a larger idea. Known-answer questions position me comfortably as the seat of knowledge in my classroom. These formats are also easy to reproduce in packaged textbook series—to incorporate into gradable tests and standardized curricula that cleanly sort the achievers from the nonachievers. This sorting, however, is not a product of successful teaching and learning; often it is simply a result of turn taking patterns, habitual classroom procedures, and ways of speaking that are not habitual for certain children.

The kinds of interactional innovations described here cannot be packaged and sold. Talking about the tacit rules of Science Talks will never be developed as a sleek boxed set of textbooks, workbooks, and assessments. The kind of imaginative play, the stories it produces, and the probing questions Vivian Paley asks about those stories will not end up in a glossy boxed set. The personal memories Tom shared after reading a Betsy Byars story will never be included in a Cliff's Notes version of the text. Each of these interactions is in part unpredictable—and abundantly creative. These interactions cannot be manufactured along a cost-effective assembly line. All the innovations described here only require recognition of the rich human resources filling every classroom.

Recognizing the human resources in our classrooms and acting on that recognition is an act of agency. Discourse analysis of interaction in our classrooms gives us the agency to see how these nontraditional interactions are functioning. Vivian Paley did not go home every night and look at the lesson plans outlined in a published Teacher's Guide. Each night, she went home and transcribed a tape of classroom interaction. This kind of analysis encourages continual re-examination of how turn taking is patterned: Who is asking questions? Who is answering them? Whose voices are excluded and why?

PUTTING IT ALL TOGETHER: MULTIDIMENSIONAL ANALYSIS OF CLASSROOM TURN TAKING

This discussion of turn taking resources brings a new set of tools to bear on the analysis of any transcript. Now we can sharpen those initial analytic questions that were introduced in the analysis in chapter 4 into a set of questions that focus our analysis on turn taking and its effects. Interactionally, we can ask,

- Who is asking the questions?
- What is the turn taking pattern?
- How is it functioning?
- What kinds of questions are being asked (known answer? open ended?) and who has the answers?

The answers to these questions also implicate social context outside of the focal interaction because the kinds of questions asked, who asks them, and the kinds of sequences they are a part of will function differently depending on the kinds of interactional habits students have when they come into the discussion. Therefore, while developing an understanding of the interactional patterns driving classroom talk, also ask analytic questions that train your analysis on how students' variable social backgrounds affect their participation in those patterns:

- Whose experiences are included?
- Who is systematically left out of these turn taking sequences?
- Why?

Much of turn taking is simply a product of unthinking classroom tradition, so look at your transcript and ask:

- What aspects of turn taking are for turn taking's sake only (procedural display)?

These questions begin to illuminate how interactional patterns and social context outside of school can interact in ways that can make some students seem more competent than others. As agents, discourse analysis allows us to investigate how interactional and social context may be controlling our actions and our classrooms in ways that are counter to our goals. Therefore, taking up a role as agents of learning in our own classroom involves asking whether turn taking patterns in our classroom are effective on our own and our students' terms—not those of a publishing company or a political agenda:

- Do turn taking patterns ensure that learning is challenging and inclusive? Why or why not? (Whose goals are they accomplishing?)
- If so, what precisely makes them work? Could I use this type of turn organization in more classroom events?
- If not, what changes in the organization of turn taking could I make?

These analytic questions are included in the following summary analytic table.

Analytic Table: Analyzing Turn Taking Sequences

EVENT	SEQUENCE	INTERACTIONAL CONTEXT	SOCIAL CONTEXT	INDIVIDUAL AGENCY
Group Story Reading	Question sequence about picture	Who is asking the questions? What is the turn taking pattern? How is it functioning?	Whose experiences are included? Who is systematically left out of these turn taking sequences? Why?	Do turn taking patterns ensure learning is challenging and inclusive? Why or why not? (Whose goals are they accomplishing?)

Analytic Table: Analyzing Turn Taking Sequences (continued)

EVENT	SEQUENCE	INTERACTIONAL CONTEXT	SOCIAL CONTEXT	INDIVIDUAL AGENCY
		What kinds of questions are being asked? (Who has the answers?)	What aspects of turn taking are for turn taking's sake only (procedural display)?	If so, what precisely makes them work? Could I use this type of turn organization in more classroom events?
				If not, what changes in the organization of turn taking could I make?

Turn taking patterns are a fascinating point of entry into the discourse in your classroom. As you begin to transcribe and consider the effects of question types, you will be surprised by the way a slight change in questioning patterns can alter a classroom environment. You will also begin to notice more nuances within the discourse in your classroom. Sometimes a single word, a borrowed phrase, or a change in voice quality or intonation can affect how a classroom event proceeds or how you interpret what a student knows. These subtle cues and their effects are the subject of the next chapter, "Analyzing Contextualization Resources" (chap. 6).

QUESTIONS AND ACTIVITIES

Critical Reflection

1. Based on your current experiences, do you agree with the claim that "turn taking still unfolds in most classrooms, most of the time, in traditional, teacher-centered sequences"? Which of your experiences run counter to this claim? Which support it?
2. Think about the ways you use IRE sequences in your classroom. In what event do you think IRE sequences are most frequent? Why?
3. In the classroom, what kinds of questions do you most like to answer? What kinds of questions do you think your students most like to answer? What kinds of questions do you ask most often in your classroom? Compare your responses to all these questions and reflect on the differences and/or similarities.

4. Have you ever been inhibited about providing answers to open-ended questions? Why? Do you ever notice students displaying similar inhibitions? What are some possible explanations? How can classroom patterns be changed to invite genuine responses to open-ended questions?
5. Have you recognized a situation of "procedural display" in classes you teach or have taken? How much of "procedural display" is a necessary part of classroom life? When does it interfere with learning?
6. Think of some typical evaluation statements you make in a class. Would it be possible to transform those into feedback statements instead? Add your examples to the following chart:

EVALUATION . . .		. . . FEEDBACK
Your pictures are great.	. . . could instead be formulated as . . .	Your pictures helped me to enjoy your story. How did you think to include the little anchor?
That's correct.	. . . could instead be formulated as . . .	That's correct. How did you get that answer?
Example:	. . . could instead be formulated as . . .	
Example:	. . . could instead be formulated as . . .	

7. Are there events in your class that could be transformed from traditional IRE events into nontraditional turn taking patterns? Why try this transformation? Why not?

Reflective Activities

1. Observe three different classrooms for 20 minutes each. As you observe, think about whether these classrooms are organized more like the Science Talks described by Gallas (teacher silent) or the traditional university classroom described by Blommaert (teacher centered). Who does most of the talking? How do turn taking patterns differ?
2. Return to the Train Hats excerpt analyzed in chapter 4 (reprinted next). Now, reanalyze this excerpt in terms of turn taking. Use the questions in the turn taking analysis chart in this chapter to guide you. Do you see IRE sequences? What kinds of questions are asked? Whose experiences are being included? Whose experiences are being excluded?

Train Hats

Teacher:	What do all the men have on their heads?
Tiffany:	Ha[ts
Rene:	[Hats
Teacher:	Hats. Do men wear a lot of hats now?
Danny:	Some don't. The train dudes- the train people wear they wear these like, big ol [things that
Teacher:	[The train people, that=
Tiffany:	Like this ((*Pointing to the picture emphatically*))
Teacher:	=that drive the train (0.2) wear hats.
Danny:	And somebody better put on some um things for um there little thing cause they hurt their ears. ((*pointing into his ears*))
Teacher:	Ah,
Danny:	Because, the noise is come in the air and (0.4)
Teacher:	But do men, do a lot of men wear hats now?

3. Now use the same questions to guide your analysis of Tom's discussion with his peers about Betsy Byars' book. Do you see IRE sequences? What kinds of questions are being asked? Who asks the questions? Who provides the answers?

Tom:	I felt like that one time because my brother—he was allergic to strawberries and chocolate and stuff like that and I fed him Froot Loops and he ended up in the hospital.
Joyce:	((to Tom)) What happened?
Tom:	Well, my brother's allergic to strawberries—strawberries and chocolate. My little brother, he's allergic to like tall grass, dust, mold, chocolate, strawberries . . .
Joyce:	((impatient)) Okay.
Tom:	Well, I fed him Froot Loops and the next think I knew he ended up in the hospital.
Bobby:	You knew that it had something in it that he was allergic to, so, yeah . . .
Tom:	Yeah, that's why we had to move out here [to Arizona] because if he had went into the hospital one more time . . .

4. Be Vivian Paley for a day: Record a classroom interaction. Go home that night and transcribe. Develop some loose hypotheses about the students' interactions. In Paley's words, the next day, your "reality will be measured alongside the children's." What do you discover?

SUGGESTIONS FOR FURTHER READING

Readers interested in a detailed, canonical discussion of turn taking within classroom events should read Hugh Mehan's (1985) article, "The Structure of Classroom Discourse." Shirley Brice Heath's (1982) article, "Questioning at Home and at School: A Comparative Study," illustrates how children in different households are socialized into different questioning patterns. For analyses of turn taking in second-language classrooms, Karen Johnson's (1995) book, *Understanding Communication in Second Language Classrooms*, is an excellent starting place. Lorrie Verplaetse's (2000) chapter on Mr. Wonderful is also an inspiring account of how dialog in the classroom can be opened up for new English speakers. Vivian Paley and Karen Gallas are excellent examples of teachers using the discourse analytic process to explore nontraditional turn taking in their primary school classrooms. For those seeking new ideas on how to break out of IRE forms, Peter Johnston's (2004) *Choice Words* provides examples of dozens of questions and turns of phrase that teachers can draw on to open up learning conversations.

6

ANALYZING
CONTEXTUALIZATION RESOURCES

PREVIEW QUESTION Consider the following examples. What do they have in common? What are the cues in each that lead to misunderstandings?

A teacher dismisses a young mother of one of her students (and a speaker of a distinct Appalachian variety of English): "I knew she was ignorant just as soon as she opened her mouth" (Purcell-Gates, 2002).

A teacher interprets a child's downward glance as an act of disrespect: "Look at me when I talk to you!"

A teacher assumes a 9th grader's graffiti-covered paper is meaningless and offensive: "Why are you writing that nonsense? It won't help you get anywhere. You can't write this stuff on your college applications!"

Now think of the ways of speaking/acting that go on in your classroom. Do the ways people talk influence how you interpret what they are saying?

As the examples in this chapter's preview question illustrates, within any classroom interaction, subtle cues—an accent that differs from our own, a downward glance, a graffiti-covered paper—trigger assumptions about how words may be functioning and what to say next. Sure-fire, one-size-fits-all meaning is not built into our statements, questions, or responses. In every interaction, we draw on layers of knowledge to interpret—and possibly make premature assumptions about—what is going on. This chapter illustrates these subtle cues and suggests ways to analyze their classroom effects.

Guiding our analysis will be the Four "C"s: contextualization cues, combinations, context, and consequences. Contextualization cues are those subtle interactional features (like ways of speaking and choosing words, posture, intonation, wait time, and speaking volume) that, in combination with other features of the individuals interacting (clothing, hairstyle, race, and other cultural artifacts such as computers, backpacks, notebooks, iPods, or Blackberries), act as clues to how words are functioning. These combinations are interpreted differently in different *contexts* and lead to different consequences for classroom learning. A discussion of what the four Cs look like and operate in classrooms continues next.

CONTEXTUALIZATION CUES

The sociolinguist John Gumperz originally coined the term *contextualization cues* to describe the extralinguistic features that we use as clues to understand how words are functioning. "Oh ↓great," for example, spoken in a lowered tone and downward intonation (as indicated by the conventional transcription symbol of the downward arrow) might function as a sarcastic complaint. The same words, "Oh ↑GREAT," spoken with rising intonation (as indicated by the upward arrow) and increased volume (as indicated by the capital letters) might function as a joyous exclamation. Often these cues function below our level of conscious choice. Like breathing, we do not usually focus on how we are using contextualization cues until there is a change of context. However, we notice how important breathing is in our lives if we are thrown into a swimming pool and, submerged, cannot breathe anymore. Likewise, we might not notice how important our own particular set of contextualization cues are to our lives until we are submerged in a new cultural context—and, for example, someone takes our downward intoned "Oh great" literally.

Gumperz and Indian English

John Gumperz has spent a career analyzing precisely this kind of cross-cultural immersion and how communication can break down in such encounters. Gumperz's original studies analyzed the discourse of Indian English speakers in Great Britain. He wanted to understand why it was that immigrants from India, who spoke impeccable English, seemed, nevertheless, to have so many misunderstandings in conversations with British English speakers. His research suggested that, although Indian

English speakers' English was grammatical and fluent, there were more subtle differences in intonation and rhetorical organization ingrained in their talk that led to these misunderstandings. British English speakers could understand the perfect vocabulary and grammar of Indian English speakers in conversation, but they could not understand how it was supposed to function. For example, a bank teller who heard the following from an English person apologized and corrected his mistake:

British English Speaker: Oh, oh. This is the wrong form.
                            My account's in Wembley.
            Teller: Oh, oh, I see.

The same interaction with an Indian English speaker proceeded differently:

Indian English Speaker: No. No. This is the wrong one.
            Teller: Why? What's wrong with it?

In the first interaction, the comment of the British English speaker clearly functions as a polite correction and the teller politely corrects his mistake. In the second interaction, however, the teller seems to take offense after hearing almost the same correction from the Indian English Speaker. In Gumperz's analysis of these interactions, intonation made all the difference. The Indian English speaker's lilting intonation emphasized "no" and "wrong":

Indian English Speaker: No, ↓no. This is the ↑wrong one.

This slight difference in intonation, it seems, led what could have functioned as a polite correction to function as a criticism and prompted a defensive reaction. In interaction after interaction, Gumperz illustrates that these differences in intonation are not a matter of intention: The Indian English speakers are not trying to be rude; their intonation in English is simply transferred from their native language environment and would be considered perfectly polite among other Indian English speakers. This slight variation, however, can sound rude and abrupt to British English speakers.

Again, just as we are usually unaware of our own breathing, British English speakers may not be aware of their expectations for British-like contextualization cues. That is, they are unaware until they are immersed in a different cultural context—in this case, in face-to-face encounters with Indian English speakers. Unfortunately, sometimes speakers are not aware that many of these sorts of misunderstandings are caused by only subtle differences in contextualization cues. Instead, people may attribute such uncomfortable encounters to more static personality traits. In the bank teller situation, the teller may even come to think of Indian people as generally bossy or disrespectful. This is racism—produced, unwittingly, through contextualization cues (Gumperz, 1970).

Contextualization Cues in the Classroom

The connections to classroom discourse are clear: In classrooms, many functions are accomplished through the subtlest of cues. The teacher carefully orchestrates these on the first day to convey the identity of her classroom. Consider, for example, how prize-winning teacher and author LouAnne Johnson (2005) recommends delivering instructions to students on the first day:

> How you deliver instructions is very important. Remember, your students are going to form their opinions of you and your teaching style within the first few minutes of your first meeting. You will project a very different persona depending on whether you are seated at your desk, perched on a stool, roving about the room, or standing in the doorway. Students will respond to the pitch, volume, and tone of your voice, your choice of words; especially your facial expression. (p. 73)

Johnson recommends that we control these initial, not-so-subtle contextualization cues consciously and carefully to create an impression in the first 5 minutes of the first day of school. She also emphasizes that students are attuned to these cues. However, not all students or teachers read these kinds of cues in the same ways.

Common Contextualization Cues

Facial expression, pitch, volume, tone of voice, word choice, and body position—Johnson mentions all of these as critical communication tools. There are many more nonverbal forms of communication you probably use to cue your students about the best ways to respond in your class, when a new event is beginning, when an event is over, when someone is trying to tell a story, and what counts as a relevant form of participation—even what is serious and what is a joke. Fred Erickson's (1996) research on "turn sharks" also brilliantly analyzes how, within the chaos of multiparty talk, students tune into the rhythms and lilts of a teacher's speech to match the rhythms, sneak in, and go for a turn—like a jazz musician going for a solo.

Students may also use the teacher's intonation to tune in to right answers, as in the following example from my own recording of a second-grade reading group I recorded:

Teacher: What is wrong with that. Is there anything wrong with that?
Sara: No.
David: No.
Rene: No.

Here the teacher's intonation (the first version of her question—"What is wrong with that?"—does not conclude with rising, question intonation, but with lowered intonation, suggesting closure) and quick rephrasing (the second version transforms it into an easy-answer yes/no question) signals this is a rhetorical question with only one right answer. This kind of cued interaction is the backbone of procedural display (see chap. 5).

As students read teachers, teachers also read students and their uses of contextualization cues. Body language that matches changes in volume, tone, and intonation can signify growing or waning interest, anxiety, anger, or myriad other possible stances. As an instructor of evening classes, I can read the not-so-subtle body language of a class that is tuning out, their bodies drooping, ready to go home. In the heat of a good class session or a good discussion, I can also see a group that is engrossed in learning—leaning in, contracting like a multiperson flexing brain.

Systematic Contextualization Cues:
Social Variation

As Gumperz's examples of Indian English suggest, contextualization cues can also collect in systematic ways to comprise recognizable forms of language variation. When language varies across a distinct demographic, the distinct variety (sometimes called an *accent* or a *dialect*) becomes associated with a certain group of people. An *accent* here refers to only the phonological features of a person's talk, that is, pronunciation (e.g., I say tomato, you say tomahto). A *dialect* includes phonological, grammatical, lexical (word choice), and discourse features. The prosodic qualities of English spoken by South Asians in London, for example, are systematic enough to be considered a variety of English—Indian English. In African-American English, pronunciation, grammar, word choice, and discourse patterns all vary systematically, and these features collect to form a social variety.

Of course, not all South Asians in London speak Indian English at all times, and not all African Americans in the United States speak African-American English at all times. However, once certain features collect into a recognizable social variety, shifting into and out of that variety can cue certain functional effects. For example, the applied linguist Ben Rampton (1995) has studied the effects of shifting into Indian English in contemporary youth culture. His research illustrates how high school students (both Anglo and Indian) used the variety to affiliate with peers who listen to *bhangra*, an India–Pakistani border genre of folk music. Among the youth Rampton studied, Indian English became a social resource and not necessarily a liability, as it was decades earlier in the studies Gumperz conducted.

Language varies in similar ways across demographics in the United States and in every school classroom. There are marked differences in the vocabulary, grammar, pronunciation, and prosody of the English spoken by students in U.S. schools: Varieties of African-American English, Appalachian English, Asian English, Chicano English, and suburban Los Angeles English all sound different. Students and teachers draw on these varieties as resources in some contexts, but experience them as liabilities in other contexts. Teachers and students have different levels of awareness of these varieties, the cues that comprise them—and how they function (cf. Rex, 2006).

Systematic Contextualization Cues:
Situational Variation

Contextualization cues also vary across situations (e.g., formal, informal, professional, or casual); the different varieties that result are called *registers*. As teachers, we may expect a relatively formal register in the classroom. Students may use a less formal register in other events—on the playground or at home. Students will also vary, however, in how they perceive what comprises a "formal register." In this way, issues of register intersect with issues of variety and can lead to miscommunication. In Georgia, for example, many students are brought up to say "yes, ma'am" and "no, ma'am" when speaking to their teacher. In other words, in a certain southern variety of English, responding with ma'am and sir to adults, comprises a formal register. In Philadelphia or Los Angeles, however, the use of "sir" and "ma'am" in schools is not required or expected as an emblem of respect or formality.

Although "yes, ma'am" is an obvious marker of formality, other features of register are more subtle. Moreover, features of language that initially strike us as emblematic of race or ethnicity may functionally be more a matter of register difference. In her research on race in the classroom, for example, the classroom discourse analyst Lesley Rex (2006) discusses the use of "signifying" in two different high school classrooms. Signifying is a characteristic discourse feature of African-American English, in which participants use verbal artistry to put down one another. As Rex reports, this discourse feature is considered a playful norm by students, but emblematic of "disrespect" by some teachers. Her research suggests, however, that for teachers the use of "signifying" in the classroom is less an emblem of race than of a less respectful register. An experienced White teacher and an experienced Black teacher both sanction signifying in their classrooms when it counters what they perceive as a respectful baseline register of respect.

Nonverbal features of interaction also contribute to register variation and its classroom effects. A downward glance, for example, is in many Native American and Latino communities considered to be a sign of respect and formality (cf. Honig, 1991). For many teachers, however, this lack of eye gaze may indicate a lack of attention or suggest that a student is treating a teacher's remarks casually. Jumping to conclusions about what this look means and acting on them ("Look at me when I'm talking to you!") can lead to a vicious cycle of misunderstanding. Moreover, in all these cases, because register features overlap with features of social variation, lack of respect can be conflated with ethnic or racial demographics and lead to systematic cross-cultural conflict.

Analyzing Contextualization Cues

As you look at your own classroom discourse, you will begin to see your own idiosyncratic use of contextualization cues, as well as the more systematic collections of contextualization cues that comprise different registers and social varieties. The following chart summarizes some of the possible cues you may find in your analysis. This is by no means an exhaustive list. You certainly will not be able or need to transcribe every single contextualization cue in your transcript.

As you analyze contextualization cues in your transcript and video, ask yourself how they are functioning and for whom. Although contextualization cues can be used as a productive resource for orchestrating relationships in your classroom (as Johnson illustrates in her discussion of teachers' first impressions), they are not always interpreted in the same ways by all students or all people, for that matter. Even among friends. So initially focus your analysis on what you perceive as classroom misunderstandings and investigate how contextualization cues are functioning within those interactions. As Gumperz's research illustrates so well, we are always negotiating, and we may often be misunderstanding. Rex's research illustrates how these same misunderstandings can occur in the classroom. Use your analysis of contextualization cues to understand the roots of those misunderstandings in your own classroom and how they can be remedied through changes in discourse.

Possible Contextualization Cues

COMMON CUES:

Non-Verbal:	Gesture, facial expression, eye movement, eye gaze, eye contact (and lack of eye contact or shifts in eye contact), posture, body movement, facial direction, style of body movement, body position (and how close you get to someone)
Paralinguistic/ Prosodic:	Volume shifts, tone shifts, rhythmic shifts, stress, stress patterns and stress pattern shifts, velocity shifts, pausing, intonation patterns

SYSTEMATIC CLUSTERS OF CUES:

Register shifts	(e.g., formal to informal)
Variety shifts	(e.g., Indian English, African American English, Appalachian English to Standard English)

(Adapted from Bloome et al., 2005)

COMBINATIONS

As you begin to look at contextualization cues, it may start to become clear that they are not working alone. Usually, they act in partnership with other features of an interaction. Understanding how this partnership functions is critical to understanding how language functions in our classrooms. James Gee (2001) has described this partnership between contextual cues and other features as a *combination*. In combination with other clues—how one dresses, one's skin color, and how one uses objects such as computers or other cultural tools—contextualization cues become powerful resources affecting how our language functions. But in the wrong context, combinations can also become liabilities.

Combinations as Resources

Any of the isolated contextualization cues discussed earlier work in combination with other features of interaction. LouAnne Johnson (2005), for example, describes not only the kind of body language, tone of voice, and facial expression that teachers might use effectively on the first day, but also encourages teachers to "dress the part":

In the search for my most effective persona, I discovered an interesting student response to my clothing: they perceive some outfits as more serious than others, and they behave accordingly. If the lesson for the day requires creativity, spontaneity, and lots of student input, I wear more informal clothing: corduroy jeans and a sweater, perhaps. On days when I want to limit the amount of spontaneity, during an important exam or a lesson that will serve as an important building block for future lessons, I wear a suit. (p. 13)

Different combinations convey different identities, and they also cause our words to function differently. When Ms. Johnson wears a suit, she feels students hear her words as being more authoritative. I suspect this suit operates in combination with the variations in body language and intonation she also recommends.

Of course, teachers are not the only ones who learn to "dress the part." Students, too, rely on combinations to convey identities and to ensure their language functions in particular ways. High school hallways are a good place to witness combinations in action. Severe black eyeliner and lacy, Victorian-style, dark-colored clothing can be paired with lowered pitch and volume and minimal smiles. This combination might be designed to convey a sensitive, introverted—but aesthetically fine-tuned—personality. This overall look and sound potentially changes the function of an ordinary Monday morning greeting—"Hi. How was your weekend?" ((*spoken in low, nasal pitch with minimal affect*))—to a personal statement layered with knowing cynicism, emblematic of the Gothic youth persona.

Combinations as Liabilities

Combinations can be deployed as resources—tools we use to try to make language function in ways we want it to. But combinations can also be read by others in ways we never intended. As nervous parents might assert as they watch their teens leave for school, the same Gothic appearance that functions powerfully in high school hallways may not function effectively when greeting the science teacher. Natsuki Fukunaga's (2006) research with college-level Japanese students has shown how cues and combinations function differently in the language classroom than outside the language classroom. These days, many students are interested in Japanese language because of their interest in Japanese popular culture—and these students often choose to dress the part. Some Japanese students change their appearance to match that of a Japanese popular singer or a character from well-known Japanese animation. Knowing Japanese words adds to their enjoyment of Japanese popular culture forms, and among their peers this combination functions as, among other things, a sign of affiliation and in-group membership. However, in the Japanese-language classroom, Fukunaga has found that teachers do not read these students' combinations favorably. Traditional Japanese-language teachers perceive these "*anime* students" as knowing *too much* colloquial Japanese and as less likely to do well in the classroom.

Combinations in Delicate Balance

Because we all wear clothes, drive cars, eat food, and use cultural tools, and because we all simultaneously speak in distinctive ways, combinations powerfully affect us regardless of whether we try to control them. The nonvoluntary function of these combinations is especially vivid when it comes to variations in language across demographic groups. For example, certain varieties of English are not necessarily stigmatized in isolation. However, when they occur in combination with other features, they become stigmatized. Sadly, I have heard elementary school teachers saying about certain students, "He doesn't even speak English!" They are not talking about a recently arrived immigrant; no, this is something I have heard teachers say about Black children who speak a distinctly African-American English. These same teachers, however, will listen to and understand a well-dressed Black Professor as he uses an African-American variety of English in his Black Masculinities class at the university, accepting fully that, in this combination, this variety counts as English. Register differences also act in combination: A White teacher dressed in a suit can "get away with" speaking frankly and colloquially (even using minor swear words), whereas a sloppily dressed teacher or a racial minority using that same way of speaking might appear disrespectful.

Analyzing Combinations

As these examples suggest, our identities in the classroom are matters of details (Blommaert, 2005). General cultural categories like male, female, Latino, African American, and so on are less functional than how those categories are made real in combinations in interaction. General characterizations of language like Black, Chicano, or Southern English do not function in isolation either. Their functionality is a factor of their combination with other nuanced aspects of appearance and ways of speaking. So, a professor speaking African-American English is recognized as an authority, whereas a Black child speaking African-American English is deemed barely understandable.

In your transcript and video, as you locate ways of speaking, also attend to how they act in combination with other, nonverbal features of talk and with an entire visual presentation of self. Think about these combinations as you view and transcribe your tape. You now have the resources to look not only at what people are saying, but also how they are saying it, what they are wearing, how close they are standing to each other, and what expressions they have on their faces. All these features of an interaction influence how the talk is functioning. Your analysis provides you with an opportunity to reflect on what contributes to your judgments of your students, their capacities, and their identities.

CONTEXT

Combinations are interpreted differently in different contexts. These different interpretations can have lasting consequences. Certain combinations function beautifully in one context, but are troublesome in others. Certain meanings just do not travel well across contexts. When a high school student uses African-American English with his friends after school, he will be heard. However, back in school, some of his teachers may lament his "lack of English." Teachers may see certain contextualization cues as part of a world that does not belong in the classroom. Different words invoke different worlds. If we don't know about each other's worlds, words may also provoke misunderstandings.

Because combinations function differently in different contexts, it becomes important as we analyze discourse to understand how contexts outside the classroom may inform how cues and combinations are used inside the classroom. Students and teachers are all, always, importing new ways of using words into our classrooms; we can use discourse analysis as a sort of archaeology of language—a way of chipping into other ways of life and understanding. A tiny detail, like the rising intonation on "wrong" in Gumperz's bank-teller example, provides a window on an entire lifetime of socialization into an Indian way of communicating in English society. By studying cues like these in our classrooms, we can potentially make multiple worlds available to all participants in classroom discourse—the global can become local. A useful tool for understanding multiple cues and their functional differences across contexts is the concept of *communicative competence*.

Communicative Competence

From rising intonation to global implications? How did we just make that connection? Simply by avoiding the common assumption that our way of speaking is the only way of speaking in the world. Oddly enough, the field of linguistics in the United States has historically maintained a significant strand devoted to discovering "language universals" by studying mainly White middle-class English speakers (Johnstone, 2000; Kulick & Schieffelin, 2004). In the 1970s, however, the linguistic anthropologist Dell Hymes (1972), reacting to what he perceived as overly universalistic claims of mainstream linguistics, developed a methodology to explore how different societies use language functionally in different ways. He then sent his anthropology students out across the globe to investigate how speech events are accomplished in different societies—and what language tools are needed to communicate competently in those events. He coined the term *communicative competence* to describe not language universals, but the culturally specific communication tools needed to participate appropriately in culturally specific speech events.

Language Socialization

The field of language socialization developed from the early work of Hymes' students and has been referred to already numerous times in this book. The work of Elinor Ochs in Samoa and of Shirley Brice Heath in the Piedmont Carolinas built the early foundations of this tradition. These scholars explore how communicative competence is developed over a lifetime of participation in speech events. This work investigated the kinds of language routines and collections of contextualization cues that children are socialized into through participation in those language practices.

From the perspective of language socialization, we are socialized through language to use language in socially appropriate ways. That is, many critical aspects of socially appropriate language use are not explicitly taught to children, but are passed on through participation with children in ordinary daily activities. For this reason, subtle features like contextualization cues are built into our language practices, but usually below our level of conscious awareness. We learn to use language in culturally appropriate ways not because we are explicitly taught, but because over a lifetime of practice these ways just feel "normal." These habits, however, are often not universal norms. For example, language socialization research conducted by Elinor Ochs and Bambi Schieffelin has also revealed that the sing-songy baby talk intonation, so common among White middle-class mothers, is nonexistent among the residents of Samoa and Papua New Guinea studied by Ochs and Shieffelin (1984). This and other patterns of parent–infant interaction, previously perceived to be universal—and necessary—to the language-acquisition process, are actually specific to White, middle-class, English-speaking mothers.

These global differences become locally relevant in a multicultural society. Gumperz's Indian English studies indicate how these socialized ways of speaking persist over a lifetime and across changes in a sociocultural context. Indian English, for example, includes features of an Indian's native language intonation. These are developed early and are functional in an Indian cultural context. However, they seem to function differently in a British English-speaking context. Similarly, language socialization studies began to reveal the ethnocentricity in early child language development studies, which would have predicted that childrearing practices in Western Samoa would lead to abnormal language development (which, obviously, they do not). By viewing language development in Western Samoa (and anywhere) as part of a cultural system, the language socialization perspective illustrates that forms are functional in specific ways in specific contexts. Contextualization cues like the dramatic pitch variation of baby talk are not a necessary part of childrearing. They are a cultural phenomenon. Lack of those cues does not indicate "bad mothering," but simply a different set of mothering practices that are functional in their own cultural context. Similarly, taking a lens informed by language socialization into the classroom can help us to avoid ethnocentric interpretations of misunderstandings there: A child who uses an African-American variety of English is not speaking "bad English," but a kind of English that is functional in another context.

Classroom discourse analysis can help us to see that varieties that seem new to us may have functional origins outside the classroom, in contexts in which those cues are communicatively competent. Many features of the contextualization cues that are unconsciously embedded in classroom talk are new to students. "Yes, ma'am" is not functional as a politeness form in my home, just as looking adults eye to eye is not functional in other households. We can use classroom discourse analysis to investigate how different forms of communication—like a downward gaze—function for their speakers. The ways that words and other features of language in use connect to culturally situated meanings is called *indexicality*.

Indexing

Cues and combinations are nouns. Indexing is the action that puts those nouns to work: It describes the work that cues and combinations do to make communication function in context. Just as a word in a book's index points to its contextualized location in a book, a word in conversation "indexes" by pointing to the functions that word is associated with in a certain context. For example, the phrase "Go Dawgs!" in combination with a Georgia cheerleading outfit indexes the function of fan support. Indexing is always contextually contingent, however. That same combination, on Halloween, might index trick-or-treating. Developing an understanding of how certain cues and combinations index certain functions or identities happens over a lifetime of socialization into certain patterns of language use in a community. Although an Appalachian accent spoken by a troublesome child's concerned mother may only index "ignorance" in the context of school, that same accent, in the context of home, may index comfort—the consoling voice of mother for a child. Try as she may, however, this mother may not be able to convey her concern to her child's teacher. All the teacher hears is the "ignorance" that accent indexes for her.

Similarly, a diamond-shaped hand sign held out by a 15-year-old Latino boy may index something different to his teacher in school than to a peer in his neighborhood in Los Angeles. For the boy, that cue in combination with gang attire and in the context of his neighborhood can index loyalty to other members of the Diamond Street gang. It may index a willingness to give up everything to protect a friend. In the context of school, that same combination will also index gang affiliation, but for school staff, gang affiliation indexes "criminal activity," not "loyalty to friends." In some schools, an index of gang affiliation may even be grounds for expulsion. So, certain cues and combinations have different functions in different contexts. As classroom discourse analysts, we can raise awareness of how those cues index differently in different contexts.

Developing communicative competence involves learning how to draw on the multiple available indexical properties of cues and combinations in a socially appropriate way in a certain context. Ideally, through awareness of the many ways of speaking and the worlds they index, the classroom becomes a multicultural context in which students and teachers become communicatively competent in multiple forms of speaking. Learning becomes a process of language socialization into multiple social contexts. This does not mean learning entails abandoning worlds and the words that are functional within them. Instead, it means learning new ways of speaking, participating in, and understanding the possible indexical values of words, grammars, and sets of contextualization cues and how they work in combination with other social features.

Analyzing Cues and Combinations in Context

Analyzing contextualization resources in context in our classrooms involves understanding the multiple forms of communicative competence that coexist. Classroom discourse analysis provides the tools to become familiar with how cues and combinations work differently in different contexts. As you look at your focal misunderstanding and identify cues and combinations at work within it, ask yourself what those combinations are indexing. Is it a world outside your classroom? To develop an understanding of the possible indexical values of words, grammars, and sets of contextualization cues and how they work in combination with other social features in your classroom, you may need to draw students into your analysis. Investigate what a diamond-shaped hand sign means to your students, talk about an eye gaze you misinterpreted, or investigate why a question you asked led to instant silence in the classroom. Like a lifeguard pulling a drowning child from the bottom of the pool, your analysis of combinations in context should proceed with the straightforward goal of rescuing students from being submersed and silenced in classroom culture.

CONSEQUENCES

Negative Evaluation

When certain ways of speaking do not work, that drowning sensation returns. Immersed in a different set of cultural norms, our contextualization cues—the combinations that are meaningful for our students in a home context—simply may not work anymore. In the classroom, students may find it impossible to display that they are competent people. Accordingly, as we begin to analyze the consequences of multiple ways of speaking, it becomes clear that in studying discourse in our classrooms, we are studying inequality. This is because different *cues* and *combinations* are interpreted differently in different contexts and lead to different consequences for classroom learning.

When students' ways of speaking are repeatedly misunderstood or, worse, denigrated in the classroom, school does not seem relevant anymore. It is impossible to care about doing well in school when school seems not to care about who you are or denigrates your knowledge or experiences because of how you are talking. It is often high-pressure testing or evaluation situations that seem to bring out these arbitrary distinctions and lead to unfortunate consequences. The tools of discourse analysis can be used to raise our awareness of these conditions. By being aware of unfair discourse practices that evaluate and perhaps ultimately silence our students, we can use that knowledge to hear students' ways of displaying knowledge and give them voice in classrooms.

From Negative Evaluation to New ways of Talking about Knowledge

Sometimes simply not being able to talk about something using the right words sets a child up to be evaluated as not knowing. Freire (1998) tells the story of a boy named Gelson who was flying a kite in a park one day.

His mathematical sense was, by chance, noticed by a mathematician who happened to be walking through the park on break from a scientific conference. The mathematician began talking to Gelson about his kite-flying:

Mathematician:	How many meters of line do you usually let loose to fly the kite?
Gelson:	Fifty meters, more or less.
Mathematician:	How do you figure out that you have let loose more or less than 50 meters of line?
Gelson:	Every so often, at about 2 meters more or less, I make a knot in the line. As the line is running through my hand, I count the knots and so I know how many meters of line I've released.
Mathematician:	And how high do you think the kite is right now?
Gelson:	Forty meters.
Mathematician:	How do you figure?
Gelson:	According to how much line I let out and the bow that the line is making. If the kite were high, well over my head, it would be the same number of meters high as of line that I let loose, but since the kite is far from my head, leaning down, it is lower than the loose meters of line.

This mathematician returned to the conference he had been attending to remark on this boy's use of trigonometry in his understanding of how high his kite was flying. Freire goes on to remark: "Ironically . . . Gelson had failed mathematics in school. Nothing of what he knew had any value in school because what he knew he had learned through his experience, in the concreteness of his context. He did not talk about his knowledge in a formal and well-composed language, mechanically memorized, which is the only language the school recognized as legitimate" (p. 73). Unfortunately for Gelson, his way of speaking had serious consequences in the classroom because he could not express his mathematical knowledge in ways the teacher would recognize. Because Gelson could not make his mathematical sense recognizable to his teacher, he was evaluated as a failure at math.

Does this mean that all math should be concretely contextualized? Isn't part of math an exercise in learning how to represent ideas in the abstract? This may be true. But from a discourse perspective, learning how to make these more abstract representations is a process of learning new ways of speaking. Students do not automatically know mathematical ways of speaking when they enter school. If they do, they have learned this out of school, through a process of socialization many children will not have had. From a discourse perspective, learning is an interactive process through which learners gain the use of tools necessary to participate in their multiple social worlds. In a math lesson, for example, students are not only learning new content, they are also necessarily and *simultaneously learning how to talk mathematically.* Learning this kind of talk is a large part of learning how to do math.

Understanding whether students are familiar with ways of speaking mathematically involves, first, understanding how they represent math ideas on their own terms. This mathematician's conversation with Gelson illustrates a math discussion that could work well in a classroom—and could begin a process of understanding the multiple ways of talking about math that can coexist. Look at the way this presumably sophisticated mathematician questions Gelson:

Mathematician: How many meters of line do you **usually** let loose to fly the kite?

Mathematician: **How do you figure out** that you have let loose more or less than fifty meters of line?

Mathematician: And how high **do you think** the kite is right now?

Mathematician: **How do you figure?**

These questions do not have the traditional ring of formal math instruction. Granted, Freire has translated these questions from their original Portuguese, but nevertheless it is reasonable to presume that this mathematician's casual register is represented in the translation through approximating words and phrases like "usually" and "do you think "and through the repeated, abbreviated probe, "How do you figure?" This change in register may have several functions: It downplays the fact that this mathematician knows a lot about math and that he may know the "right" answers to the questions he is asking. Like Mr. Wonderful, the science teacher discussed in chapter 5, who used the conversation starter "I wonder how . . ." to spark students' curiosity about genetics, this mathematician takes on a tone of wonder to draw out Gelson. Taking this tone might function as well in a math class as it does in a park to bridge different ways of speaking and in-class and out-of-class mathematical contexts. By taking on this register, in a way, Freire's mathematician transformed the kite-flying experience into a mathematics inquiry lesson for Gelson.

In this context, the mathematician recognized Gelson's contextualized understanding of trigonometry: By recognizing how Gelson represented his ideas, the mathematician was able to accurately (and positively) evaluate the concepts that Gelson understood.

From Silencing to Giving Voice

Apparently, while the mathematician gave voice to Gelson, the evaluation Gelson's classroom teacher gave him potentially silenced him in school math class. Whereas Gelson could speak freely with a professional mathematician, he could not express his math sense in the language of school. Again, when certain ways of speaking do not work anymore, it becomes impossible not only to display that we are competent people, but also to give voice to any of our needs and concerns in the classroom. All the examples given at the start of this chapter illustrate that cues in combination can, in the context of the classroom, lead to the consequence of silencing. Let's go back and rethink how these misunderstandings are generated.

Purcell-Gates talks about a young mother whose Appalachian accent indexes, to her daughter's teacher, that this woman is ignorant. This mother, Jenny, had been to the school repeatedly, asking why her son, Donny, was not reading and what could be done to help him. Because Jenny's speech was socially marked (in combination, probably, with other social features), she was never taken seriously. Despite her frequent visits to the school to ask about Donny's lack of progress, the school continued to send notes home to her about her son's problems as if she had never been there. Eventually, Dr. Purcell-Gates approached the administration on Jenny's behalf. Instantly, the son's situation was addressed. Until Purcell-Gates spoke for Jenny, this concerned mother was silenced.

In the second case, a teacher interprets a child's downward glance as an act of disrespect: "Look at me when I talk to you!" Why was the child scolded for looking down? Countless stories of teaching among Native Americans include accounts like these. For some Navaho Indians, eye contact can index anger. White middle-class Americans, in contrast, crave eye contact, and as teachers may look favorably on those students whose sparkly eyes closely monitor their every word. So, for Navaho children in the classroom, a silence that is meant to communicate respect at home potentially becomes a dysfunctional silence in the classroom. These differences lead to a vast chasm of miscommunication and silence, when again and again a student's downward glance indexes respect to him and disrespect or ambivalence to a teacher (Honig, 1991).

In the third case, what prompted such an outburst over the graffiti on a piece of paper? When I began teaching seventh, eighth, and ninth grade in Los Angeles in 1990, I believed in my students and, above all, wanted to see them succeed academically. When I saw some begin to write graffiti on their papers, I was heartbroken. To me, this graffiti represented their doom and my failure as their teacher. In a panic, I would berate them—try to shame them into my way. I was the one who would say, "That won't work on your college applications!" It took about 5 years for me to realize that these students had numerous and complex reasons for beginning to affiliate with gangs or graffiti-tagging posses. Only by talking to students, without snap-judging them on the basis of a graffiti-strewn paper, could I begin to learn about what was important to them— not just tell them what was important to me. Many of my students perceived gang affiliation as their primary link to friendship, security, and safety. My proclamation about college prospects was not going to convince them otherwise. Gang writing, although indecipherable to the novice teacher, may be the most meaningful and functional literacy these students use. Connecting to students through this medium can be a powerful tool for drawing them out of their silence in the classroom.

Unfortunately, in each of these situations, cues and combinations index differently for different groups of people. As long as these differences remain unspoken, they remain misunderstood: Jenny, the young Appalachian mother, is only as ignorant as the teacher who does not understand her; a Navaho child casting his eyes down before the teacher is no more disrespectful than the teacher who misinterprets that glance; and the graffiti on a piece of paper is no more destructive than the teacher who condemns its author. In each of these cases, silence across these lines of discourse difference perpetuates inequality.

Breaking such patterns of inequality necessitates giving voice in each of these situations. Conducting classroom discourse analysis potentially raises awareness of moments of silencing—and provides tools to make those explicit connections across lines of discourse difference.

AGENCY THROUGH AWARENESS
OF CONTEXTUALIZATION RESOURCES

How, exactly, is discourse analysis going to help us here? How could we possibly see, in a transcript or a video, the infinite possible variations in contextualization cues and what they index? We do not need to see every nuance of difference in our classrooms. But usually there are some differences that are easy to see—as easy to see as the angry exchange between Gumperz's bank teller and the Indian English speaker or a misunderstanding between an impatient teacher and a resistant student. Misunderstandings are easy to spot. Getting to the source of that misunderstanding is our responsibility as teachers. Classroom discourse analysis is our tool.

As we begin to look carefully at discourse in our classrooms, we inevitably find that studying classroom discourse is about studying inequality. Discourse-level inequality in the classroom is in large part produced by long-standing inequalities present in society outside the classroom. Taking a position of agency in our classrooms involves finding ways to subvert these inequalities, rather than reproduce them.

Augmenting Our Agency as Teachers

In any misunderstanding, our agency is automatically augmented through awareness. Seeing the force of a simple contextualization cue can give us more control. When we discuss Gumperz's examples of cross-cultural misunderstanding in my classes, students' jaws drop in sudden recognition. Inevitably, at least one student recalls a misunderstanding in which a slight variation in contextualization cues created an unsettling interaction. As if predicting these reactions, Gumperz provides some advice at the end of his film, "Crosstalk," that can apply to any misunderstanding:

1. Think about your everyday assumptions
2. State your everyday assumptions
3. Be explicit
4. Talk about discrimination
5. Listen to the END
6. Give extra time

This advice, meant to apply to any cross-cultural encounter, is equally applicable to the classroom. Two of these pieces of advice emphasize timing: listen to the end, and give extra time. Each of these features is critical in classrooms. We have already discussed the need to wait and listen. In chapter 5, we discussed how, when teachers wait after a child's reading miscue (rather than instantly correcting it), children often self-correct, leading to a greater sense of self-efficacy on the part of the child and potentially enhancing their identity as a successful reader. Noticing when we do not listen to the end and where we need to give extra time are important outcomes of discourse analysis—and areas where teachers have the potential to make powerful changes.

The other four pieces of advice mentioned by Gumperz cluster under two fundamental processes: (a) recognizing our assumptions, and (b) talking explicitly about them. Assumptions are notoriously difficult to access and discuss because assumptions about language and its functionality, like the air we breathe, are ever present and, usually, invisible. However, discourse analysis potentially makes those assumptions visible, tangible, and subject to discussion. Discourse analysis, by involving the recording and transcribing of real instances of interaction, turns our cultural assumptions into something concrete to talk about—as Gumperz recommends, "explicitly." In the classroom, talking about our assumptions through a discussion of actual transcripts and/or recordings of interaction can directly involve students—and augment their agency as well by giving them awareness of their linguistic choices and the consequences those choices may have in different contexts.

Augmenting Students' Agency

Once we begin to talk about assumptions with our students, being explicit is an important way of augmenting our own and our students' agency. Judith Baker, a high school teacher from the Boston area, illustrates this process in a chapter she wrote about teaching her students about trilingualism. By *trilingualism*, Baker does not mean learning three languages with national borders. Instead, she calls on her students to recognize that they are already becoming trilingual. As she points out to her students, they all are developing—and need to know—at least these three different "languages":

- "home" English or dialect, which most students learn at home, and recent immigrants often learn from peers, and which for first and second generation immigrants may be a combination of English and their mother tongue
- "formal" or academic English, which is learned by many in school, from reading and from the media, although it may also be learned in well-educated families
- "professional" English, the particular language of one's profession, which is mostly learned in college or on the job, or in vocational education (pp. 51–52)

Making these three languages explicit is the key to making students aware of their different possible functions. Instead of suggesting to the students that the language students use at home is wrong, she lets students know (and helps them to discover) that this language is a powerful resource. In the process, she illustrates how different ways of speaking can be resources, but only when used in certain combinations and in certain contexts.

Becoming communicatively competent in multiple contexts then involves learning how our words index differently in different contexts. Knowing how our ways of speaking indicate different things to different people can provide us with a powerful communication tool. Once students are aware of the different possible combinations and their effects, students can make choices about how they want to deploy these resources. Baker, in fact, devises role plays for her students and has them test out which of their three languages they want to use and to think about the consequences of their language choices.

Baker's work with high school students puts into practice the advice that Freire has given to teachers who want their students, like Gelson the kite-flyer, to have a stronger voice in school. Like Baker, Freire (1998) stresses that school register should be taught explicitly to all children, but he also be stresses the following:

1. Children's home languages are as rich and beautiful as the educated norm and that therefore they do not have to be ashamed of the way they talk;
2. Even so, it is fundamental that they learn the standard syntax and intonation so that

   a. they diminish the disadvantages in their struggle to live their lives;
   b. they gain a fundamental tool for the fight they must wage against the injustice and discrimination targeted at them. (p. 74)

By incorporating explicit activities and discussion about contextualization resources in the classroom, students and teachers alike make their assumptions about language and identity clear. By making such assumptions explicit, students and teachers both achieve agency by gaining the interactional tools to understand and participate in multiple social worlds.

PUTTING IT ALL TOGETHER: MULTIDIMENSIONAL ANALYSIS OF CONTEXTUALIZATION RESOURCES

This chapter and the analysis suggested within it now make it clear: Discourse is not just language in context. Discourse is also a site of inequality (Blommaert, 2005). Analyzing discourse gives us insight into that inequality and the option to refuse to perpetuate it in our classrooms. In the previous chapter, we noticed the imbalance of turn taking. In this chapter, our analysis turned to how microscopic cues in our interactions are embedded in a context of inequality. Understanding how our classroom interactions reproduce or challenge this inequality involves looking at the multidimensionality of discourse. Looking at contextualization resources—cues, combinations, context, and consequences—adds another layer of analysis within those dimensions.

To proceed with analysis of your own classroom discourse, locate a source of misunderstanding within the speech event you have chosen to analyze. It may be a question you have asked that never gets the answer you were looking for. It may be a student answer you never expected, a disagreement, a derailed discussion, or a student who is suddenly participating or suddenly silent. Locate a sequence that interests you and that seems worthy of further investigation. In a sequence like this, you can begin to see how the four Cs function.

Interactional Context: Cues and Combinations

Our first entry point is to look at the interactional context. Interactional context comprises the sequential or other patterns of talk within an interaction—like systematic deployment of contextualization cues—that influence what we can and cannot say and how others interpret it within classroom discourse. At this level of analysis, it is important to notice how contextualization cues are functioning in combination with other features of the interaction. As you watch a sequence you have selected as an example of "misunderstanding," ask yourself the following:

1. What contextualization cues are functioning here and how?
2. Are cues noticeably different for different people? (e.g., Are the students reacting differently than the teacher is? Who is misunderstanding whom?)
3. Are certain other features of the interaction (e.g., dress, appearance, objects) influencing how cues are functioning? Are they perpetuating the misunderstanding?

Social Context: Consequences in Context

Your answers to the questions about interactional context may likely lead you into considerations of social context. Social context comprises the social factors outside the immediate interaction that influence how words function in that interaction (in contrast to interactional context of classroom discourse, which involves sequential or other patterns of talk within an interaction). This is where indexing comes into the picture. For example, if you cannot make sense of a student's response, but everyone else is displaying a certain understanding, the students may have some contextual information you do not have. Ask yourself questions about how contexts outside the classroom may be informing how cues are functioning and what their relationship is to this particular misunderstanding:

1. How might cues (including shifts in register and social variety) be indexing relationships outside the classroom? For example, could certain ways of speaking be clear in a peer or family context, but not in a school context?
2. How are these variations contributing to this particular misunderstanding?

To answer these questions, you may need to talk to the participants. For example, if there are words constantly in use and which you do not understand (e.g., *roll dog* and *nube* are two examples I have encountered in my own research), ask students what these words mean to them. Such words may have immense functionality outside the school context.

Agency: Changing the Consequences

Finally, analyzing contextualization resources in our classrooms may give us insight into inequality in discourse that we do not want to perpetuate. Misunderstandings always involve at least two different perspectives. When the teacher's perspective is always the right one, nobody is learning. However, when we investigate the multiple worlds and ways of speaking that contribute to misunderstandings, we augment the agency of our students and ourselves. After looking at your transcript, how will you redo interactions to augment student voice and student choice? Ask yourself and your students:

1. In this misunderstanding, who has voice and why?
2. Whose assumptions are guiding different understandings?
3. How can we change this situation?

Taking up agency as a classroom discourse analyst involves understanding how cues, combinations, and context work together to construct consequences in our classrooms; and using that awareness to change the negative consequences of different ways of speaking.

The following analytic table should give you some guidance as you embark on an analysis of the four Cs and how they feature in a particular misunderstanding in your classroom.

How we express ourselves and how our students express themselves, down to the stretch of a vowel or the pitch of a question, can have lasting consequences in our classrooms. But these features of our interactions also function as powerful resources to make points, question our students, and convey disdain, approval, moral authority, or infinite other possibilities. As features of our talk that develop over a lifetime, contextualization resources are also quite often features we use unconsciously. However, through awareness, we can come to use them in powerful and conscious ways. Analysis of classroom discourse can be a first step toward learning how contextualization resources can indeed be resources and not liabilities for learning. In the next chapter, we begin to investigate another powerful and universal interactional resource—the power of narrative.

Analytic Table: Analyzing the Four Cs

		INTERACTIONAL CONTEXT	SOCIAL CONTEXT	AGENCY
Event	Sequence	Cues and Combinations	Context and Consequences	Changing the Consequences
e.g., Group Story Reading	Something you perceive as a mis-understanding	How are cues functioning? For whom? In combination with what?	How might cues (including shifts in register and variety) be indexing relationships outside the classroom? How are these variations contributing to this particular misunderstanding?	In this misunder-standing, who has voice and why? How can we change these consequences?

QUESTIONS AND ACTIVITIES

Critical Reflection

1. LouAnne Johnson describes specific combinations—options for how to talk, act, and dress on the first day of school. Do you have specific ways you consciously talk, act, and dress on your first day of school? How do they compare to Johnson's advice?

2. Throughout your teaching, how do you use contextualization cues in your classroom to signal different events, your expectations for a certain event, and your assessments of student responses?

3. Do you have a student in your classroom who seems "perfect"—who always does the right thing, knows the right answer, and so on? If so, how do contextualization cues contribute to this impression? If not, can you imagine such a person? Or an entire class of perfect students? Is this the kind of class you want to teach? Why or why not? What are the implications for the investigation of contextualization resources?

4. Apply what you've learned about "combinations" in this chapter to Gumperz's research on "contextualization cues." Do you think a phe-notypically White person using Indian English intonation would also be perceived as pushy or impolite? Why or why not?

5. In your life, think of an example when cues, combinations, and context have conspired to yield positive life consequences (i.e., what cues, combinations, and contexts make you feel most powerful?). Then think of a case in which cues, combinations, and context have con-

spired against you (i.e., what cues, combinations, and context make you feel powerless?). How have these experiences shaped the opportunities you've had and who you are today?

Reflective Activities

1. Combinations detecting: What combinations do you witness in your classroom and school? How do they influence your judgments of students and colleagues? At first, try looking exclusively for language/clothing combinations and weigh their effects in the following chart (add rows as necessary).

WAYS OF SPEAKING (Contextualization Cues)	WAYS OF DRESSING	FUNCTIONAL EFFECT

2. Classroom analysis: Look at your videotaped classroom event and isolate a single case of misunderstanding. Within this sequence, how do contextualization cues, combinations, and multiple contexts affect the participants' interpretation of how language is functioning and how they should participate? Who has voice in this misunderstanding and who does not? Use the summarizing analytic table at the end of this chapter to guide your analysis.

Suggestions for Further Reading

Those interested in more details and a theoretical discussion of contextualization cues might look at one of John Gumperz's (1977) foundational articles, "Sociocultural Knowledge in Conversational Inference." The film I have mentioned throughout this chapter, "Crosstalk," is now long out of print, but many of the same concepts are discussed in his book, *Discourse Strategies* (1982). For a detailed description of "combinations" and how they function, see Gee's (2001) review article, "Identity as an

Analytic Lens for Research in Education." Readers interested in language socialization have a wealth of ethnographies from which to draw: I have already drawn many examples from Elinor Ochs's (1988) *Culture and Language Development* and Shirley Brice Heath's (1983) *Ways with Words*. Bambi Schieffelin's (1990) *The Give and Take of Everyday Life* describes socialization practices on Papua New Guinea, Marjorie Harness Goodwin's (1990) *He Said, She Said* describes the after-school language practices of Black children in inner city Philadelphia, and Ana Celia Zentella's (1997) *Growing Up Bilingual* describes bilingual language socialization within Puerto Rican families in New York City. Delpit and Dowdy's (2002) volume, *The Skin That We Speak*, contains beautifully written essays that testify to the power of multiple ways of speaking and how to recognize these as resources within the classroom. Judith Baker's chapter in this volume provides descriptions of exercises she has used with her high school students to draw out discussion about multiple ways of speaking and their varied uses. Those interested in reading more about how high school students can explore their own languages should also look into the work of Bob Fecho (2000), starting with his article, "Critical Inquiries Into Language in an Urban Classroom."

7

ANALYZING NARRATIVE RESOURCES

PREVIEW QUESTION Before you read this chapter, think about the stories you have heard in your classroom and in your school.

How do stories come out in your classroom discussions?

What have you learned about students from the stories they tell?

What stories have you told in class and how do you think they affect students?

Schools are filled with stories. Once we start listening to them, our classrooms explode with both the profound differences between individuals and our universal humanity.

Once upon a time . . .

Federico, a young man attending City School Alternative Charter School, told the story about why he left Belmont, a notoriously rough Los Angeles high school:

Federico: Our neighborhood started having shit with that
neighborhood down there? So I went over there to the
bus so they came and hit me up.
I said my neighborhood and they said fuck that so they
socked me?
↑Everybody rushed me.
Then the next day we, we and the homeboys went down
and they got me. So that's it.

Once upon a time . . .

A three-year-old girl named Vinnie hugged her Teddy Bear upside
down and told the class her first story (Paley, 1990, p. 18):
Vinnie: There was a bear that he standed on his head.

Both of these stories came out in classrooms: one from a 15-year-old
boy with a police record who had attended several schools, and one from
a 3-year-old girl with a Teddy Bear attending school for the first time.
Profoundly different—but universally human: Both storytellers are vulnerable and alone, and for both, their words present a possibility to connect to a teacher and a set of peers. This chapter looks at how stories like
these emerge in classroom discourse, how peers and teachers respond to
those stories, and what follows these storytelling sequences. I call this the
Into-Through-and-Beyond of narrating in classroom discourse.

All three dimensions of discourse we have been analyzing—social
context, interactional context, and individual agency—affect the Into-
Through-and-Beyond stages of narrating. Through narrative, we traverse
interactional and social contexts, and we call on our own agency to infuse
our life's experiences with meaning and relevance. This chapter includes
examples of different kinds of narratives to illustrate that your exploration of narrative in your classroom should not be limited by overly
strict notions of narrating or the worthiness of a particular form or style.
However, you will need a focused lens to begin to notice the significance
of narration in your classroom. As you analyze the Into-Through-and-
Beyond stages of narrating in your classroom, use the dimensions and
summative rubrics explicated in the sections that follow to focus your
questioning and analysis.

INTO-THROUGH-AND-BEYOND:
THE INTERACTIONAL DIMENSION

First, we focus on how the interactional context affects how tellers get
INTO a story (or what instigates it), what interactionally carries them
THROUGH the telling, and, finally, what happens in interaction after the
story is told (BEYOND the confines of the narrative). The following table
summarizes the analytic questions discussed through examples in the
sections that follow. As you analyze your own classroom interactions, you
can also use this table to focus your attention on interactional context.

Analyzing Interactional Context

INTO   What question or object is this narrative a response to?

              What event is the narrative embedded in?

              Is the narrative on the border of an event?

THROUGH	What is the form of the narrative?
	How do word choices shape the protagonist and antagonist within that form?
	How is this narrative co-authored during telling?
BEYOND	What happens in that interaction when the story finishes?

INTO: *What Question or Object Is This Narrative a Response To?*

In interaction, certain questions instigate classroom narratives: "Tell us about your birthday party," "How did you get that cut?", "How did you end up at this school?", and "What just happened to you?" Just as questions take on a range of functions, their responses can range from perfunctory statements to elaborate narrative journeys. Just as "How are you?" functions as a typical greeting, but also sometimes as a genuine question, there is a functional give and take, a dialectic, between the question (or any instigating remark) and the narrative: The question instigates a certain kind of narrative; at the same time, how the question functions is retroactively measured by the narrative that follows it.

Question ↔ Narrative
instigates

It may seem obvious that questions instigate narrative. But how could a narrative retroactively instigate a question? If students enter our classroom having just fought with a peer, won a prize, worked all night, and so on, no matter what we ask them, our question may lead to a story about those experiences, retroactively transforming even the most school subject-oriented question into a question about human experience. A question such as, "What was the theme of last night's reading?" can turn instantly into the functional equivalent of "What just happened to you?"

Even when questions are not designed to incite them, narratives emerge, apparently unbidden. On these occasions, it becomes clear that students are bursting with stories to tell—and they will use any questions to make their storytelling possible. Consider Danny's Train Hats narrative (more fully analyzed in chap. 4):

Teacher: Do men wear a lot of hats now?

Danny: Some don't. The train dudes- the train people wear they wear these like, big ol [things that

Teacher: [The train people, that=

Tiffany: Like this ((*Pointing to the picture emphatically*))

Teacher: =that drive the train wear hats.

Danny: And somebody better put on some um things for um
           there little thing cause they hurt their ears. ((*pointing
           into his ears*))

Teacher: Ah,

Danny: Because, the noise is come in the air and . . .

Danny reconstructs this teacher's known-answer question as a bid to tell his own story. He uses "Do men wear a lot of hats now?" to launch a narrative about hats that train dudes wear. Train hats are compelling for him. Why? No one will know unless someone asks for more. Listen for these stories in your class one day and note how you respond. What happens when you follow the thread of a student narrative—even one that seems, at first, to unravel your intended lesson? You may find students' stories can be a new and renewable classroom resource.

You may also find that not only people and questions instigate stories: Objects instigate stories as well. In Vivian Paley's (1990) *The Boy Who Would Be a Helicopter*, for example, the preschool-age boy Jason weaves a year-long story about his helicopter—sometimes with broken wings, at other times hiding, in battle, aloft—making its way with Jason through the daily give and take of classroom life. Paley gradually uses Jason's helicopter to pull him into dialogue with his classmates and fuller engagement with school. As Paley remarks, "Helicopters and kittens and superhero capes and Barbie dolls are story telling aids and conversational tools. Without them, the range of what we can listen to and talk about is arbitrarily circumscribed by the adult point of view" (p. 39). High schools may not have kittens and superhero capes, but instead have graffiti notebooks, pencil cases, posters, purses, microscopes, globes, bookstands, coffee thermoses, and so on. Every classroom is full of these storytelling aids—make note of them, and watch how they instigate and, in turn, are brought to life by student narratives.

As you begin your analysis of narratives, look back to the surrounding questions, remarks and objects and consider the relationship between the story told and the circumstances that prompted it.

INTO: *What Event Is the Narrative Embedded In?* (*How Is It Reshaping That Event?*)

In addition to an instigating question or object, we need an event (sharing time, current events, and math review) within which we can tell our stories. As illustrated next, the functionality of a narrative intertwines not only with the remark or object that prompted it, but also with the event within which it is embedded. In classrooms, students gradually learn to fine tune their narrating to a learning event and the kinds of questions within it.

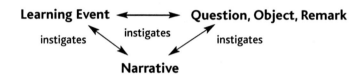

Certain events lend themselves to certain kinds of narratives: Federico's story at the beginning of this chapter is embedded in a group discussion about leaving schools, in which students are building on each other's responses, leading to more questions that in turn lead to more stories. His story fits in perfectly with this event design and foments more discussion of school departures. Similarly, Vinnie's one-sentence story, "There was a bear that standed on its head," is part of a designated story-acting portion of Vivian Paley's preschool classroom. In this event, stories are heard, probed, and catalogued in the group's collective memory. They will be recycled and elaborated on in future events.

Show and tell, a perennial classroom event, is not only a "show," but also a "tell" that involves a narrative about a favorite toy, a dinosaur bone, or a pet rat. Like the give and take between stories and the questions that prompt them, an object is reshaped, brought to life, by the "telling" that goes on around it while the narrative is simultaneously shaped by the "showing." This showing and telling is an ideal medium for classroom learning—bringing objects in our world to life by imbuing them with human understanding and connection.

Unfortunately, "show and tell"—like a story about a Teddy Bear or Train Hats—is often treated as a detour from curriculum—something to fit in if time permits. In the meat of traditional classroom events, narratives are often constructed as distractions, not focal interactions worthy of more probing. However, as Vivian Paley (1990) has remarked, these interruptions can be bids to join into an instructional conversation. It is those who do not interrupt that we must be wary of: "Those who never interrupt may be withholding too much. Until they tell us more of what is on their minds, they may not be able to listen to what *we* have to say" (p. 39).

When students interrupt, we must be able to hear them so that they will be able to understand us. So, as you listen to narratives, two questions become relevant: (a) What about this event made narrating possible? and (b) How is this narrative reshaping classroom questions and events? A close look at narrative discourse may begin to illustrate when narratives are necessary interruptions or welcome departures from lessons that can be returned to, if necessary, much more fruitfully later.

INTO: *Is the Narrative on the Border of an Event?*

Sometimes, however, narrative interruptions of classroom talk do not emerge or cannot be heard during formal classroom events. Along the margins of a traditional lesson, when the structure of events suggests that we are no longer being held accountable for learning or teaching, I have found that teachers and students may come back to narratives that could not be told during a lesson. We might catch up with students while still in each other's presence, a few minutes before class officially ends, but when a learning event has come to a close. What do we talk about with our students while we are all packing up our books? What do we tell while we wait for the bell to ring? Is it necessary for these to be silent moments? I found the few minutes gap between the end of an ESOL pullout event and the return to mainstream classes to be a fertile territory for impromptu narrating, as when this ESOL teacher turns to Rene:

> Teacher: Tell us about your birthday party. You were trying to tell
>   me earlier and I couldn't listen to you . . . .

On this simple prompt, while waiting to go back to his class after this pullout ESOL session, Rene tells the lengthiest story I had heard him tell in 2 years. Moreover, his classmates joined in, and the teacher learned more about all the students as they offered and contested each other's feelings about birthday traditions.

Students will also, unbidden, launch into their own stories on the borders of events. At City School, I recorded heated narratives embedded in arguments about gang membership, the price of friendship, and the definition of a real friend or an honest person. These narratives were not part of class, but part of life. These stories, however, informed what these students cared about—where their moral commitments were, and how, in the midst of chaotic childhoods, they made it through every day on top of going to school. These are the kinds of stories that can inform classroom lessons and make connections between students' worlds and commitments.

In these cases—chatting after a pullout session or arguing with peers between classes—the end of a lesson, not the lesson itself, incites student storytelling. Don't miss these border narratives as you record; as you analyze these stories, reflect on how the margin of an event contributes to what goes on in a story among students or between students and a teacher.

THROUGH: *What Is the Form of the Narrative?*

What carries us through a narrative? In talk—whether a conversation at recess or a discussion in class—stories represent a break in the routine back and forth of turn taking. Interaction is suspended as someone indicates with a clearing of the throat, a "once upon a time," a "so this guy," or a wistful pause that he or she is about to begin narrating. What compels us to keep listening or to keep telling in this suspended moment? Sometimes the prototypical form of narrative—problem, response, and consequence—can compel our attention and shape our telling. Although questions incite narrative, the form also shapes what narratives look like. While Federico, in the narrative that began this chapter, was responding to "What made you leave Belmont?", the narrative that followed, in many ways, justified his choice, as he portrayed himself as a protagonist who fought and against all odds survived an unfair attack from a group of enemies. In part, narrative *form* affords this narrative portrayal. As shown next, Federico narrated himself as a protagonist in a typical narrative form as he faced a problematic event and stoically took the consequences. His narrative contains prototypical narrative features—a problematic experience, his response to that problem, and the consequence, which was the departure from school.

PROBLEMATIC EXPERIENCE	Federico:	Our neighborhood started having shit with that neighborhood down there? So I went over there to the bus so they came and hit me up I said my neighborhood and they said fuck that so they socked me? ↑Everybody rushed me. hn.
RESPONSE		Then the next day we, we and the homeboys went down
CONSEQUENCE		and they got me. So that's it.

As you begin to analyze narratives in your focal event, see how those narratives fit into these prototypical divisions. Usually that problematic setup includes a setting—and that setting may even cue the pending trouble. These narrative setups are often routinized; if you hear "Woke up this mornin' . . ." while listening to the radio, for example, you know The Blues are coming. If you hear "A guy walked into a bar . . . ," prepare for a joke. Like 3-year-old Vinnie's "There was a bear . . . ," these formulas help get stories going and cue listeners that more action is coming—". . . that he standed on his head." Because of these formulaic expectations, we may also expect more than what we get: "Well then what happened?" In this way, the form kicks stories along as an audience listens and expects certain kinds of events to follow. Have you ever thought you were finished with a story only to find your listeners still waiting for the conclusion? Did you think fast to add some kind of conclusive punch (or mutter nervously, "Heh, heh, guess you had to be there . . .")? Although our own idiosyncratic experiences may compel us to tell, the form of narrative and the expectations it creates can often force those experiences out in a certain predictable way.

Expectations brought on by a narrative form can also give an author control over how to portray a personal story. In Federico's story, for example, the form magnifies the problematic event (neighborhood gang rivalry) and minimizes his reaction (self-defense). In this way, the form helps to craft his position in the story: The problems he faced as a student in that neighborhood were big. The way he confronted them and the consequences he met were inevitable—almost not worth detailing: "They got me." Federico uses the form here to construct a sympathetic portrait of himself as the protagonist in his own story.

THROUGH: *How Do Word Choices Shape the Protagonist and Antagonist Within That Form?*

Within those story forms, word choice is another powerful tool for making sense of our experiences in the presence of others. The single word we choose to call a threatening enemy, for example, can create immediate impact. Oddly enough, a seemingly vague word like the pronoun *they* can function as a powerful tool to repeatedly assert the presence of some unknown other. In Federico's story, he uses the pronoun *they* in combination with *everybody* without explicitly naming an enemy to convey the ominous and powerful presence of "that neighborhood" as he narrates the initiating problematic event:

> "**They** came and hit me up."
> "**They** said fuck that."
> "**They** socked me."
> "**Everybody** rushed me."

Taken together, these globalizing pronouns portray a formidable, although nameless, antagonist. Moreover, everything *they* do is directly violent or offensive:

> "They came and **hit me up**."
> "They **said fuck that**."

"They **socked me**."

"Everybody **rushed me**."

In contrast, Federico's statements about his own actions are comparatively placid:

"I **went over to the bus**."

"I **said my neighborhood**."

When Federico does retaliate in his response to this victimization, he does not act alone. Now he is a "we."

"**We** and the homeboys went down."

This verb phrase "went down" is so ambiguous I had to ask later what "We and the homeboys" did that was so bad. What he describes as "went down" refers to a lot: He returned to the rival gang hotspot with his gang and retaliated. This time a presumably better-matched fight ensued, one that also included people getting hit up, rushed, and socked. The word choice of "went down" to describe this fight contrasts vividly with the explicit fighting words used to describe the rival gang in the problematic event.

Finally, Federico voices the consequences he faced. Again, the pronouns are ominous, but ambiguous:

"**They** got me."

Here, *they* is the enemy. *They* could be the police, the school officials, or the other gang. It doesn't matter. What matters is that *they* got him, and he could not go to Belmont anymore. Federico did not leave Belmont by choice—he left because he had been pushed into fighting by rival gangs. The *they* who got him to leave school in the end is not much different from the *they* who socked him. These pronouns and the actions they commit build a narrative genre that was repeated by Federico's peers and recurs in published gang narratives. This genre always includes a pre-existent threat (e.g., "that neighborhood") that leads to conflict that leads to leaving school. The consequences are inevitable. A letter by a 24-year-old former gangster, Dana, echoes the dynamics narrated by Federico and his peers: "School was the enemy to me. I was bullied and tormented. I got into a lot of fights and started running with gangs" (Johnson, 2005, p. 299).

"School was the enemy." When school might have reached out to students like Federico or Dana, school pushed them farther away. Why don't we as teachers listen more closely and carefully to these stories? Exploring the word choices within narratives like this can be a form of listening and appreciation. As you look at narratives in your own transcript, highlight the words that are being used to describe the protagonist and the antagonist(s). Pay close attention to pronouns like *I*, *they*, and *we*. Then look at the verbs that co-occur with those pronouns. Share what you find with your students. Together these simple combinations can make powerful impressions.

THROUGH: *How Is This Narrative Coauthored During Telling?*

Many times these word choices and formal arrangements, although spoken by the individual storyteller, are influenced strongly by the audience for that story. A good story can cause a suspension in the usual back and forth of turn taking, but usually conversational narratives have multiple tellers: Audiences make silent contributions—rapt attention or drifting gaze—that indicate a story is compelling or needs to wrap up. Audiences also make spoken contributions that redirect, completely undo, or fine tune a narrative in progress. In this way, every narrative is coauthored by the others present.

In classrooms, as Courtney Cazden (2001) has noted, narratives are often told for a "dual audience"—as students tell their stories, they tune into both the student perspective and the teacher's perspective. In their classroom discourse analyses, both Karen Gallas and Vivian Paley also note how students carefully monitor both their peers' reactions and those of the teacher, as their eyes shift from the storyteller to her. When 5-year-old Charles tells a disturbingly vivid story, for example, Gallas (1994) writes, "The other children became visibly restless, glancing nervously over at me" (p. 68). Paley explains to one of her assistants why she watched quietly as a student interrupted every student's story: "The rest watch. And especially, they watch the teacher to see if that unsettled child is safe from harm. That's all they want to know." In other words, children are acutely aware of how peers and teachers are responding to their actions. When students make themselves vulnerable by telling a dangerous story, interrupting a story, or simply listening to these stories or interruptions, they need to know they are safe.

Without this assurance of safety, narrating will cease. Negotiating this dual audience—teachers and peers—not to mention the multiple kinds of peers in any classroom, will always entail personal risk. While I spoke with students like Federico at City School, I could sense them carefully crafting their stories in a way that recognized their life experiences were becoming part of public knowledge. These teenagers told their stories about leaving the school in a way that simultaneously made them look good to me and seemed accurate to their listening friends. This dual audience would become apparent in Federico's stories when, on occasion, his friend Manny would join in the telling to modify how exactly Federico framed the events. After Federico told the Belmont story, for example, I was confused, and I asked him exactly how he could get kicked out when, according to my understanding of his story, he hadn't really done anything wrong. Manny provided the answer:

Betsy:	Did you start the fight, er-
Federico:	No, <u>they</u>- they did.
Betsy:	So how did you get kicked out?
Manny:	**'Cause [the next day <u>he</u> started it.**
Federico:	[Cause the next day I went down. The next day I started a fight.

Federico is quick to concur after Manny more fully articulates what went on in the next day's fight. Manny was also always quick to offer other tempering perspectives on his peer's narratives with direct interjections such as, "He just says that because he thinks that looks cool." He would not let his peers tell a story to me, a naïve listener, without filling in the blanks.

Manny's presence prevented his peers from crafting a one-sided story for my benefit. Generally, students absorbed Manny's viewpoint and narrated on. This dual audience dynamic, however, can also silence students: Some may not want their story to be co-opted by a peer or a teacher. If a narrative provides a way to make sense of our own complex experiences, opening that narrative up to the possibility of being shaped publicly can be threatening. But this coauthoring is also precisely why storytelling in the classroom can be so powerful. When narratives are shared publicly, they potentially create a common narrative—one that is owned, shared, and elaborated by everyone.

Coauthoring in the following excerpt, for example, brings a teacher and her students, who usually maintain a traditional IRE back and forth, into dialogue as Rene remembers a birthday event he did not like:

Rene:	I had—I'm gonna have a cake. But I don't like when they stick my face in there.

This mention of getting his face stuck in a cake strikes a chord for everyone in the group. Immediately, they all begin to coauthor Rene's story. His peers Nancy and Roberto immediately join the storytelling, but, unlike Rene, they say they *do* like the face sticking:

> Rene: I had—I'm gonna have a cake. But I don't like when they
>   stick my face in there.
> Nancy: I do.
> Roberto: I do.

The teacher, however, is confused:

> Teacher: They stick your ↑face in the cake?

Rene and Roberto both smile and nod at the teacher's question.
Already, Nancy and Roberto have taken this story on as their own as
much as Rene's. As the storytelling goes on, Rene dances delicately
between explaining the tradition to his teacher and justifying to Nancy
and Roberto why he does not like having his face stuck in cake. The
teacher appeals to Nancy, checking, it seems, to see whether this is just
Rene's idiosyncrasy. Nancy joins in to help Rene explain the tradition:

> Teacher: Do they stick your face in the cake too at your party?
> Nancy: Yes.
>   Some people cry=
> Teacher: Yeah.
> Nancy: =when they stick their face in the cake.
> Teacher: Why do they cry?
> Nancy: I don't know ((*laughs slightly*))

Here, Nancy seems to legitimate this practice as a common one. But her
general statement, "Some people cry," both generalizes the tradition and
suggests that certain people do not take it in stride. Although Nancy says
she knows all about this tradition, she does not know why some people
cry. Her little laugh even suggests she is indirectly laughing at Rene, who
has already said he does not like having his face stuck in the cake. The
coauthoring influences of Nancy's laugh, Roberto's smiles and nods, and
the teacher's questions all incite Rene to elaborate on his initial narrative:

> Rene: 'cause they say "take a bite, take a bite" and then- and
>   then- The first time I did it I was like four years old. And
>   then I took a bite, and then my dad stook my whole face
>   in the cake ((*laughs slightly*)) and then I started crying.

This is the end of Rene's story. He took a risk starting it—he was
nearly framed as a cry-baby and a practitioner of strange and unusual
birthday rituals. But through Nancy and Roberto's cotelling, he has legit-

imated this face-in-the-cake tradition as a shared practice and explained it to the teacher. He has also clarified that he was *4 years old* when he cried. A long time ago for an 8-year-old! He seems to imply that he cried because he was young—not because he is currently babyish and not because there is anything wrong with this tradition.

Sharing stories like these—in a roomful of eager coauthors, including a teacher who may not understand—is risky. But it is precisely this risk that makes conversational narrating compelling. This story is now a story shared by the group. It is a story that can generate more stories, more sharing, and more talk that links learning to these students' lived experiences. In contrast to the back and forth teacher–student ping-pong of IRE sequences, narrating is an invitational medium that can permeate a classroom, inviting multiple voices and perspectives. Watch for cotelling as you analyze your narratives, and look for the webs of connection that stories can bring out. Recognize the risks that storytellers take in stepping up, that coauthors take by stepping in, and how classroom talk can create a safe place for that risk taking and the learning that comes with it.

BEYOND: *What Happens in an Interaction After a Narrative Is Finished?*

In interaction, we have talked about how narratives are instigated by questions, objects, and events. During the telling, they are shaped interactionally by form, word choice, and coauthorship. But how do narratives in turn influence the interaction after they are told? For Vivian Paley, in her classroom, narratives are installments in an ongoing classroom drama. Remember Vinnie's story?

> Vinnie: There was a bear that he standed on his head.

This is a start—potentially insignificant. But Paley's teaching tapped into the potential significance. From Paley's (1990) perspective, Vinnie's first story made her present in the classroom: "Now she is known" (p. 18).

In Paley's (1990) classroom, children's stories also provide material for their classmates to be "known" and known in relation to each other. On one occasion, another girl in the classroom, Lilly, tells a story about the Paw Paw patch and her words trigger a hopeful response from Jason:

> Lilly: A little girl is losted. The mother finded her.
>
> Jason: Losted losted losted ((*covering up his helicopter*))
> Finded finded finded ((*holding it aloft*)) (p. 71)

Jason is an introverted boy who plays primarily with his own toy helicopter, a boy whom Paley tracks all year, investigating how to pull him into the classroom community. In this interaction, he seems to leap onto Lilly's choice of "losted" and "finded" and the reassuring narrative they create. Paley comments that Jason does not usually use these forms of lost and found. But "losted" and "finded" were powerful narrative tools for Jason to lift his helicopter aloft. As Paley (1990) writes, Lilly's story does not drift into the margins of classroom talk. Instead, "Lilly has given Jason usable material" (p. 71). Paley has recognized the value of this conarration for Jason: By narrating together, students in her class are also building a supportive community for each other.

To understand narratives' potential beyond the moment of their telling, as you analyze classroom discourse, watch for the ways that narratives are taken up into the classroom dialogue and how, in turn, the narrator becomes part of the classroom community.

INTO-THROUGH-AND-BEYOND: THE SOCIAL DIMENSION

In contrast to the interactional dimension of narrating discussed earlier, which involves sequential or other patterns of talk within an interaction, attending to the social dimension of narrative invokes questions about the social factors outside the immediate interaction that influence how words function in that interaction. As you analyze a narrative you have recorded, questions about how the social context outside that interaction influences that narrative will likely come up. The following table, like the analytic table for the interactional dimension, summarizes the analytic questions discussed through examples in the sections that follow. As you analyze your own classroom interactions, this table can focus your analysis of social context by directing your thinking to how social context affects the start of the narrative (INTO), how it is told (THROUGH), and what might happen after it is told (BEYOND).

Analyzing Social Context

INTO	What broad social conditions is this narrative a response to?
THROUGH	What does narrative form indicate about the broader social context?
	What does narrative word choice indicate about the broader social context?
	How do features of broad social context (like institutions) coauthor narrative?
BEYOND	What might be the broader social consequences of this narration?

INTO: *What Broad Social Conditions Is This Narrative a Response To?*

Although narratives may immediately be instigated by classroom questions, narratives are more deeply instigated by concerns that precede and will extend far beyond the classroom. Vivian Paley uses storytelling as the foundation of her preschool curriculum precisely because narratives are the way her students bring their outside-the-classroom experiences and their associated emotions into her classroom. These are concerns that cannot be cast aside for more concrete teaching goals. These concerns need to be addressed by teaching. Similarly, as Elinor Ochs (an anthropologist) and Lisa Capps (a psychologist) have written, conversational narratives are not just responses to questions in the moment; they build our very existence (2003). Through conversational narratives, human beings reconcile the chaos of lived experience with the order of daily life. Narratives are, in classrooms and conversation, a way of knowing ourselves and others and a way of knowing the world. The developmental psychologist, Jerome Bruner, has discussed narrative as a form of logic— a way of making sense of events on a human scale. Understanding the world in narrative terms, he argues, is critical to healthy human development (Bruner, 1986). Across all these understandings of the role of narrative, one thing is clear: Narratives are incited by a need to understand both our own lives and the relationship between our experiences and the world and people around us.

In a classroom, however, unlike a typical family dinner conversation, social contexts are not all shared. Each individual comes into the classroom with a different set of stories he or she needs to tell and a different set of unanswered questions about them. Promoting narrative in the classroom, then, can be much more complicated than storytelling at the family dinner table. Classroom stories can be a profound form of learning because students' narratives potentially bring universal primordial concerns as well as a range of individual and social differences into the discussion. Three- and 4-year-olds in Vivian Paley's classroom, for example, experience the world differently than Paley does; their stories make it possible for her to enter their worlds. Paley (1990) imagines the immense context that may be driving a simple statement and turns crayon, paper, and scissors into a narrative that can encompass universal fears:

> "A crayon comes, a paper, a scissors" may be taken as: "Pretend I am a crayon and I color on a paper and the scissors tries to cut me and I roll off the table." (p. 7)

Crafty stuff—scissors, paper, and a crayon. These tools become a medium for bringing worlds and worries from outside the classroom into the classroom. Each day, recorder in hand, Paley follows her children's journey through the classroom by paying attention to her students' most profound existential concerns as they emerge through stories. Narrative can bridge the vastly different concerns of an adult and a 3-year-old as well as other kinds and degrees of difference. Through narrative, a White, middle-class 20-something can potentially enter into the concerns of a Latino teenager; through narrative, teachers of myriad backgrounds can begin to understand how students experience reality culturally. In short, narrative promises the possibility of culturally relevant teaching (Ladson-Billings, 2001).

However, when differences and misunderstandings overwhelm the narrative worlds of students within the classroom, learning can stop. In contrast to Vivian Paley's meaningful account, the teacher-researcher Vivian Vasquez (2004) remembers her own experiences as a 5-year-old, involving scissors, paper, and crayons—and a teacher with a different plan:

> I took the red circle, traced it onto the black sheet of paper and pro-
> ceeded to cut along the line. "Stop! Is that what I told you to do? You
> are doing it all wrong." (p. xiii)

In one classroom context, scissors, paper, and precut shapes can insti-gate a narrative that releases questions and fears about the broader con-text of a child's life. In another, that narrative is silenced—these shapes were supposed to become a stoplight. Little Vivian cried: "The tears that welled in my cheeks and streamed down my face blurred my vision" (p. xiv). Vasquez's narrative was silenced and her vision blurred in favor of one perfect stoplight project.

Analyzing students' narratives in our classrooms allows us to recog-nize not only how our questions or our carefully planned events incite narratives, but also how experiences, ideas, fears, and expectations from outside the classroom are the underlying and most profound induce-ments to narrate.

THROUGH: *What Does Narrative Form Indicate About the Broader Social Context?*

Although narrative form is powerful, it is in no way fixed. The "Problem, Response, Consequence" frame (introduced in the section on interac-tional dimension of narrating), although a useful analytic starting point, is not a universal formula for narrating. Narrative form is infinitely variable. As the developmental psycholinguist Courtney Cazden (2001) asserts, "Narratives are a universal meaning-making strategy, but there is no one way of transforming experience into a story" (p. 19). Conversational narratives, especially the kind we are looking at in classroom discourse, are not formed or unformed—they range widely in how much they orient to structure, linearity, tellability, coauthorship (Ochs & Capps, 2003), and even the "truth." Depending on how children are socialized into language, their narratives will widely traverse this range.

Heath (1983) has described these differences in her characterizations of stories told in the towns she called Trackton (largely White, working class) and Roadville (Black, working class). She found that families in these two communities had different ideas about what made a good story. The residents of Roadville believed a good story was a factual rendition of an event. For Trackton residents, "a 'true story' calls for 'talkin' junk' and only after one learned to talk junk could one be a good storyteller" (p. 189). "Talkin' junk" involves layering exaggeration, compliments, and vivid comparisons within the telling of an event. A good story in Trackton was a story embellished with all sorts of fictional "junk." Whereas Roadville residents considered stories as a factual retelling of events, Trackton residents would consider this presumably factual version just one side of a story that could be told many different ways—some involving and provocative, some boring and "junk"-free. "In short, for Roadville, Trackton's stories would be lies; for Trackton, Roadville's stories would not even count as stories" (Heath, 1983, p. 189).

These kinds of different socialization into storytelling can lead to differences in how storytelling is heard in the classroom. Sarah Michaels (1981), for example, found that even in an event like "sharing time," in which students are expected to tell stories, certain stories were frequently interrupted and cut off. When she investigated these stories further, she found that stories told by the Euro-American children in the classroom featured a topic-centered pattern, whereas those of the African-American children featured a series of storied episodes that was difficult for the Euro-American teacher to follow. In a follow-up study, Michaels and Cazden (1986) found that when they played these stories for a diverse group of adults, these differences in understanding corresponded to differences in ethnicity: Euro-American adults found the episodic stories difficult to understand, whereas the African-American adults were impressed with their complexity.

It is precisely this kind of classroom discourse research on narrative styles that, in combination with her own classroom discourse analysis, led Karen Gallas to change her teaching approach—to take less control in the classroom and offer more opportunity for her students' narratives to unfold, to let students be drawn into storytelling by their peers rather than the exclusive and possibly ethnocentric prompts of the teacher. Sometimes listening will be difficult for teachers and students. Once Gallas started relinquishing control of storytime in her class, for example, some of the children began telling stories that she labeled *fantasy*. To be sure, children could distinguish between these two discourse styles; the class developed the labels *true* and *fake*. In Gallas' class, the fake stories became captivating stories and beloved of most of the students—even the initially reluctant participants expanded their discourse styles in the end to include both fake and real storytelling (Gallas, 1998).

The broader implications of Heath's ethnographic description of storytelling in the Piedmont Carolinas is clear: Everyone comes to school needing to tell stories, but they will tell them in different ways. These differences are related to but also extend beyond race, class, ethnicity, and gender. They are existential differences between each child in our classrooms. We will all run across a story in our classrooms that seems to be illogical, inappropriate, or just not true. How do we respond? In her forward to Vivian Paley's book *Wally's Stories*, Cazden (1981) writes,

> Teachers are usually counseled to respond to such stories with some version of what might be called "confrontation pedagogy": rub the children's mind in the errors of their thoughts by providing arguments against their inconsistencies. . . . Although that advice seems plausible, there is reason to believe that this approach is more comforting to the adult than helpful to the child. (p. i)

In classrooms, the bottom line is that as teachers we must be able to hear all our students' stories—not just those select few that correspond to our expectations. The process of recording them, looking back, and contemplating their forms is one way of understanding what stories can mean for our students.

THROUGH: *What Does Narrative Word Choice Indicate About the Broader Social Context?*

Word choices like the pronouns and associated actions (described earlier in the section on interactional context) operate within the story world to create powerful impressions. Some word choices, however, are more broadly indexical. As described in chapter 6, certain words act in combinations with other features of an interaction to index certain functions. The same is true with a narrative. Certain words used inside narratives index worlds beyond the narrative. For example, stories I heard at City

School about gang days—especially stories told to convince peers to leave gangs—were often punctuated with shared address terms like *roll dog, homes, esse,* and *chucho,* which indexed an awareness of gang norms and created a backdrop of peer-group authority that students could draw on to convince wannabes to avoid gang involvement. These words, although not necessarily considered Standard English or Spanish, were nonetheless important resources for making life-and-death arguments at City School.

As you analyze narrative, make note of words and their combinations (e.g., what *they* did) within the story, but also those words (rolldog, *chucho*) that index worlds and connections beyond that single story. Ask yourself (and, when possible, your students) how those words are functioning.

THROUGH: *How Does Social Context Coauthor Narratives?*

Just as narrators are attuned to coauthoring individuals as they tell their stories, they are also influenced by the broader social context within which they are telling their stories. In addition to individuals who coauthor our stories by chiming in, nodding, or looking aghast, bored, or perplexed, social context coauthors how we tell our stories. Classrooms, for example, are embedded in certain societal expectations that demand a certain kind of narrating. In most school contexts, stories about fights and gang allegiances would be unlikely to emerge in the classroom. In most preschool contexts, a year's worth of stories about Jason's helicopter would have been left to the purview of the children, whereas the "real" stories would be the official talk in class. Social contexts dictate what we can safely hear.

In both of these contexts, teachers were taking risks by hearing these stories. Social norms for classroom talk suggest that Jason's helicopter story is an "aside" and that Federico's fight story is criminal. However, because listeners took risks by listening to these stories, students were able to develop their voices. Both of these contexts are also innovative institutional settings that facilitated that risk taking. City School was a charter school that was not subject to the usual surveillance and standardized curriculum of other public high schools. Vivian Paley worked in a Lab school—a preschool setting associated with the University of Chicago that respected her choices and fostered her creativity. In both of these cases, the larger social context, therefore, also coauthored the developing narrative voices in these school settings. As you analyze your narratives, also ask yourself: How is the setting co-authoring stories in my classroom?

BEYOND: *What Might Be the Broader Social Consequences of this Narration?*

The stories that students tell in our classrooms can also lead to broader social consequences. What are the social consequences of how students tell or don't tell stories and how they are coauthored?

In Paley's classroom, David Elkind (1991) writes, "the end product of her year's work is a group of children who can live comfortably with themselves and with one another." Paley's classroom goals are simultaneously modest and momentous. On the one hand, her modest goal is to create a classroom in which students respect each other and move through the day comfortably. Given the multiple viewpoints that come together in a classroom, even this modest goal is no small task. It would be rare to find a group of twenty individuals—of any age—who could move through the day comfortably together.

Paley's more momentous goal is to have this mutual respect go beyond the classroom walls. To this end, Paley resists labeling tendencies of the social context outside her classroom: She wants her classroom to be a place where multiple stories are told, not a place where labels—African American, learning disabled, English-language learner—are affixed: "None of these labels apply in a classroom that sees children as storytellers. These labels don't describe the imagination. A storyteller is always in the strongest position; to be known by his or her stories puts the child in the most favorable light" (p. 54). Resisting labels and fostering students' development on their own terms is an act of resistance that will have implications that extend far beyond her classroom walls. These children are constructing narrative futures for themselves that do not include limiting labels.

Older students can also resist societal labels by telling their own stories. The stories told at City School by Federico and his peers put them in a favorable light. Without the opportunity to tell these stories, instead of projecting their favorable role within them, the experiences these stories depict can become a psychological burden. But when teachers listen, storytellers can project a future for themselves—and move beyond their stories to future experiences. Someone has to listen before a teller can move on. This listening needn't be complicated. For example, looking back on being kicked out of schools after three fights in which she defended herself, Dana, age 24, writes:

> If I had had just one teacher who cared, I would have actually gone to high school instead of having to get my GED at seventeen. Most gangsters I grew up around were just like me. Lonely, feeling there's

> nothing out there, no place to fit in, and no one who wants to give
> them a chance or view them as a person. (Johnson, 2005, p. 299)

It is hard to find a willing ear for gangsters' stories at school. In many schools, even admitting gang membership can be grounds for dismissal. But when no one hears those stories at school, students will take themselves away to search for a place where they have voice. Rather than telling kids to "just say no!" to gangs, listening to students' stories about why *they just can't say no* may keep many more in school.

When students of any age do not find that "one teacher" who will listen, school becomes a place full of misunderstanding—not growing understanding. Instead, just as Jason found a place within Paley's classroom, many students at City School found their voices there. Teachers connected to them through their stories. Students who ordinarily wouldn't carry a pencil, not to mention a book, walked around with the novel *Always Running: Gang Days in L.A.* by Luis Rodríguez under their arms. This story spoke to them—because teachers knew that this story was their story. Students who ordinarily ran from police dragged their parole officers into the art room to show off their paintings. Students afraid to read, big 18-year-olds who could barely sound out words, dared to try. This context not only fostered student narratives, it potentially gave these narratives futures. Because our narratives portray us in our best light, they can, if heard, also give us something to live up to.

INTO-THROUGH-AND-BEYOND:
INDIVIDUAL AGENCY

What is the role of individual agency into, through, and beyond classroom narratives and how do we analyze it? Launching a narrative, telling it in a group, and following up on narratives after they are told can be an act of individual agency that resists controlling interactional and social contexts. The analytic questions in the following table guide the discussion in this section. You can use these questions to guide your analysis of the role of agency in classroom narrative.

Analyzing Agency

INTO	How did an individual instigate this narrative—regardless of question, event, and social context?
	Who created the conditions for agents to narrate?
THROUGH	How do narrators frame who has agency in the story?
	Who co-authors the story and what are the effects?
BEYOND	Are tellers aware of the effects of their narratives? (Ask them.)

INTO: *How Did an Individual Instigate This Narrative?*

Although questions, events, and social contexts all instigate narratives, we also have the capacity, as individual agents, to launch our own narrative when and where we choose. I may seem odd if I want to tell a story about my grandmother at a formal meeting of the University Council, but I can. By doing so strategically, I may make a point about authority or its abuse, for example. I, as an agent, can choose to butt heads with interactional expectations for turn taking and event structure. Because as a professor I already have some measure of legitimacy at my institution, it is likely that some of this head butting will affect interactions in ways that I want. These little tweaks at interactional expectations can gradually make change. I will get to tell my story.

However, when students in classrooms take these initiatives, they may be silenced. Their bids to tell stories out of turn or in unlikely contexts may be treated as disruptions to something more important. However, until our students can tell their stories—their versions of events—they cannot be agents of their own learning. Instead, like Vivian Vasquez, they may be left to passively paste together a stoplight designed by an unknown teacher.

INTO: *Who Created the Conditions for Agents to Narrate?*

As teachers, we can provide those openings, instigating narratives, so that students can have a voice. As you listen to the narratives or nascent narratives in your own classroom recordings, think about how you can give voice to the unknown storytellers in your class.

Sometimes students' stories emerge on the heels of stories told by their teachers. Even teachers' humdrum recollections of their own school days, challenges, or triumphs can act as incitements for others to tell their stories. Kindergarten teacher Karen Hankins, for example, connected with an initially hostile parent of one of her most troubling students by telling about her own family and about the troubles her sister, who had a severe learning disability, faced in school (Hankins, 2003). As you look back at your transcripts, notice how your own stories—or even the simplest of statements—can break the silence and get others talking. If, by breaking the silence, we give others voice, we have given them agency. What happens if you let yourself be known by your students? This may make it possible for them to be known by you. Investigate these questions by looking at your narrative transcripts.

At other times, students realize their narratives are important when they witness other students being allowed to take the floor. I have struggled to include those vociferous students in class discussions without silencing the rest: As one student tells story after story that seems barely related to our discussion topic, I have battled with inner panic as I see the faces of other students and the slightest hint of rolling eyes as they wait through these lengthy turns. Considering narrative and student agency in my own classroom has helped me to adopt a counter-intuitive approach. Lately, I resist those rolling eyes, and I focus intently on the narrating student. Respecting this narrator awakens the rest of the class to the possibility that their stories might be important too: This narrator is safe here. Their stories can be safe here. This attention, in turn, makes the dominant student weigh carefully the import of their stories. Their stories are *important* here. Their words become more measured. The whole class is witnessing the potential agency their narratives hold. If by being silent but attentive we can listen to the inconvenient intrusion, we have let students know they are worthy of that agency.

Discourse analysis can help us to listen to the inconvenient intrusions and to notice those silent students—and possibly help us facilitate those conditions within which students can become agents of their own narratives. As you analyze, notice openings for narratives, watch how they are instigated, and try to determine whether and where there is space for narrative to develop. Look at your transcript to see how arrangements allow student agents to tell their own stories. Notice who makes those arrangements. Is it you?

THROUGH: *How Do Narrators Frame Who Has Agency in the Story?*

No matter what happened to an individual, narrating that event provides the opportunity to frame those experiences in a way that seems right to the teller—they provide a chance for people to show themselves in the best possible light. Although Federico had been kicked out of several schools, he framed his position in this narrative as one of a loyal friend who would stand up for his peers. When Rene told the birthday cake story, he could frame his emotions about the event by placing his crying in the distant past. These agentive narrators draw on story form, particular words, and the way those words connect to particular worlds to shape the way their narratives function. Through narrative, an agentive individual makes claim to the opportunity to state one's case.

THROUGH: Who Co-authors the Narrative and What Are the Effects?

Consider this paradox of agency and narrative: Although a narrative provides an individual the opportunity to state one's case, a narrative, told in public, also brings one individual's experiences into dialogue with others. Narratives would not exist without coauthors, and these coauthors can either diminish or augment our agency as narrators.

As teachers, we have a great responsibility as we coauthor our students' stories. We can listen for stories, and for the moment we are needed to clarify or contest. Sometimes the stories we hear will not match our expectations or our moral order. Sometimes stories raise issues we would rather not examine. These stories call for dangerous listening—and may be appeals for coauthorship. When we listen through a story of violence, dramatic emotion, or failure, we can foster our students' agency by working with students to understand these stories on their own terms. We can also add another perspective.

Students' stories give teachers insights into how our students place themselves in the world. These insights will, most likely, change our own narratives as well as our students'. Classroom discourse analysis is a tool to bring these processes to light—the goal is to understand how we can use classroom talk to pull our students and ourselves through our stories to new places and ways of thinking.

BEYOND: Are Tellers Aware of the Effects of Their Narratives?

Narratives are potentially powerful vehicles for agency. However, it is likely that agency can remain ensconced in the narrative frame. For narrators to live up to their storied roles, they may need to reflect on their stories and what they mean for the future. Although narrators may create agency for themselves in the way they frame themselves in their stories, if stories rest uncontested and unexamined, their value for ongoing agency is minimized. Don't let those stories sit unmoved. After narrating ends and after you've transcribed the discourse, show students their words and give them awareness of social and interactional contexts that shape their stories. Students will revel in their own words—and they will be their own best critics. As teachers, we can participate in this analysis with our students. What did you mean here? Who told you to say this? What was Manny talking about? Do you think you are equally culpable?

As early as a child can say "Fall go boom!" narrative framing is at work, and it doesn't cease. To ensure narrative futures, we need to foster critical minds that can use the tools of narrative—and understand how they work. Along with our students, we need to hone our skills and learn, together, to discern which narratives will resist social labels, which will protect our lonely souls, and which will foster positive futures.

PUTTING IT ALL TOGETHER: A MULTIDIMENSIONAL ANALYSIS OF CLASSROOM NARRATIVES

As you think through a single narrative sequence, use the questions introduced in this chapter to guide your analysis. The following analytic table summarizes these questions and includes a space to record your focal event and sequence.

As always, discourse analysis and, more specifically, the analysis of narratives cannot be conducted by following a recipe. Instead, the process of discourse analysis is the process of asking certain questions of a speech event and a sequence within that event. As such, these questions are meant to guide your entry into classroom narrative; once there, you will find multiple possible paths to take in your analysis—and in your future actions as a teacher. You may also begin to experiment with new ways of arranging your classroom events so that you can promote student narrative in your classroom. In the next chapter, we look into the analysis of how classroom arrangements for participation influence what kinds stories are told, as well as what questions are asked and answered and by whom.

Analyzing Narratives in Classroom Discourse

EVENT	SEQUENCE	NARRATIVE STAGE	INTERACTIONAL CONTEXT	SOCIAL CONTEXT	AGENCY
				DISCOURSE DIMENSION	
e.g., Boundary Transition Time	e.g., Rene's Birthday Story	1) INTO	What question or object is this narrative a response to? What event is it embedded in? Is it on the border of an event?	What conditions is this narrative a response to?	How did an individual instigate this narrative—regardless of question, event, social context? How can we create the conditions for agents to narrate?
		2) THROUGH	What is the form of the narrative? How do word choices shape the protagonist and antagonist within that form? How is this narrative coauthored during telling?	What does narrative form indicate about the broader social context? What does narrative word choice indicate about the broader social context? How do features of broad social context (like institutions) co-author narrative?	How do narrators frame who has agency in the story? Who co-authors the story and what are the effects?
		3) BEYOND	What happens in the interaction when the story finishes?	What might be the broader social consequences of this narration?	Are tellers aware of the effects of their narratives?

QUESTIONS AND ACTIVITIES

Critical Reflection

1. Have you ever had a story you simply had to tell? Did you find a way to get it out even when no one was asking you about it? In the same way, do narratives emerge unbidden in your classroom?
2. What events are fertile ground for narrative in your classroom? What kinds of questions are asked in these events? What kinds of narratives do students tell?
3. How would you respond if, in response to a specific question, a student launched a lengthy story? In what ways are these unbidden stories interactional problems? In what ways are they opportunities?
4. Do you notice a "dual audience" in your classroom? How do you see students orienting simultaneously to each other and to the teacher? Compare your students in your classroom and your classmates in a university classroom. Is the "dual audience" present in both contexts?
5. Compare the effects of interactional and social contexts on narrating. Which do you think is more influential in your setting? What are the implications for your own and your students' agency as narrators?
6. How does your setting coauthor stories in your classroom? How do you resist this coauthorship?

Reflective Activities

1. Students as discourse analysts: Find several narratives in your classroom transcript that you think you could share with your students. Talk about narrative form and word choice with them. Then have them highlight the words that are being use to describe the protagonist and the antagonist(s) and the verbs that co-occur with those actors. Talk about the impressions made by narrative from these combinations of actors and actions.
2. Read the Rene's birthday story transcript in its entirety. Then think through the analytic questions in the table for this chapter. What is a possible narrative future for this story? What if it were told in your classroom?
3 Select a narrative sequence from your transcript and think through the analytic questions in the table for this chapter. What narrative futures do you see?

END OF ESOL PULLOUT SESSION:

Teacher: Tell us about your birthday party. (.) You were trying to
            tell me earlier and I couldn't listen to you.

Rene: My birthday party is on Sunday.

Teacher: What are y'all gonna do?

Rene: I: don't kno:w.

Teacher: You were trying to tell me.

Rene: Well I got- I- (.) stuff that I got from my dad (.) that's
            what I told you, the stuff.

Nancy: Oh [(the watch?)

Teacher: [Are y'all gonna- Are y'all gonna have a party?

Rene: Yes. On Sunday.

Teacher: Are y'all gonna have a pinyata (.) or anything=

Rene: [Yes.

Teacher: [=fun.

Rene: I had- (.)I'm gonna have a ca:ke. (.) But (.) I don't like
            when they stick my face in (there).
            [(   )

Nancy: [I do.

Roberto: I do.

Teacher: They stick your <u>fa:ce</u> in the ca:ke?

Rene: Yeah. ((nodding and smiling))

Roberto: Uhn-huh. ((*yes*))

Teacher: I wouldn't like that either.

Nancy: I [(would)

Rene: [I know cause the people (that) can't eat that piece.
            ((*laughs*))

Teacher: Why can't they eat it?

Rene: Cause my germs are on it [(my face goes in it.)

Teacher: [(((*laughs* . . .)) That's ri:ght.
            (.) Do they stick your face in the cake too ((*to Janet;
            Janet nods*)) your party.
            (3.0)

Nancy: Some people cry:.

Rene: Yeah.

Nancy: When they stick their face in the ca:ke.

Teacher: Why do they cry? (.) Cause they don't like it?

Nancy: I don't know. ((*laughs slightly as she says this*))

Rene: Cause they say (.) take a bi:te, take a bi:te and then-
and then   [(   ) The first time I did it I=

Roberto: [(go there   )

Rene: =was like four years old. And then I took a bite, and
then my dad stook my whole face in the ca:ke. ((*laughs
slightly*)) And then I started crying.

Teacher: O:h, I would not like that <u>ei:the:r</u>. That is sa:d.
(3.0)

Rene: ((*Rene makes a mistake shuffling*)) Woops.

Teacher: Are you gonna bring anything to school like cupcakes or
anything like that to share with the class?

Rene: No. ((*softly*))

Teacher: No.
(1.0)

SUGGESTIONS FOR FURTHER READING

Elinor Ochs and Lisa Capps' (2003) *Living Narrative* is essential reading
for those interested in further discussion of conversational narrative, as is
Jerome Bruner's (1986) *Actual Minds, Possible Worlds*. I've mentioned
Ways with Words (Heath, 1983) many times, but once again this classic by
Shirley Brice Heath is full of fascinating descriptions of the different roles
narrative plays in people's lives and how those narrating styles come into
conflict with classroom norms. Sarah Michaels' (1981) original research
on "sharing time" in the classroom is a vivid portrayal of different storytelling styles in the classroom and an insightful discussion of the effects
of sharing time differences on literacy development. Or course, Vivian
Paley's books, especially *Wally's Stories* (1981) and *The Boy Who Would Be
a Helicopter* (1990), are brilliant portrayals of how stories and children's
fantasy play can shape classroom curriculum.

8

ANALYZING FRAMING RESOURCES

PREVIEW QUESTION Before you read this chapter, think about *how voices outside* your classroom (opinions of principals, parents, peers, even *your* parents and peers, etc.) influence how you and your students participate and what you all can say. How do different procedures within your classroom, ways of grouping students, or arrangements for interaction affect how people participate, what language(s) they use, or how competent they appear?

Our classrooms contain an intense meeting of minds. Each mind brings with it habits, memories, fears, desires, and relationships that frame our talk and often unwittingly influence the twists and turns of our interactions.

In a second-grade reading group in Georgia, for example, a discussion prompted by a picture book is framed by ideas about what can and cannot be said (Rymes & Anderson, 2004):

Sally: ((*pointing to a picture in the book*)) They're White and everybody else is Black.

Teacher: Oh, so her friend is White and everybody else is Black in the picture?

Danny: Hey don't you be talking about that.

Teacher: What is wrong with that?

Danny: Nothing. ((*Danny shakes his head*))

Sally: Nothing.
Teacher: Is there anything wrong with that?
Students: No. ((*Sally shakes her head*))
Teacher: No, I didn't think so either.

In an alternative high school in Los Angeles, LaTasha begins to talk about her own recent trip to LA County Jail. She frames her ideas in the context of what her peer group might say (Rymes, 2001):

LaTasha: Everybody was like "I'm going to j̲ail, all my homies in jail."
           Whatchu wanna go to jail fo̲:?

Frames, the interactional and social contexts that surround individual utterances, can be both resources and liabilities for understanding what is going on in our classrooms. Our statements are framed by larger social contexts that give meaning and functionality to our words, but which can also create interactional constraints we may want to resist. What led the teacher in the second-grade excerpt above to close down a discussion of race? What led LaTasha to claim that "everybody" wants to go to jail? The social and interactional frames surrounding these interactions offer explanations for these turns in classroom discourse. As these excerpts begin to illustrate, and as is elaborated on in this chapter, frames surround and influence all the analytical resources we have discussed in the previous chapters—how we take turns, how our contextualization cues are interpreted, what counts as a narrative—and what counts as knowledge in our classrooms.

This chapter, perhaps more than any others, will highlight the *critical* component of your classroom discourse analysis. That is, you will notice how the way we do things and what we talk about—or think we *can't* talk about—are framed by social norms and interactional habits that are usually left unexamined. As you recognize this framing, you will become a critic. You will start asking critical questions: "What is it about this context that permitted that statement?" "What is it about this context that made that statement seem important?" Sometimes we are so blind to the frame within which we are acting that we do not realize that our classroom commitments—even some that seem so important to us—are not necessary or productive for student learning.

The examples in this chapter introduce the tools to analyze framing resources more broadly and systematically in classroom interaction. In what follows, you will learn how social context frames classroom discourse, how frames are constructed interactionally within classrooms, and how an awareness of how we are *being framed* by interactional and social contexts can augment our agency to *break frame* and conduct classroom discourse in new and unexpected ways.

HOW FRAMING RESOURCES EMERGE
FROM SOCIAL CONTEXT

Students are often more likely than teachers to draw our attention to how social norms arbitrarily frame our actions and words. Remember George's reaction to the "Farm and Zoo Animals" unit (see chap. 2)? As a first grader, he called attention to the arbitrary nature of this framing curriculum. Interactionally, he *broke frame* to make his point. As a consequence, his teacher broke frame and listened to what George had to say, rather than what she should do to fulfill the typical teacher role. Fortunately, George had the wherewithal to see the arbitrary nature of his curriculum and to name an alternative. Fortunately, his teacher recognized his voice as *pro*ductive, rather than *dis*ruptive. Other times, however, larger social processes keep us obediently and, at times, obliviously within a frame. An analysis of framing resources in classroom discourse can be a useful analytical tool to make these larger social processes visible when a student like George is not there to make them visible for us.

Production Format

The sociologist Irving Goffman spent his career studying institutional talk and the frames that guide it. In any situation, according to Goffman (1981), a speaker is framed by implicit participation structures that offer different degrees of participation status. He named three distinct status roles for speakers:

Animator: The individual physically saying the words—the "sounding box in use"

Author: The creator of the spoken words

Principal: The institution or individual whose beliefs are being represented—the party ultimately responsible. (pp. 144–145)

Collectively, these roles (in addition to the roles of listeners, discussed later in this chapter) comprise the overarching frame that Goffman calls the *production format*. In any given interaction, the same speaker, different speakers, or a combination can occupy these roles. In a U.S. Presidential State of the Union address, for example, these three roles may be very distinct. The president is the animator, or the "voice box" for the words, most likely authored by a team of speechwriters. The principal is the institution that constructs his platform—say, the U.S. Government. As a democratically elected official, he may even claim to speak "for the people" of the United States and their beliefs. This production format—the president as animator, the speech writer as author, and the U.S. government as principal—frames the presidential address as indicated in the following table:

EVENT	ANIMATOR	AUTHOR	PRINCIPAL
Presidential Address	The President of the United States	Speechwriters	The U.S. Government

In other cases, the roles of animator, author, and principal may fluctuate within a single utterance. When I taught at a Los Angeles junior high school, for example, all students were to rise and say *The Pledge of Allegiance* out loud, hands over hearts, reciting from memory along with the voice of the assistant principal, Ms. Alonzo, broadcast over the public address system. After days of hearing the same formula for this event, my students rarely finished reciting at "with liberty and justice for all." Instead, they would continue right along with Ms. Alonzo through "You may be seated" so that the pledge would sound, in its entirety, like this:

> Students: ((*standing with hands on hearts*)) I pledge allegiance to the flag of the United States of America and to the Republic for which it stands, one nation, under God, indivisible, with liberty and justice for all. You may be seated.

Although the animators—students reading along with the vice principal—are the same for the entire reading, author and principal change at "You may be seated," a command presumably authored by the vice principal to enforce school-based routines—not national pride. The following table illustrates these fluctuations in participant status.

UTTERANCE	ANIMATOR	AUTHOR	PRINCIPAL
I pledge allegiance . . . with liberty and justice for all.	Ms. Alonzo and students	Author of the Pledge of Allegiance	The Nation— U.S.
You may be seated	Ms. Alonzo and students	Ms. Alonzo	The School

When the principal role changes at "You may be seated" from the United States (and its need to reinforce national allegiance) to the school (and its need to reinforce routine obligations), this makes for a mildly irreverent joke. To this day, I have a hard time not silently tacking on "You may be seated" at the tail end of a recitation of the pledge. This joke—in its capacity to negate the solemnity of all that came before "You may be seated"—also illustrates how powerfully a frame can influence the meaning of our words.

Production Formats in Classroom Discourse

These distinctions among author, animator, and principal are powerful tools for understanding classroom discourse and its institutional origins (a component of what we have been calling *social context*). For example, in the classroom interaction that started this chapter Danny, a second grader, commands "Don't you be talking about that" after his classmate mentions the race of characters in a picture book. Danny's discourse seems to be framed by something outside that interaction. We find ourselves asking, "Who told you we can't talk about these issues?" In Goffman's terms, who is the principal of these beliefs you are voicing? Who is ultimately responsible? In Danny's case, perhaps his mother told him not to talk about the relationships between Black and White people at school. However, he also may have absorbed this message from the school, interactions in his neighborhood, television, or, most likely, all of the above.

The Same Principal Across Utterances

As the interaction unfolds, it seems that the demand Danny initially voices permeates and is even reinforced by every subsequent question and answer. Danny's utterance "Don't be talking about that" is functionally not so different from his teacher's utterance "What is wrong with that?" Both are uttered in the context of a potential discussion about race, and together they function to close that discussion down. Each of these statements obviously has a different animator: Danny animates, "Don't be talking about that," whereas his teacher animates, "What is wrong with that, is there anything wrong with that?" Each is authored, most directly, by its distinct animators. However, the principal they are both bringing voice to is functionally the same. Oddly enough, although the teacher disagrees with Danny on record, her yes/no question closes down dialog; she maintains the unspoken norm, "Don't talk about race in the classroom." The underlying belief that the class is not a place for a discussion on race may even originate in their shared orientation to parental understandings and school-wide norms for what is appropriate.

UTTERANCE	ANIMATOR	AUTHOR	PRINCIPAL/BELIEF
Don't you be talking about that.	Danny	Danny	Mom, school, society at large /Don't talk about race in the classroom
What is wrong with that ... is there anything wrong with that?	Teacher	Teacher	Danny's mom, school, society at large / Don't talk about race in the classroom

Multiple Authors and Principals Voiced by the Same Animator

As the "You may be seated" addition to the *Pledge of Allegiance* illustrates, even within a single utterance, participant statuses can switch. This kind of switching happens routinely when we tell stories and quote the speech of other people, animating words (presumably) authored by someone else. In LaTasha's single sentence about jail that started this chapter, for example, she voiced both the perspective of some of her peers who endorsed jail ("Everybody was like, 'I'm going to jail, all my homies in jail'") and her own perspective that jail is no fun ("Whatchu wanna go to jail fo?").

UTTERANCE	ANIMATOR	AUTHOR	PRINCIPAL/BELIEF
I'm going to jail, all my homies in jail.	LaTasha	Peers	Peer Group/Going to Jail is cool.
Whatchu wanna go to jail fo:?	LaTasha	LaTasha	LaTasha/Going to Jail is no fun.

These framing distinctions afford LaTasha a certain power in the discourse. Although she knows that peers may want to go to jail or think that it is a cool option, her friend has just experienced it and knows, first hand, that she does not want to be there. She speaks authentically from this position, but simultaneously recognizes and displays her awareness of other perspectives. By using framing conventions to her advantage, she makes a potentially convincing argument with "everybody" about staying out of jail.

Endorsed by the "Principal": Frames that Increase the Impact of Discourse

Although LaTasha's words may be uniquely hers, and powerful among her peers, this discussion is also framed by the institution within which

LaTasha is speaking. Ultimately, the City School context is also responsible for LaTasha's words and potentially adds weight to her voice. Because she is in a class discussion, talking in front of a teacher (who is not censoring her talk), this context may make it easier for her to articulate this perspective. With this in mind, the production format for her question of her peers might be revised to look like the following table.

UTTERANCE	ANIMATOR	AUTHOR	PRINCIPAL/BELIEF
Whatchu wanna go to jail fo:?	LaTasha	LaTasha	*City School /* *Jail is no fun.*

Instead of speaking just to her own peers from her singular experience, she is speaking with the backing of an institution. When LaTasha is given the floor at school—in part by the school, in part by her peers—she has something to say, and she may have convinced a friend or two that day to stay out of jail. In fact, keeping kids in school and out of jail is part of City School's institutional mission: "To reduce the high cost of school failure."

Were a student like LaTasha to be given the presidential podium and allowed to talk "for herself" in front of a large audience, her words could have an even more powerful institutional principal behind them. Some people, who ordinarily would not consider listening to LaTasha, might start thinking about jail, youth, and race in new ways. If LaTasha is speaking from the presidential podium, under the auspices of the highest elected official within that government, her words will have more weight than those of someone voicing her own personal opinion among peers. Sometimes a fancy frame around a humble picture can transform the mundane to the powerful.

The frame, then, is a specified context for our words that can imbue them with meaning and make our listeners look for more meaning. Frames can force us to reserve judgment and give other voices the benefit of the doubt. In this way, "framing" is an ideal metaphor: The frames around talk function a lot like frames around pictures. As parents and preschool teachers know, an elegant frame can render even the most humble toddler scribbles functional as art and instill deeper appreciation of the toddler's talent. Frames around talk can also function to make us notice the import of the framed message. This means the frames we, as teachers, bring into the classroom and put around our students' talk and writing can play an important role in bringing students' concerns into the foreground—transforming their humble voices into powerful ones that can affect the world.

Admittedly, frames can also function to imbue certain discourse with more meaning than it may deserve. There are certain horrible things I would never consider framing. Still—as Andy Warhol's Campbell's soup series of paintings illustrated—even something as humble as a soup label can be dressed up and put in a museum. Likewise, frames in discourse can transform acts that would look ridiculous in another context into important statements of loyalty, silly words into important ones. Consider the following "Bushisms":

George W. Bush: The vast majority of our imports come from out-side the country.

George W. Bush: Natural gas is hemispheric. I like to call it hemi-spheric in nature because it is a product we can find in our neighborhoods.

George W. Bush: I believe we are on an irreversible trend toward more freedom and democracy—but that could change.

Were these brash statements to appear in a high school social studies essay, they would likely meet with their share of red ink. In an ordinary job interview, they might disqualify their speaker from a job. Even at a friendly dinner with family, they might meet with some ribbing. At the word level, they simply do not make sense: They suggest the speaker does not know the normative meaning of *imports* or *irreversible*, for exam-ple. Within the frame of a 21st–century presidential address, however, they function quite well. They not only go by with little condemnation, they may actually bolster the reputation of our president as a humble man, working tirelessly for the good of the nation (Silverstein, 2003). If he tosses in "our neighborhoods" while using a potentially intimidating word like *hemispheric*, that just might connect with someone. His words operate within a cultural frame that not only legitimizes this way of speaking, but turns it into a political asset. The policies promoted by these words are rendered negligibly relevant to the immediate listener. What is he saying anyway? In the words of the 1960s-era media critic, Marshall McLuhan (1964), "the medium is the message."

Another case in which frames glorify—or justify—words and behav-ior that would be inscrutable in any other context is fall football season on many university campuses across the United States. Would face paint, hats with huge foam chunks of cheese on them, bare chests smeared with letters, or, in Georgia (home of the "Bulldawgs"), *human barking* be appropriate in any context outside of a football stadium? Speakers would have to work at it. These behaviors, words, and actions require a particular frame for them to make sense. Even in context they do not make much sense. But they do get their supportive point across—anyone willing to dress up, paint up, and stand yelling (or barking) for

4 hours in the hot sun must be devoted to the team. Again, "the medium is the message."

That same power of a frame to bring new forms of functionality to a soup label, the words of a president or a football fan's barking can also bring arbitrary functionality to the words of a teacher, a professor, or a visiting important person. Often we listen to a formal, organized lecture simply because of the external, institutional trappings that frame those words. In discussions with teachers and students, what role do these trappings play? As you listen to teachers and students talking, think about each participant and the production format that frames their words: Who is animating, who is the author, and what is the principal supporting these contributions? Because a teacher is saying it, does that mean a statement is true or a statistic is meaningful? On whose terms is it true? The principal? Our state? Whose beliefs and interests are being served? Why does it matter? These are the critical questions provoked by a frame analysis of talk in your classroom.

What is the "Principal?" Frames that Demean Discourse

Frames have the power not only to elevate discourse, but also to demean discourse. The *Pledge of Allegiance*, for example, has largely been absorbed by the schooling frame. As my students tacked on "You may be seated" to the end of the *Pledge of Allegiance*, they also slyly illustrated how, in that context, *The Pledge* is not necessarily a statement bolstered by our national principles, but one enforced by the school principal. How much do the words of that pledge carry meaning for the children who recite them day after day? The school frame in which they occur—which mandates that they occur—may actually be draining their desired affect.

Unfortunately, after the pledge is over and the school day begins, institutional frames like this can also stagnate our thinking on other subjects. Just as students mindlessly mouth the pledge, students often mindlessly repeat the routines of schoolwork. The frames that perpetuate these activities allow us to continue them without asking, "Why am I saying this? Why am I learning this? What am I learning?" For example, as a parent, I receive notes home in all capitals TO ALL FIRST-GRADE PARENTS from FIRST-GRADE TEACHERS reminding us about spelling tests on Fridays. A worksheet with sentences to practice comes home with the reminder, "THEY WILL BE TESTED ON THIS." My son does his homework, practices his spelling words and looks over his Daily Oral Language (DOL) sentences. But he writes his spelling words correctly the first day they come home—as well as on the test a week later. Still, all his successes on school tests will be framed as a product of

school routines (and school-enforced home routines) that have little to
do with his achievement. I know he already knows all these words and
his DOL sentences because he practically lives and breathes reading and
writing—not because he has been practicing lists of spelling words since
birth. He will do well on all the tests despite, not because of, all these
notes home and the practice writing he does in class. *I hope*, after years
of spelling and DOL tests, he will not forget why he loves to read and
write.

Although these practices frame reading and writing as painful exercises, aspects of kids' leisure experiences can frame reading as interesting
and powerful. Discourse analysis can help us as teachers capture the
abundant evidence of this. Often interactions between peers or on the
borders of classroom events highlight how important reading is to children. Recently, I overheard a boy in the hall of an elementary school talking to a younger schoolmate who had just received a Hot Wheels car,
which was still in its packaging. The older boy read the package to his
young schoolmate: "Hot Wheels. Super-charged, turbo-drive command-
er!" Then he commented, "See, Joshua—when you learn to read, you will
be able to read all this great stuff."

When we as teachers start noticing moments like this and framing
them as important, nearly everything students do every day in and out of
class can become a literacy event. My 8-year-old son, Charlie, for example, writes purposefully but randomly and often humorously—he'll slide
a note under his big brother's door accompanied by a neglected veg-
etable from dinner: "Yum, green peppers!" He'll leave a note on the pillow next to a sleeping Mom on early Saturday mornings: "Get up! You
are in big trouble!" Or he'll break my heart by leaving a note under the
covers for me to discover when I pull them back at night: "I love you
Mom." He reads everything in sight. Even the seemingly mundane
becomes a curiosity: odd words from TV commercials, the cases of DVDs,
the ingredients in cereal, the captions in the newspaper, the facts in the
Ripley's Believe It or Not comic: "Did you know Poison Dart Frogs become
poisonous by eating ants, Mom?" "Did you know our eyeballs are the
one part of our body that never grows?" I learn a lot of unexpected information from this young reader's meanderings.

In many traditional classrooms, it is hard to find the important
frames for peers talking about words in the halls, the random reading of
candy ingredients, or the odd note to big brother. Instead, 10 spelling
words and five correctly punctuated sentences get framed as the important reading. When educational policy mandates yearly testing and
schools orient to this as THE goal of schooling, they give the fancy frame
to noncollaborative, nonfunctional, discrete skills. In the world, however,
as these early readers grow, they will need to use skills collaboratively
and in creative combinations to accomplish projects and make change.

Politically motivated policies that frame only discrete, testable skills as the end point of reading threaten all children's literacies. By closely examining how discourse frames talk in our classrooms, by doing some important kid-watching (Owocki & Goodman, 2002), we can resist the externally framing principals that could demean the discourse in our classrooms. Through discourse analysis, we can seek out those multiple literacies and document them—and resist social and political practices that demean classroom learning, turning it into procedural display. The next section discusses in more detail how to do precisely this kind of analysis.

Doing It: Analyzing Frames as a Feature of Social Context

Resisting frames that demean our discourse—and embracing frames that foster dialogue and engagement—can begin with an analysis of the production formats behind talk in our classrooms. To analyze how utterances are framed within a production format, begin by looking carefully at an utterance and asking, Who is the animator? Who is the author? Who or what is the principal? In some cases, this framing may be visible in the words. For example, at first it seems that, in her narrative about jail, LaTasha does all the framing work of what "everybody" says.

UTTERANCE	ANIMATOR	AUTHOR	PRINCIPAL
I wanna be in jail	LaTasha	Everybody	Peer Group that wants to go to jail

LaTasha animates "everybody" as saying they want to go to jail. Like the *everybody* that needs $100-dollar-sneakers ("everybody" has them), this sounds like LaTasha's peer group talking. This peer group could be seen as the principal behind the view that jail is a desirable place to go. This assignment of animator, author, and principal is only an initial hypothesis about the relevant frame for LaTasha's story. This initial hypothesis, however, provides an entry point for more investigation. Do you really think LaTasha's peer group wants to go to jail? Why is she making this kind of claim?

Through the process of classroom discourse analysis, we can go back and ask students; we can also gather evidence from other interactions and from what we see around the school. At City School, evidence abounded that at least some students did want to go to jail—and were proud of it when they went. Some students even wore "LA County Jail" uniform shirts to school once they got out. Others would talk proudly about going to jail for each other. Certain students told me that substituting yourself for a friend at a crime scene was easy and commonplace—

LA Police, sadly, would gladly take in any brown or black potential per-
petrator without following up on the details of who actually performed a
crime. Students at City School absorbed this practice into their own framing system: Going to jail—because it may have been done on behalf of a
friend—could be an act of friendship and a demonstration of loyalty.
Follow-up discussions at the school and an accumulation of evidence and
observation suggest that this "going to jail" ethos is indeed the product
of a peer group principal behind LaTasha's words, "Everybody's like, 'I
wanna be in jail.'"

This follow-up discussion, however, also uncovered some other
framing institutions. When friends go to jail for friends, and when police
don't care who they arrest, when racial minorities are racial majorities in
jail, this peer group norm also appears to be a product of a racist society
and a police force that sees all black and brown children as equally jail-
worthy. When students see half of their friends in jail, they may want to
go there. In the context of society at large, they are literally all *framed* as
criminals. So our revised framing chart might look more like the following table.

UTTERANCE	ANIMATOR	AUTHOR	PRINCIPAL
I wanna be in jail	LaTasha	Everybody	Peer Group *Police Force* *Societal Racism*

This is an analysis that students need to hear and talk about—and debate.
This is the kind of background that needs to inform how we analyze
what students say. In wanting to go to jail, in wearing their jail uniforms
as a badge of honor, are they, in a way, complicit with the racist police
force that puts them there? But what are their options? In classroom discourse analysis, in many cases, *the process is the product.* We need to use
the analysis as an opportunity to ask students and peers, principals, and
other staff about the principal behind their words. In many cases, this act
of thoughtfulness may encourage some critical examination of hitherto
unexamined assumptions held by you and/or your students. In the prior
case, at City School, teachers struggled to combat this student culture
that glorified jail. With years of hindsight, I realize now that talking with
students about their own words and worlds (rather than silencing talk
about this topic) was the best approach to working through this issue.
LaTasha was already critiquing "everybody's" pro-jail viewpoint when
she commented on her friend's experience: "I couldn't be in jail," was her
conclusion.

Although LaTasha and her friends scoff at the pro-jail attitude, the
principal behind the pro-jail discourse at City School may in part be the

LA Police Department (LAPD) and the institutional racism with it. Who would have thought being "cool" was actually playing into the hands of the LAPD? But students are not the only ones in classrooms whose words are backed by principals their authors and animators may not condone. Analysis of the production format for the other interaction that began this chapter affords a closer look at how a teacher's words are framed by another external principal (and often the principal at the school). Within this interaction, the teacher asks, "Is there anything wrong with that?"— in effect, is there anything wrong with discussing "Black" and "White" characters in a book? On an initial analysis, it may appear that she is animator, author and principal of her own words.

UTTERANCE	ANIMATOR	AUTHOR	PRINCIPAL
Is there anything wrong with that?	Teacher	Teacher	Teacher

Obviously, as represented by this transcript at least, the teacher spoke these words and authored them as spontaneous speech on the spot. Although "Is there anything wrong with that?" and the answer it receives ("no") voice a belief that there is absolutely nothing wrong with discussing race in the classroom, this exchange simultaneously functions to shut down all talk about race. By shutting down talk about Black and White, this teacher agrees with Danny, effectively saying to her students, "It is not okay to talk about race here" or, in Danny's words, "Don't you be talking about that."

Is this something she really believes? I asked her. She does NOT want to silence talk about race and ethnicity in her classroom. She believes in multicultural education and in discussing issues of racial and linguistic difference—and in using multicultural literature in her classroom. In fact, that is why she chose to discuss a book (*My Little Island*) that, unlike many picture books in classrooms, contains mostly Black characters.

So why did she shut down the talk? Who is controlling her discourse? I have asked her and many of the teachers in my university classes about this hesitancy to talk about race. Overwhelmingly, teachers fear they will be flooded by phone calls from irate parents if they talk about race in the classroom. The school principal, whatever his or her feelings about our multicultural society, will not look kindly on negative parent phone calls; as a result, teachers feel their jobs are threatened when they speak about race. In Georgia, teachers have no recourse. There are no unions; there is no teacher tenure. Many worry that controversial content in their classrooms could threaten their own livelihood.

So who, then, really, in this case, is the principal behind the teacher's words? A new analytic chart might look like the following.

UTTERANCE	ANIMATOR	AUTHOR	PRINCIPAL
Is there anything wrong with that?	Teacher	Teacher	*Students' parents School Principal Georgia State Govt. banning teacher unions and teacher tenure.*

Because the principal within this frame—parents, the school principal, the Georgia state legislature—is so powerful compared with the voice of a single classroom teacher, a teacher who has studied how to use multicultural literature in the classroom and who is pursuing a graduate degree focusing on multicultural education in the classroom interactionally silences student talk about race. This example illustrates the power of *unexamined* social context to shape our classroom discourse. Classroom discourse analysis can start the process of examining these powerful frames—and begin countering unsavory principals who may be shaping our classroom talk.

In our classrooms, however, we also have more immediate interactional recourse. The next section introduces an analytic tool for understanding and reshaping classroom talk in its own interactional context: the analysis of participant structures.

FRAMING RESOURCES IN INTERACTIONAL CONTEXT: HOW PARTICIPANT STRUCTURES FRAME CLASSROOM TALK

The two classroom examples discussed earlier—one from a second-grade reading group, and one from a high school discussion facilitated by the teacher—are different not only in terms of content, but in terms of participation. Goffman's production format can be useful for noticing the broad social conditions that may be shaping our classroom discourse (what we have been referring to in this book more generally as "social context"). In a single interaction, however, the habituated flow of turns (e.g., teacher–student–teacher–student) or what we have been calling "interactional context" can also be a profoundly influential framing resource, shaping who has voice and what they get to say.

Reframing Student Talk Through Shifting Participant Structures

Participant structures, or "ways of arranging verbal interaction with students" (Philips, 1972, p. 377), are honed over years of teaching and teacher training. Often our class agendas, written hastily on the board, projected on a screen, or handed out before class are outlined in terms of these structures: (a) group check-in; (b) small groups, jigsaw; (c) whole-group discussion; (d) individual quick writes; and (e) group sharing. Throughout a class or a day, we move from talking to single students, to addressing the group, to working with a small group, to listening in on a small group that is working more independently. We take on different talking roles accordingly. Each of these kinds of configurations can lead to different interactional patterns and different kinds of language.

While we become familiar with these routines over years of experience, we may nevertheless be unaware of the fundamental but subtle effects they have on who gets to speak and how. In her ethnographic work as a linguistic anthropologist on the Warm Springs Indian Reservation, Susan Philips (1972) researched how certain participant structures shaped student participation there. She described four distinct participant structures widely practiced in the Warm Springs schools:

1. The teacher interacts with all the students.
2. The teacher interacts with only some of the students (e.g., in reading groups).
3. Students work independently at their desks.
4. Group project work.

Although these are standard formats, probably recognizable by most teachers in many school contexts, Philips noticed some distinct differences in how the Warm Springs Indian students participated in these different structures. Indians were most unlikely to participate in the first two. They were far more active participants in the second two. Why?

The key words are *"teacher* interacts." Within both the first and second structures, students direct their talk primarily to the teacher. In the first structure, the teacher interacts with all students, and all students' attention is directed toward the teacher. Sometimes, this structure might be in the form of a student presentation or show and tell. Still, even if a student, rather than the teacher, is standing in front of the class, the student presenting often orients primarily to the teacher—who, after all, will be evaluating the report. In the second structure (teacher-fronted, small-group work), students still orient primarily to the teacher. However, in this small group, the students may have more frequent and less interrupted teacher attention.

By contrast, in the third and fourth participation structures (independent desk work and group project work), students' activity is not directly addressed toward the teacher. Students are either working independently on a task, or directing their work toward peers. In group project work, the Warm Springs children were vociferous and active.

Gradually, teachers on the Reservation learned that "spending as little time in front of the class as possible" (Philips, 1972, p. 382) was the best possible way to encourage Indian participation in learning. Teachers gradually learned not to expect Indian students to present in front of class—or even to ask questions of the teacher in front of others. Teachers began to make themselves available privately to answer questions.

Philips found that these differences in participation corresponded to differences in language socialization in Warm Springs Indian homes. At home on the Reservation, children are given considerable autonomy and are usually supervised by older siblings, rather than parents. When children learn new skills, they learn them through silent but attentive observation of adults. During adult conversations, children are expected to listen attentively, but again silently. Indians try out their skills among peers when adults are not around.

Silent observation among elders and practice among peers: This listening and watching, peer-to-peer practice approach to learning differs starkly with staged performance of skills and the "learning through public mistakes" (Philips, 1972, p. 281) approach practiced in some traditional classrooms. As teachers accommodated to Indian norms, they found more Indian participation. However, when these students went on to high schools where teachers were unaccustomed to Indian participation norms, the Indians were again minimal participants. Many dropped out. One participation structure framed Reservation students as competent classroom participants, while another framed them as difficult students and reluctant learners.

Philips' work draws attention to the relationships produced by different participant structures—and the differential access to participation these structures might create unless explicitly addressed. Her study suggests that different frames for participation—as much as different ways of speaking—can limit students' voice in the classroom. Just as Baker's exercises in "trilingualism" began to get students and teachers thinking about the value and functionality of different ways of speaking in different contexts (see chap. 6), it is likely that involving students and teachers in talk about different forms of participation could give them the resources to have voice within both the participation structures of the Reservation and those of the public school.

Pinpointing Participation

The first step toward understanding how participant structures are shaping interaction in our own classrooms is to map participation within an event. Begin by mapping the pattern between teacher (T) and student (S) turns (cf. Cazden, 2001). In the teacher-fronted lecture, for example, the pattern might look like this:

T-T-T-T-T-T-T-T-T-S-T-S-T-T-T

As this pattern displays, in a lecture, the teacher carries on uninterrupted, but for the occasional flurry of student questions.

Even when a student is presenting in front of the class, the pattern might indicate a singular orientation to the teacher, as the teacher co-authors a presentation:

S1-S1-S1-S1-S1-T-T-T-S1-S1-S1-S1-S1-T

In this case, labeling the student "S1" also illustrates that only one student is talking here. Students 2–25 remain silent.

Even in a full-class discussion, the teacher may be the addressee for most student remarks:

S-T-S-S-T-S-T-S-S-S-T-S-T-S-T-S-T-S-S-T

Sometimes, however, a teacher is able to relinquish some control of the talk and let student voices more fully permeate a discussion. The discussion at City School, in which the teacher's voice is minimal, would look different in terms of participation compared with a discussion in the second-grade reading group in Georgia, in which the teacher is front and center:

EVENT	PARTICIPATION PATTERN
City School Jail Discussion	T-S-S-S-S-S-S-S-S-S-S-S-S-T-S-S-S
Georgia Elementary Book Discussion	T-S-T-S-T-S-T-S-T-S-S-T-S-S-S-T-S

The difference in participation in these two events illustrates the value of making these participation maps rather than giving events a participant structure name such as "small-group discussion." These events might both be labeled as "small-group discussions," but this title glosses over critical differences in participation within them. Simply pulling students aside to talk about a book with the teacher does not ensure students will be doing most of the discussing.

After you have mapped your focal event, reflect on how much talk is produced by teachers and by the students, and how that talk is functioning. Does the pattern reflect the kind of classroom you want to be teaching within?

Ratified and Unratified Participants

In classrooms, as we move from participant structure to participation structure (e.g., lecture to discussion, group work to break), how much we speak and what we say is framed largely by the changing patterns of participation across these structures. How people listen also changes from event to event. During a lecture, all students are expected to be listening to the teacher. Goffman calls the student listeners in this case *ratified participants*. In contrast, during small-group work, students are meant to be talking to each other while the teacher becomes the listener. But a teacher listening to small groups is in a different listening position than students listening to a teacher. As we listen in on a group talking with each other, we are, in Goffman's terms, *un-ratified participants*—also known as bystanders. Depending on whether bystanders admit they are trying to hear, they can be called "overhearers," who presumably accidentally listen in (as in, "I *couldn't help* overhearing . . . ") or eavesdroppers, who more intentionally listen in on an interaction not directed to them. When teachers listen in on student group work, we are bystanders, not fully ratified participants. However, this does not mean we are not influential.

As Goffman (1974) points out, the presence of bystanders often shapes the talk—and bystanders often enter more fully into the talk they are listening in on, eventually becoming full participants. In the classroom, ratified or unratified status fluctuates constantly. As we move from group to group during project work, for example, we are "permitted" by the participant structure to simply stand outside a group and eavesdrop on this discussion. As would be expected, however, when the audience changes, the kind of talk in those small groups changes. Students may modify their language when they spy a teacher hovering nearby. When we as teachers listen in on group work, we are often acknowledged and incorporated into the talk in some way. With strategies verging on spy tactics, some teachers even pose as eavesdroppers on one group while doing undercover eavesdropping simultaneously on another more distant and unsuspecting group. As teachers and discourse analysts, we have the tools to reflect on and negotiate our role as bystanders and to monitor its effects on classroom discourse and classroom learning.

Underlife

As you begin to eavesdrop deliberately on student talk, and especially as you record talk (another form of eavesdropping) in your classroom, you may recognize that a great deal of talk is not meant to be heard by teachers. Even during a presumably teacher-directed lesson, talk in classrooms is layered: In one layer, students and a teacher may be discussing social studies or current events, while in another, simultaneous layer of talk, students are planning their weekend, discussing a popular YouTube clip, or debating a point mentioned by another student 5 minutes earlier and long dropped from the official T-S-T-S-T-S back-and-forth layer of the classroom strata.

Goffman names this talk beneath the expected institutional talk *underlife*. Although underlife often spins off a statement that was initially part of official discourse, its participation pattern differs drastically, adding another layer "under" the official lesson:

T-S-T-S-T-S-T-S-T-S-T-S-T-S-T-S-T-S-T-S- T-　} *Official Lesson*

S-S-S-S-S-S-S-S-S-S-S-S-S-S-S-　} *Underlife*

While the official T-S-T-S discourse proceeds, students may maintain another (or multiple) productive conversations simultaneously. Although this looks chaotic, underlife is often muffled. It may even be taking place in the form of notes or other unspoken communication. These days, even cell phones can be used to carry on underlife via text messaging. Underlife conversations are often started when a student's response within the teacher-led discussion is interesting to other students—but just tangential enough from the teacher's agenda that he never takes it up. By definition, underlife remains beneath the surface as official class talk flows along, as in the following example during a current events unit at a Los Angeles high school.

TEACHER-LED DISCUSSION	UNDERLIFE
T: What did the Supreme Court decision in *Brown v. the Board of Education*, have to do with?	S: James Brown? S: James Brown? S: James Brown? S: Shut-up S: You shut up S: James Brown?
T: Ye:::s?	S: Al Green

James Brown? Al Green? These musicians have more meaning to these students at the moment than a distant Supreme Court case. What would happen if this teacher pulled these voices into the official participant structure? When underlife is reframed in this way, it can potentially take the classroom learning in productive directions.

Ratified Underlife

Underlife is often generated by teacher talk, but, as the James Brown example illustrates, if left alone by the teacher, it can swiftly run far afield from the teacher-led discussion. It is as if students have started recess early. However, some teachers have noticed, as eavesdroppers on underlife, that they can reframe it as part of official classroom discussion—and that doing so can build relevance into curriculum. An official classroom discussion on the school barbeque, for example, prompted some ruckus in Vivian Vasquez's (2004) classroom:

> As the children came into the classroom, the air was filled with excitement about the school barbeque. . . . Stefanie was interested to know whether there were more people who ate hamburgers or more people who ate hot dogs. To do this, she stated that she was "going to do a hand-count survey." A quiet whisper could be heard from the back of the group followed by what seemed to be agitated conversation. Anthony, one of the boys in the class, had said to some of the children sitting beside him that he didn't eat at the barbeque because he is a vegetarian and therefore he could not participate in Stefanie's survey. (pp. 103–104)

Rather than being construed as a diversion from the real work of school, attending to the whisper of underlife at the back of the classroom prompted an entire inquiry unit on vegetarianism. Students began to work toward a vegetarian option at the next barbeque. In the process, they wrote letters, read books about vegetarians, surveyed the school about the barbeque and vegetarianism, and gave a more prominent frame to the marginalized whisper in the back of the class. Underlife, then, for Vasquez became the relevant medium for curriculum involving reading, writing, researching, calculating, and reporting—as well as a vehicle for social action. These students realized, at 4 years old, that learning is related to their concerns.

At City School, a school designed for students who were just about to give up on the idea that school-based learning had any relevance to them, underlife often was reframed as a building block for class discussion. In the conversation with LaTasha, excerpted in this chapter, one of the students had arrived to class late—having literally just been sprung from jail. Rather than taking this as a distraction, or leaving the jail discussion to build on its own as underlife beneath the surface of his lesson, the teacher took LaTasha's experience as an opportunity to reframe student underlife as significant life lessons, endorsed by the teacher. Talking about jail within the context of his class may be different than the kind of talk about jail that would go on outside his class. Noticing underlife became a tool for fostering dialogue between school-sanctioned views and the urgency that drives peer choices.

Border Talk

Border talk, or the impromptu talk between classes or classroom events within the cracks of institutionally sanctioned discourse, is another form of underlife. However, when teachers join in—as when the City School teacher joined in the telling of LaTasha's jail story—border talk gets reframed as relevant to the entire classroom community. Border talk provides another opportunity to pull students' worlds into dialogue with classroom concerns. For example, although I have characterized the participation structures in the second-grade reading group in Georgia as regularly following a traditional T-S-T-S-T-S pattern, the primary exception to this pattern was the Border Narrative discussed in chapter 7. Once the teacher opened the conversation for Rene's birthday story, more and varied student participation snuck in between each teacher turn. Although the teacher still largely influenced the direction of the conversation, Rene's peers, Nancy and Roberto, were legitimate and influential participants, as this segment illustrates:

T	Teacher:	Why do they cry? (.) Cause they don't like it?
S	Nancy:	I don't know. ((laughs slightly))
S	Rene:	Cause they say (.) take a bi:te, take a bi:te and then-and then
		[( ) The first time I did it I=
S	Roberto:	[(go there)
S	Rene:	=was like four years old. And then I took a bite, and then my dad stook my whole face in the ca:ke. ((laughs slightly)) And then I started crying.
T	Teacher:	O:h, I would not like that ei:the:r.

This T-S-S-S-S-T pattern of participation was distinctly different from the usual T-S-T-S-T-S this group participated in during their ESOL session.

The participant structure along the borders of events often contrasts dramatically with the activity within a formal lesson, in both content and structure. The most noticeable contrast may be the prevalence of student voices. By eavesdropping occasionally on underlife and border talk, we may be able to reframe these voices as relevant not just to the teacher's agenda, but also to students' lives and futures.

Framing and Reframing Talk,
Word by Word

As we have seen, contextual frames around talk render certain discourse appropriate or not. Even if the same person is the animator across situations, the language will be different in a lecture, a second-grade picture book discussion, or a first date. Each event frames language in certain ways. However, language helps construct these frames, defining these events. I do not need to say, "I am giving a lecture now." Using language in a normative lecture way gives students clues that I am giving a lecture—and that they should click their pens into action and dutifully take notes. Using language in certain ways also can transform certain participant structures (a lecture) into others (a discussion). Students who are bent on getting their concerns into my lecture can figure out ways to ask questions that will change the participation pattern. Just as language is controlled by normative frames, language also can be used in new ways to resist those normative constraints. In other words, discourse and its frame are in a dialectical relationship:

Contextual Frame ↔ The Language We Use
constructs

The following sections illustrate how discourse analysis that focuses on peer language and language variety, affective and epistemic language, and the use of pronouns can help us to recognize how language is shaped by and is shaping participation patterns in the classroom. By understanding how these language resources work, we can practice using them as tools to reframe talk and modify participation patterns in our own classrooms.

Peer Language Versus School Language

When peers converse, on their own, they choose the language that functions for them—the discourse that best communicates with a peer. This discourse may include a combination of multiple registers, varieties, coinages, and national languages. I am broadly labeling this kind of talk *peer language* here, instead of *home language, Spanish, African-American English,* or anything else because we are looking at the language students use when they turn and talk to each other. This peer language is more readily afforded by certain participant structures. You will probably hear peer language in classroom underlife and group project work, for example. I know I am much more likely to hear "This guy is an ass!" when eavesdropping on group work than when conducting a class discussion, where "I have some problems with this author" would be more likely. We saw evidence of this kind of language monitoring in the example analyzed in chapter 4, when Danny corrected his use of *dudes*:

Teacher: Hats. Do men wear a lot of hats now?

Danny: Some don't. **The train dudes—the train people** wear they wear these like, big ol things that-

Why this correction? What made him think that *people* was a more appropriate word than *dude*? His self-correction suggests there are external norms guiding what he deems as appropriate talk in a teacher-directed group. In this example, structure seems to control what kind of language is used.

However, depending on the participant structure and the established classroom norms, peer language may be regularly and productively integrated into classroom learning events as well. Some students boldly use language to change participation norms. Compare Danny's self-correction to LaTasha's statement at the beginning of this chapter:

LaTasha: Everybody was like, "I'm going to jail, all my **homies** in jail."

Homies is at least as distant from school English as *dude*, but LaTasha needs that word here; it is functional, and it is never censored—by herself or anyone else. LaTasha's use of peer language helps to construct the classroom frame as one that foregrounds student voices. Her language invites student language into the setting and, quite possibly, makes it more difficult for the teacher to jump back in. Danny's *train people* correction is constructed by the existent participant structure; LaTasha's *homies* helps construct a new participant structure.

As you look at other participant structures in your own classroom, look for how peer language is facilitated within them and reflect on how variations in the use of more peer language affects participation patterns.

Affective and Epistemic Language

Different participant structures also construct the degree to which emotional statements or factual evidence guide contributions. In classrooms in general, the classroom discourse analyst Courtney Cazden (2001) has found that affective or emotional language is hard to find. Instead, epistemic or knowledge-related language dominates. The focus is frequently more on what students know and how they know it than on what students are unsure of or their feelings about it. When making a teaching point, talk usually orients not to students' emotions but to the facts and the evidence that support our ideas. When discussing this point with peers, however, students may back off the factual claims, begin to question them, and infuse their arguments with emotional language. In each participant structure, participants will use different kinds of language to communicate affective and epistemic stance. The following table illustrates some examples of language that indicate how "sure" of something someone is (epistemic stance) or the way they feel about it (affective stance) (Ochs, 1993).

POSSIBLE MARKERS OF EPISTEMIC STANCE	POSSIBLE MARKERS OF AFFECTIVE STANCE
DISCOURSE MARKERS: e.g., *uh, well, I mean, okay, so* (these usually function to weaken epistemic stance—to show we are not quite so sure)	**ADDRESS TERMS:** friend, liar, homey, man, sweetcakes, all nicknames, etc.
VERBS: Modal verbs: e.g., *can, may, must, ought to, have to*	**EXTREME EXAGGERATION:** never, always, **everyone**, no one, people (as in ALL people), forever, etc.
Modal lexical verbs: e.g., *order, urge*	**VERBS:** *I... can't stand, dread, fear, hate, regret, resent, enjoy, hope, like, love, prefer, seek, want, wish.*
Factive verbs: e.g., *know, think, remember*	*IT... aggravates, agitates, annoys, bothers, confuses, disappoints, discourages, disgusts, disturbs,*
Low/High certainty verbs: e.g., *I don't know, I'm wondering, I'm not sure, I think, I thought, I don't think, I gather, I imagine, I assume, I doubt, I estimate, I guess, I infer, I suppose, I wonder if, I conclude, I demonstrate, I establish, I know, I perceive, I realize, I know, I show*	*embarrasses, frightens, irritates, kills, rubs, saddens, scares, shocks, troubles, worries amazes, amuses, delights, interests, pleases ... me.*
Low/High certainty adjectives: *doubtful, possible, supposed, uncertain, unlikely, unclear, unsure, certain, evident, impossible, obvious, true, well-known, clear, sure, **real***	**ADJECTIVES:** *afraid, alarmed, annoyed, ashamed, concerned, depressed, disappointed, disgusted, disturbed, embarrassed, frightened, irritated, mad, sad, scared, shocked, unhappy, upset, worried...* *amazed, amused, content, curious, delighted, eager, fascinated, fortunate, glad, happy, hopeful, interested, lucky, pleased, proud, relieved, satisfied, thankful...*
Low/High certainty modal adverbs: e.g., *probably, always, broadly speaking, of course, arguably, conceivably,*	

POSSIBLE MARKERS OF EPISTEMIC STANCE (*continued*)	POSSIBLE MARKERS OF AFFECTIVE STANCE (*continued*)
ostensibly, supposedly, perhaps, maybe, exactly, certainly, really, definitely, absolutely, always, never, evidently, indeed, in fact, obviously, undoubtedly	IT *is/seems... amazing, incredible, interesting, natural, pleasing, significant, understandable...*
INTENSIFIERS/DEINTENSIFIERS: e.g., *so, really, kind of, sort of, just, like, somewhat, for sure, almost, DO + verb, Really + adjective, so + adjective/adverb, such a...*	ADVERBS: *annoyingly, depressingly, disappointingly, regretfully, sadly... amazingly, appropriately, funnily, happily, luckily, preferably, thankfully, ironically, sardonically...*

The examples of language in this table are just a starting point to get you comparing relative epistemic and affective stances across different participant structures in your classroom. As previous chapters have emphasized, these words do not function in isolation—their work as markers of affect or truth value is always done in context, in combination with other words and social cues. Their location in one column or the other is a judgment call—and you will need to make these judgments again and again as you identify truth claims and emotion in your own data. In addition to these linguistic features, contextualization cues like raised pitch, repeated words, or an increase in volume can elevate the affective stance of an interaction. Compare the affect of "Good morning" with "Good ↑MORNing," for example. Then throw in an address term for heightened affect: "Good ↑MORNing, sweetcakes!"

Our talk is not simply epistemic or affective. Rather, our language is always making claims and emoting in varying degrees. Statements full of heightened positive affective stance markers are expressive and emotional: "I **love** watching salamanders!" Affect also can infuse discussions when participants overlap each other's statements, jump in to agree or disagree, or escalate the level of affect: "I'm there! I **totally adore** Salamanders too!" In contrast, statements that include high certainty epistemic stance markers are distancing and objective, often marked by the passive voice and the absences of hedges: "Salamanders **have been found** to live in all habitats." Epistemic stance in published scientific articles is usually heightened. But epistemic stance within spoken scientific discussions may include more mitigating stance markers: "Er, it **may be true** that salamanders live in all habitats, but I **don't think** Salamanders could survive in Antarctica."

Exploring how stance changes across participant structures can begin to help us understand why some students prefer certain classroom events and subject areas far more than others. Why do some students love literature circles but dislike science? These two subjects may be dominated by different participation patterns and different kinds of language. Sometimes students may feel shut out of science simply because the participant structure of a science lesson seems to demand objectifying, scientific language. In contrast, some students may be resistant to the emotive language that may emerge in a student book club. But do these boundaries need to be so rigid?

On a closer look, you may find that students' emotional literature discussions are permeated with factual talk. When a fifth-grade reading group studied by classroom researchers Karla Möller and JoBeth Allen, for example, discussed a book about race relations, the girls need to clarify what aspects about this book were real in their own lives. An initially emotionally laden discussion turned into an exchange centered on getting the facts right, when a student who had never heard of the Ku Klux Klan asked her discussion group, "Who, who is K Klux? Who, who, who is that people?" (Möller & Allen, 2000):

Nicole:	White folks—people that don't like Black people.
Tamika:	And they dress up in-
Nicole:	Sheets.
	… (5 more lines describing the Klan and their activities)
Carmen:	I saw a movie about it.
Tamika:	And they'll burn a cross in your yard and put you on it and they'll burn you up.
Karla:	So you didn't know about the-
Jasmine:	**They real**?
Tamika:	Yeah.
Nicole:	It's called, it's a-
Karla:	You didn't know about the Ku Klux Klan?

As this exchange shows, finding out how "real" the Ku Klux Klan is, even today, was important to these girls—and new knowledge to at least some of them. Their desire to understand the Ku Klux Klan in terms of their own lives involves an intermingling of affective and epistemic urgency. As their talk illustrates, literature discussions can be even more powerful when they shift between fantasy and fact—when an emotion sparks our epistemic need to know.

Just as a literature group can turn to the facts, a science talk can be flush with affect. Welcoming displays of affective stance within a lesson can change participation by opening up discussion to students' passions.

Displaying hesitations in epistemic stance is another discourse strategy that can open up science to more diverse participation. "Mr. Wonderful," discussed in chapter 5, used this strategy to spark students' curiosity about genetic puzzles. Instead of firmly stating facts about biology, he wondered out loud: "I **wonder** . . ." This word mitigates epistemic stance and opens the floor to multiple possible explanations. Like the "wondering" exchanges in Mr. Wonderful's class, successful Science Talks in Karen Gallas' (1995) classroom were constructed through hesitations in epistemic stance. When students began to preface their comments with "I **think**" or "**maybe**," more classmates and a greater diversity of classmates joined in the conversation. As Gallas found, explicit work on modifying epistemic stance changed an event that was dominated by three vociferous and sure students into an event in which all students participated in science-like inquiry.

But this is the bottom line: What is it that drives our work in classrooms and our learning beyond the classroom? So often the work of a prominent doctor or scientist or other professional is driven by some emotional turning point. Developmental psychologist Lisa Capps was driven to study agoraphobia, a panic disorder found predominantly in women, in part because her own brother suffered under this condition. In the same way, students are driven to read stories that connect with emotions they are struggling with in their own lives or to study questions that do not yet have answers. This kind of emotional passion drives intellectual work. Classrooms are as much about knowledge as they are about emotions. Look for both kinds of language, and use your discourse analysis to investigate how affective and epistemic stance markers function across subjects and participant structures in your classroom.

Inclusive Versus Exclusive Pronouns

How often during the day, as a teacher, do you use the word *we*? How many times have I used it in this book? As teachers, *we* like to think we share similar perspective, goals, and even moral frameworks. When we talk as one, we can create the impression that we are thinking as one.

In contrast, what happens when we use the pronoun *they*? This small change creates a chasm between *us* and *them*. For example, consider this talk about students in the faculty lunch room: "**They** are absolutely crazy today! Is it the full moon or something?" By choosing the pronoun *they*, this teacher has immediately distanced herself from the students in her class. Might not we teachers be a bit crazy too? After all, it is *our* full moon too. In general, using inclusive language helps us to think inclusively. Exclusive language, well, excludes. I am not saying we all need to behave as if we were the same—but being aware of how we use personal pronouns can help us recognize how our words are framing our relationships.

The power of framing pronouns can affect not only our relationships with students and peers, but also the relationships between our students and the classroom material. We can use pronouns to frame questions and curriculum inclusively, bringing curriculum closer to us, rather than keeping it at an abstract and uninteresting distance.

Like modifications in epistemic stance, modifying pronoun use can be an effective tool to bring the material onto a human scale—to illustrate, for example, that a science problem is of mutual concern to us. After all, we are all affected by global warming, advances in biotechnology, mutating viruses, and so forth. Personal pronouns show how these sometimes seemingly abstract topics affect us as people.

Using personal pronouns to frame science in classrooms can also encourage more student participation. When Karen Gallas puzzled over why some of her primary school Science Talks went so well, she had an intuition it had something to do with how she had rephrased some of the topics of inquiry to personalize them. When she looked back at her transcripts, her intuition was right. The participant patterns changed dramatically when questions were asked with personal pronouns: "How do dreams get into **our** heads?" generated more student interest and discussion than an impersonally stated question such as, "Where do dreams come from?" (Gallas, 1995, p. 95).

This personalization as a tool to construct productive science talk and theorizing is not just an artifice of the primary grades. This personal way of entering into theoretical science is something real adult scientists do too. Applied linguists Sally Jacoby and Patrick Gonzales and linguistic anthropologist Elinor Ochs spent years studying the talk of theoretical physicists in their research meetings. The principal investigator who led this group routinely entered into the problems of physics by talking as if he were a molecule, thinking out loud with statements such as, "When I come down, I'm in the domain state" (Ochs, Gonzales, & Jacoby, 1996).

In summary, just as language can be limited and constrained by certain participant structures, language can, in turn, be brought into interactions to influence what kind of participant structure emerges. As soon as one student begins using emotional language, a book discussion can become a vehicle for social action. When one student uses the language of her peers to prevent them from going to jail or joining a gang, a border discussion can be a vehicle that saves lives. When we include ourselves as relevant actors in the drama of science, we enter into the learning. The next section gives specific suggestions for analyzing how words and interaction create and are restricted by frames in your classroom.

Doing It: Analyzing Frames as a Feature of Interactional Context

Understanding how language can be affected and in turn affect participant structures in our classrooms can point us, as teachers, in new directions. As we "cover the material," we can do so in new ways, with new languages, and in new participant structures. At the interactional level, our analysis can help us understand how participant structures frame who talks, what language they might use, and how language can function—and in turn point us to new possibilities for organizing classroom interaction and learning.

What is the Participant Structure?

Start by asking yourself, "What is the participant structure within this event?" In LaTasha's commentary that initiated this chapter, for example, begin by pin pointing student and teacher turns at talk. In the following longer excerpt, of which LaTasha's comment is a part, the teacher participates only once:

S Keneisha: I don't <u>NEV</u>er wanna go back.
   (0.8)
T Teacher: I hear ya.
   (2.0)
S LaTasha: Liar you just <u>said</u> that's where everybody <u>at,</u>
            you should go out and <u>do</u> somthin' <u>e</u>lse, huh.
S Keneisha: Who me?
S LaTasha: Yeah tryin' to get through [there.
S Keneisha: [Oh ↑<u>no:</u>! (0.4) I didn' care
            about anybody being there
            [I wannida go home.
S LaTasha: [Everybody was like, I'm going to <u>ja</u>il, all my homies
            in jail.
            Whatchu [wanna go to jail <u>fo:</u>.
S Vicki: [People be like ?I'm- I'm goin' to jail."
            As soon as you get there=
S LaTasha: That's STUpid.
S Vicki: =?I wanna go ho[:::me.
S Keneisha: [You be waninda go ho- I'm tellin' you
            ma:n.
S LaTasha: See I couldn't be in jail 'cause all that.

A participation map of this interaction looks like this: S-T-S-S-S-S-S-S-S-S-S. The teacher has decided to listen to this one—and wisely so. The girls negotiated a conclusion he would endorse. Now, despite peer pressure from "everybody," it seems that not one of these girls is interested in going to jail. During this discussion, the teacher learned about a particular form of peer pressure that these girls contend with regularly.

Who Has Voice?

As the teacher sits, silently, he lets the girls negotiate a conclusion in their own voice. His "I hear ya," it seems, was enough to encourage the discussion. This discussion, however, is not taking place in the language of school. In this context, it did not need to. As their language takes center stage, all the girls become eager participants.

Who Are the Ratified and Unratified Participants?

In this excerpt, everyone participates. All are ratified participants. Is it possible, however, that the teacher might be slipping into the eavesdropper role? We would have to see more transcript to see his participation unfold. What happens when, standing at the front of the class, we slip into eavesdropper position? Have you ever experienced this happening to you in your own class discussion, as students take off with an idea? This can feel either like we no longer have control or, in the best of circumstances, that our students are taking control of their own learning. Analyzing a transcript can help you make this distinction in retrospect.

What Kinds of Talk, Stance Markers,
and/or Pronouns Are Present?

This is peer-to-peer language. A brief glance at this discussion yields words and stance markers that one might not ordinarily find in classrooms. There are features of AAE and/or Youth register:

No extra copula:
> LaTasha: Everybody was like, I'm going to jail, **all my homies in jail**
> LaTasha: Liar you just <u>said</u> that's **where everybody at**

Youth-culture descriptors and address terms:
> LaTasha: Everybody was like, I'm going to jail, all my **homies** in jail
> Keneisha: You be waninda go ho- I'm tellin' you **ma:n.**

There is a proliferation of affect markers:

Raised pitch and volume:
Keneisha: Oh ↑<u>no:</u>! (0.4)
Keneisha: I don't **NEVer** wanna go back.
Overlap:
LaTasha: Yeah tryin' to get through [there.
Keneisha: [Oh ↑<u>no:</u>! (0.4) I didn' care
                       about anybody
Extreme exaggeration:
Keneisha: I don't **NEVer** wanna go back.
LaTasha: Liar you just <u>said</u> that's where **everybody** <u>at.</u>
LaTasha: **[Everybody** was like I'm going to <u>jail</u>, **all my homies** in
                   jail.

Finally, there is building opposition of individual pronouns ("**I** didn' care," "**I** don't never…") and the voice of a collective peer ("**everybody**," "**people**"). Keneisha's concluding remark, however, uses a collective, generic *you* to unify those individual voices in a collective opposition to the pro-jail perspective: "**You** be waninda go ho[me]."

Each of these features of talk indicates involvement and excitement. This is a topic of some urgency to all of these girls. Shutting this conversation down to get on with the real lesson could be disastrous for learning in this setting.

So, what do you do if you hear this kind of language in your classroom? This analysis, in combination with the analysis of the social context influencing LaTasha's statements about "everybody," suggests that letting such talk proceed with minimal teacher reframing can potentially take the curriculum in new directions. Your next step is to negotiate the balance between the teacher's voice and the students' voices within that learning—between becoming a permanent eavesdropper and carefully allowing students' talk guide how you re-enter the conversation.

Just as Vivian Vasquez listened to a side comment from a vegetarian and built an inquiry unit from it within her pre-K class, LaTasha's teacher could build a powerful inquiry unit from these students' comments on jail. This unit could involve first showing this transcript to the students and discussing it, surveying City School on their jail experiences and opinions, reading literature on jail experiences, inviting the Parole Officer to talk to the class, taking a field trip to LA County Jail, writing about that experience, writing letters to the mayor or the newspaper about personal experiences with police brutality, and even setting up a watch-dog group to monitor the LAPD. This is the kind of curricular—and social—vision that classroom discourse analysis should promote. This is how students and teachers can begin to break frame.

USING FRAMING RESOURCES FOR AGENCY

As the accumulation of examples in this chapter has begun to illustrate, frames are ideologies in practice. **Ideologies** are unstated, "tacit" beliefs or assumptions held by the general public that guide our actions. Discourse frames construct and sanction those ideologies. When David says, "Don't you be talking about that!," he is giving voice to an ideology that guides much of school talk today: Race is not to be discussed. Frames create an environment in which we can only talk in certain ways, and in which, as a result, certain ideologies are much easier to have than others. However, awareness of how we are being framed can give us the first tool to breaking frame, contesting assumed ideologies, and augmenting our agency in the face of institutional norms.

From Being Framed to Breaking Frame:
Analyzing Frames as an Act of Agency

How can we break frame?

What does it meant to *break frame*? It means to act in non-normative ways. Sociologist Harold Garfinkel (1972) used to send his students out to purposely "break frame"—violating social norms we never think about. For example, he would have them walk onto a crowded elevator and face the back or sit down next to someone on a bus, although dozens of seats were vacant. A friend of mine tells a story about how she broke frame at the doctor's office by not taking her clothes off after repeated requests from the nurse. Although she was only getting her broken finger checked and there was no medical need for her to undress, the doctor noted her behavior on his chart: "Difficult patient." Facing the back of the elevator, scrunching next to someone on a bus filled with vacant seats, staying dressed at a doctor's exam: These are ways of breaking frame that make visible some of the social norms that force us to do things.

On the bus or the elevator, you may get some odd stares when you break the frame, and in the doctor's office my friend was deemed "difficult"—in this way, people know they are breaking a norm. Frame-breaking experiments like this are revealing, but the stakes, admittedly, are rather low. I don't mind facing forward on the elevator after all.

In classrooms, however, the frames that constrain us can be damaging. Unspoken rules can lead to Friday mornings at school crammed with spelling and punctuation tests, shutting down meaningful talk, not listening to students. Taking agency is the act of resisting these frames: Don't give tests every Friday morning. (I know a group of first-grade teachers who just started this act of resistance. They are delighted with the expanses of time they now have for learning activities.) Help students to take issue not with the peers who think it is cool to go to jail, but with those institutions that construct their self-destructive attitudes. Talk about race. Read books about race. Do not flinch. These are frame-breaking acts that may reveal norms in abrupt ways. The principal may be irate, students might unearth some shocking statistics about jail in the United States, and peers and irate parents might call you (instead of the other way around). These are signs that you are running into a frame.

PUTTING IT ALL TOGETHER:
ANALYZING FRAMING RESOURCES

The analyses in this chapter have begun to illustrate how framing resources can be a tool for your classroom discourse analysis. As you proceed toward analyzing how framing is at work in your transcript, use the questions in the following analytic table to guide your inquiry.

Analytic Table: Analyzing Frames

EVENT	SEQUENCE	SOCIAL CONTEXT	INTERACTIONAL CONTEXT	AGENCY
e.g., Discussion about Jail	e.g., LaTasha's story	Who is the animator?	What is the participant structure?	How can we break frame?
		Who is the author?	Who has voice in this structure?	
		What or who is the principal?	Who are the ratified and unratified participants in this structure?	
			What kinds of talk and stance-markers are present?	

The final question we are left with, "How can we break frame?", will have multiple answers and different answers in any given context. There are critical steps to take in redoing classroom interactions to positively shape learning. This redoing is the most practical goal of classroom discourse analysis. After we break some frames down, we need to build new ones. This rebuilding process is the subject of the next and final chapter, "Creating New Learning Environments through Classroom Discourse Analysis."

QUESTIONS AND ACTIVITIES

Critical Reflection

1. Irving Goffman's concept of *principal* behind our talk and actions refers to institutions or people outside a specific interaction that nevertheless control what we say. In what ways do you think institutions or people outside the classroom manipulate your senses and attitudes inside the classroom?
2. Use this chart to think about who animates, authors, and principals each of the listed genres. The Presidential Address is filled out as an example. Compare and discuss your answers in a group.

GENRE OR UTTERANCE	ANIMATOR	AUTHOR	PRINCIPAL
Presidential Address	The President of the United States	Speech-writers	The U.S. Government
Personal testimony on a commercial for Tylenol			
Singing the National Anthem at a Baseball Game			
"PEACE NOW" written on a placard at an anti-war protest			
"I like the choices Johnny is making," said by a teacher to a silent child walking down a primary school hall.			
Others?			

3. What participant structures do you use in your classroom? What kinds of participation patterns are present in each? (For this exercise, you may take the "armchair" approach and guess at the approximate T-S pattern.) Which do you prefer? Which do your students prefer? To answer this last question, show students your list and take a vote! Fill out the following table. Then discuss the results with your students.

PARTICIPANT STRUCTURE	PARTICIPATION PATTERN	PREFERENCE (record student votes)
e.g., whole-class discussion	T-S-T-S-T-S-T-S-T-T—S	IIII

4. This chapter mentions some examples of blatantly breaking frame (e.g., facing the back of an elevator, squeezing in next to a stranger on a nearly empty bus, explicitly mentioning race while discussing a children's picture book). Think of a time when you have broken frame (or think of a way to do that today). What happened?

Reflective Activities

1. Make a participation map of your focal event. After you have mapped your focal event, reflect on how much talk is taken up by teachers and by the students, and how that talk is functioning. Does the pattern reflect the kind of classroom you want to be teaching within? If not, think about modifications—you might also show these patterns to your students and talk about modifications with them. What suggestions do they make?
2. *Students as discourse analysts*: Give students a transcript of a classroom event (you might even use their own discussion group). Have them make a participant map (e.g., T-S1-S1-T-S2). Then, regroup and discuss the implications of this map. Was this the pattern they expected to find? What was unexpected? How could it be changed for the better?
3. Analyze the interactional dimension of framing in the "Don't you be talking about that" excerpt that begins this chapter. What is the participant structure? Who has voice in this structure? Who are the ratified and unratified participants? What kinds of talk and stance markers are present?

4. Choose a sequence in your transcript and in your focal event and use the analytic chart to see what framing resources are at work within it.

Suggestions for Further Reading

Those who would like to read more about framing in the broad social sense should start with books by Irving Goffman (I find his chapter on "Footing" in *Forms of Talk* [1981] a readable and entertaining entry point). Susan Philips's (1984) book-length ethnography of her research on the Warm Springs Reservation, *Invisible Culture*, is a beautiful exploration of the ramifications of traditional schooling in a multicultural society. For an example of how children's talk is fostered and furthered in a literature group, Möller and Allen's (2000) article in the *Journal of Literacy Research* is a must-read. If you find the phrase "the medium is the message" intriguing, you may want to read more of and about Marshall McLuhan (who also penned, "Mud gives the illusion of depth" and coined the term *global village*). His *Understanding Media* (1964) is now a classic and is considered to be prophetic of the current media explosion into cyberspace.

9

CREATING NEW LEARNING ENVIRONMENTS THROUGH CRITICAL CLASSROOM DISCOURSE ANALYSIS

PREVIEW QUESTIONS Before you read this chapter, ask yourself: What is the difference between a *teacher* and a *teacher who does classroom discourse analysis?*

Brainstorm a long list—big and small differences, positives and negatives. Are these differences that matter to you? Your students?

What is the difference between being a teacher and being a teacher who does classroom discourse analysis?

You have now learned about what doing classroom discourse entails and, possibly, recorded and analyzed some classroom discourse of your own, discussing it with peers and even students. Now what? Can the same *you* just go back to the same classroom? You may find that once you start the journey of the classroom discourse analyst, your classroom will never seem the same. By becoming deliberately aware of the social and interactional contexts that shape classroom talk, you may have already begun to change talk in your classroom. Your new ways of hearing may have given students new ways of speaking.

This chapter sums up what it means to be a classroom discourse analyst—reviewing the dimensions of discourse and the discursive resources that shape discourse norms in our classrooms. Throughout this book, we have delved into the way those resources are unwittingly modified in each interaction and the way our awareness of these processes can augment our agency to foster productive learning environments. After looking at our transcripts, it becomes clear, as teacher researchers Ann Phillips and Karen Gallas (2004) have put it: "Sometimes normal teaching practice can stand in the way of seeing the complexity of children's thought" (p. 4). Looking at transcripts of classroom talk can help us see this complexity we miss in real time teaching.

But awareness alone cannot alter the conditions in our classrooms. (If only thinking made it so.) Through the kind of awareness developed through discourse analysis, we become more powerful observers. But as teachers, we also want to transform or augment our actions. How can an awareness of discourse norms prevent us from being controlled by norms by which we cannot abide? Norms that limit our students' learning? To answer questions like these, this chapter also revisits our cyclical understanding of classroom discourse analysis. Transcripts provide a medium for reflection, including dialogue with peers, teachers, and students. Discussion provides a way to think through—and even act out—ways of redoing those interactions. Then we return to the classroom. These three processes are prompted and fed by discourse analysis: (a) reflecting, (b) redoing, and (c) revisiting. They offer ways to move onward and upward into renewed possibility after that initial discourse recording. These three processes feed our classroom agency.

REVIEWING THE THREE DIMENSIONS
OF CLASSROOM DISCOURSE

Once we start on the journey of the classroom discourse analyst, there is no turning back. Talk is not inside a Ziploc bag you can zip back and forth, resealing the contents when you're finished. Discourse cannot be contained. We may need a few new tools to get at it—but once the bag is unzipped, there is no practical way to seal it up again. What's inside? The exploration begins. This book has offered you some tools to guide this exploration. We have discussed different dimensions of classroom discourse and the language resources that affect discourse across those dimensions. I have suggested some focal questions to help analyze how these resources operate across those dimensions. The following table broadly summarizes what we've covered:

	RESOURCE			
DIMENSION	*Turn Taking*	*Contextualization*	*Narrative*	*Framing*
Social Context	What are the multiple social norms for turn taking, contextualization, narrative and interactional frames that originate outside our classrooms but may influence talk in our classrooms?			
Interactional Context	How do these resources actually function in classroom interaction?			
Individual Agency	How does awareness of the social context of talk and the interactional contingencies of classroom interaction augment teacher and student agency in the classroom?			

By way of empirically summing up the journey we have taken so far, here is a true story from my own recent practice. Use this story to think through the dimensions and resources of discourse analysis in the previous table: Recently, a student named Jane, who is also a teacher of English for Speakers of Other Languages (ESOL) at a local primary school, decided to pursue a master's degree. This is pretty typical for teachers. However, because she is interested in language—particularly second-language acquisition—she chose to pursue her degree in linguistics rather than education. "What a great idea," I thought naively, "a focus on language!" As a teacher, she wanted to research the effects that older siblings had on the language learning of their younger siblings in her classroom. But, as a master's of arts degree-seeking student in linguistics, her course of study was primarily a survey of traditional linguistics. She developed some knowledge of phonetics and phonology, morphology, syntax, and pragmatics. She also took courses in second-language acquisition and first- and second-language development. As one of Jane's early professors (of first- and second-language development), I was one of three professors who sat on her committee when, upon completing her coursework, she took written and oral exams. The oral exam, in my view, was a disaster. As is the norm for this event, each professor had a chance to ask a question in writing—and then after reading the response, to follow up on that question during the oral exam.

Three sample oral questions illustrate the extreme differences represented on this committee.

Professor A: Which phonemes exhibit most variability cross-linguistically? Why?

Professor B: Diagram the sentence, "Mary hit the boy with the book."

Professor C: You've told me you've been looking at the kids in your classrooms and their siblings. Could you maybe talk

> a little about how siblings have been discussed in the
> literature on second language learning and, by way
> of example or contrast, how older siblings might be
> influencing the English language learning of younger
> siblings in your classes?

Jane was able to answer each of these questions. She listed phonemes on the board, diagramed not only "Mary hit (the boy with the book)" but also "Mary hit (the boy) with the book," illustrating that she recognized the potential ambiguity. She talked at length about siblings in her elementary school, the way she had observed them using language so far, and the ways additional language learning had been discussed in the literature. She passed her comps, and she went on to finish her research and defend her thesis successfully that summer. However, our discussion during the exam was limited. Jane did not convey that she had extended her learning into her teaching context, and there was no dialogue between professors, between questions, or between the fields of linguistics and education. I was left feeling like we were each trapped in our own framing disciplines, while Jane was caught in a double bind of procedural display—not sure which procedure was appropriate.

This example illustrates broadly the kinds of resources this book has discussed: Jane came naively into the linguistics program, seeking the linguistic information that would facilitate her work as a teacher of language. However, Professors A and B, from linguistics, were concerned with disciplinary knowledge from their field. I, as Professor C, was attempting to make bridges between disciplinary knowledge and Jane's work in the schools. Thinking about the discourse resources we used, it is clear that they were taken up differently by every participant in this interaction. In terms of turn taking, the IRE formula dramatically dominated the discourse between Professors A and B and Jane. As they asked questions, she responded, and they either nodded or looked worried, by way of evaluation. At which point, Jane would look increasingly furtive and nervous—I watched as red blotches began to appear on her face and neck. In my question, as Professor C, I tried to diffuse her nerves—and to develop a back and forth in which I was not the only one who held all the information. But this left her unsure what kind of answer I was looking for—while Professors A and B became increasingly impatient.

Our differences in questioning were also reflected in differences in contextualization and narrative. While Professors A and B asked their questions with noticeable grilling intonation, I made noticeable efforts to make my questions sound open ended, including hedges like, "Could you **maybe** talk about. . . ." In terms of narrative, although my questions encouraged Jane to tell stories about her school and the kids in her classes, this foray into storytelling clearly made Jane uncomfortable as the other professors began to shift in their seats. Although I was trying to construct narrative as a resource, these professors viewed these school stories as a side track. I was hoping to use this interaction to construct new knowledge—bridges between Jane's classroom work and the field of second-language learning. However, I may have simply lowered myself in the eyes of my linguistic professor peers. What I wanted to come across as epistemic openness and encouragement for discussion may have appeared to my peers as a feeble lack of expertise.

Finally, how was our talk framed? A look at the production format for this oral exam illustrates that my words and the words of Professors A and B were probably guided by different but equally formidable institutional "principals" (in Goffman's sense), and this master's committee meeting was characterized by a clashing of these institutional principals. As a professor affiliated with the Linguistics Program, but housed in the Department of Language and Literacy, my guiding principal was primarily the College of Education—in which teacher's voices are respected and honored in our courses and exams. However, Professors A and B, as professors of Second-Language Acquisition and Syntax, are far more central to the Linguistics Program. Their institutional principal privileges not the voice of teachers in the schools, but a body of linguistic knowledge negotiated as important within the linguistics program and the field of linguistics. Within this production format, the guiding belief is that students need to master knowledge and display this mastery in the exam. Within my home department of language and literacy education, in contrast, the guiding belief in most oral exams is that students need to make connections between their studies and their work in schools.

Of course, within these different frames, different kinds of language are used as well. Professors A and B framed their questions using strong epistemic stance markers. They were implying there is one right answer and students will know it. "Which phonemes exhibit most variability cross-linguistically?" phrased in the eternal present tense implies a static set of phonemes that must have been memorized as an adequate and singularly correct response to this question. "Diagram the sentence 'Mary hit the boy with the book'" implies one and only one way to diagram that sentence. In fact, Professor B constructed this as a "trick" question. After Jane diagramed one interpretation, Professor B dropped the punch line, "Hmmm. Is there another way to diagram that?" It became obvious that she was supposed to display two (and only two) versions. In contrast, my question is infused with language that diffuses epistemic stance: "Could you **maybe** talk a little . . ." and ". . . how older siblings **might** be influencing. . . ."

These contrasts were dramatic and, I am afraid, disconcerting to Jane. She was the victim of a strange meeting of different norms—from turn taking, to contextualization, to narrating, to framing. At the same time, I was shocked at how different my norms had become from those of my colleagues more centrally located in the linguistics program.

Our different ways of using resources had been developed in the different social and institutional contexts of our training and within our current university departments. In interaction, this clash of norms kept us all on edge during the exam. Interactionally, we were all inflexible about our norms. As Professors A and B became more insistent on pursuing their factually oriented trains of questioning, I became more insistent on opening up discussion, encouraging Jane's narratives, and infusing an open, questioning epistemic stance into my own statements. In the dimension of agency, on later reflection, I felt I had at least learned something about my colleagues. But my rigidly open-ended discourse probably did little to dissuade them from doing things their way in the future.

However, I now have the awareness to proceed more carefully next time. If I am ever on a committee of this composition again, I will talk to my linguistics colleagues beforehand and clarify the goals of the exam and the assumptions guiding our questioning. In a case like Jane's, I think I can also make the point that a master's student who will be conducting classroom research will need to talk about linguistic material in terms of her work in schools. Through such a discussion, we have the potential not only to make the next oral exam go more smoothly, but to construct some valuable interdisciplinary conversations between linguistics and language education.

This oral exam also provides a useful example in which multiple discourse resources are being used in starkly contrasting ways. The contrast is rarely so obvious, but in this case the contrast can illustrate the resources we have discussed in the book, the dimensions within which they operate, and the kinds of questions we ask about those resources as discourse analysts. What are the norms leading into an interaction? How are these norms functioning in interaction? How can an awareness of these norms and their emergent functionality in a given interaction give us more control over classroom talk?

Like the oral exam with Jane, classroom interactions can reveal a clash or dialogue among multiple sets of norms for turn taking, contextualization, narrative, and interactional frames. As teachers in classrooms, we may be able to examine and critique norms with our students to change how interactions in our classroom—and perhaps beyond our classroom—proceed. Use the chart preceding this example to focus your initial reflections.

REFLECTING, REDOING, AND REVISITING

As Jane's oral exam suggests, social context provides us with abundant "prepackaged" discourse norms—for turn taking, contextualization, and narrative—and with frames that structure what kind of language is heard and used. In the context of these powerful norms, interaction happens and can shift those norms: Turn-taking expectations can be different, contextualization cues can be variably misinterpreted, narratives can be construed in multiple ways, and frames can unexpectedly produce unlikely experts. We can analyze these affects by looking at discourse. We can augment our agency as teachers through an awareness of these pre-packaged norms and how they come together in an interaction. To make real change in classrooms, discourse analysis must necessarily be a recursive process. Reflection includes thinking about multiple ways to redo interactions, and, in turn, redoing involves revisiting the classroom with a new outlook. This is how analyzing the resources within our classrooms becomes a recursive activity. Classroom interaction is not a one-shot experience. We return each day. Because we do, reflection can become part of an important feedback cycle. You may recognize the following figure from chapter 1. Now we have equated "classroom learning" with this agentive process of reflecting, revisiting, and revising:

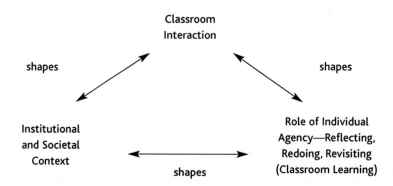

Although we return each day, we may never return to exactly the same place. Along with our students, we are learning. With new understandings, we have the potential not only to return to new norms in our own classrooms, but also to gradually challenge entrenched norms. At first pass, discourse analysis provides the tools for uncovering social and interactional context and revealing how these contexts affect language in use in the classroom. But the reflection, redoing, and revisiting of classroom discourse are the critical agentive processes that develop new knowledge in and about our classrooms—helping us return to the classroom in new and renewing ways, and helping the classroom become an empowering place for students.

Reflecting

At the end of the day—literally, at the end of every day—I can usually recall a situation in which I did not say something I wish I would have or I said something I wish I had not—as a teacher, a parent, a mentor, or a friend. In many ways, we cannot take those words back. Nor can we revive the words of others that we never heard. But on reflection, we can consider why we said what we did, why children said what they did, why we couldn't hear them, or why we couldn't hear ourselves with their ears. Teacher-researcher Steve Griffin (2004) noticed, before he began to record sharing-time events in his second-grade classroom, "the type of talk that was allowed in the classroom was constrained in ways invisible to me as the teacher." Then he asked, "What other constraints are operating in my classroom that are still unknown to me, effectively inhibiting my children's full use of their endowment of language and reasoning skills?" (p. 30).

Life in classrooms is complicated. What can we do to sense this kind of inhibition in our classrooms? When we reach an impasse? When there does not seem to be a solution for an inscrutable interaction? When we wake up the next morning, ready to face the day, we will never find a set of sure-fire "Best Practices for Every Situation" waiting under our pillow. Teachers in the Brookline Teacher Researcher Seminar joined together to puzzle over precisely those "moments in classroom practice when [an] experienced teacher's best practices simply did not work" (Phillips & Gallas, 2004, p.1). In Steve Griffin's case, a student repeatedly countered his expectations for the sharing-time routine. He was stymied. Together, in weekly meetings, the Brookline Teacher Research Seminar puzzled over possible solutions to cases like these (Ballenger, 2004). By studying the transcripts of his own classroom, Griffin was able to recognize that many of the rules guiding his sharing time—rules that were being broken repeatedly by one creative storyteller—were not necessary. The students relished the new, lengthy, creative, and funny stories. After a look at the talk, their teacher began to recognize them as important learning events.

There is no guidebook that can tell us the right way to behave so that we respect and understand everyone's words and the feelings and knowledge behind them. There is no Miss Manners for classroom interaction. Instead, I hope this book and the examples within it have offered some guidelines for being reflexive—for thinking about why we do what we do when we teach and noticing the results. This is not a recipe book for looking at a transcript and concocting an analysis—but a series of questions to frame a reflective discussion.

Redoing

What do we do if we reach an impasse? We can reflect. We can discuss. We can write about it. But what do we *do*? Sometimes, we just seem stuck. Often the reasons we are stuck are much larger than ourselves. As I sat through Jane's tumultuous oral exam, I imagined institutional discourse wrapping its octopus-like tentacles around us all, pulling us in different and contradictory directions. Although I know that I cannot single-handedly wrestle that institutional octopus to the ground, I can control how I react to it in my next interaction. When I return to a similar exam, I will need to ask myself not "How can I change those traditional linguists?", but "How can I conduct myself in a way that does not sacrifice my sense of responsibility for this student?" In class, I do not want to ask myself "How can I make the students stop seeking my approval all the time?", but instead, focusing on my own actions, "How can I return to class without blurting out an evaluative comment after every student contribution?" "How can I respect a student's demands for the floor without silencing the rest of the class?" "How can I be sure my students will hear this question as an open-ended question—not a search for the right answer?" If I feel there is a right answer, why is it important? How can I best convey that to my students? These are hard questions to simply sit alone and puzzle about.

Theater of the Oppressed

Fortunately, there are other, more active ways of approaching them. The Brazilian actor, director, and critical educator Augusto Boal (1979 [1974]) developed the *Theater of the Oppressed* precisely to work to work through questions like these. In his books and workshops, he has written about and demonstrated dozens of suggestions for theater activities that teachers and students can use to rethink their interactions within entrenched social contexts—and to practice new and resistant ways of acting them. Boal's theater developed as an alternative to traditional theater, in which audiences simply watch an unfolding drama without having to take part in it. Traditional theater allows the *spectators* to escape from reality. They can watch the drama unfold before them and then go out for a comforting desert and discussion after the show is over. In contrast to this model of theater, Boal, through the Theater of the Oppressed, encourages *spectACTors* to participate in reality—and to change it through the medium of theater by literally redoing theatrical representations of oppression. Boal referred to these reenactments as the "rehearsal for the revolution."

I like the term *spectacting* because it turns a passive spectator into an *actor* who can change the course of events. I also like the hint of *speculation* in the term. When we practice spectacting with our own classroom transcripts, we have the opportunity to act out the speculations into which our transcripts and their discussion lead us. Looking back at transcripts of our classroom discourse and reflecting on and discussing new possibilities for those interactions is another way we rehearse for the revolution in our own classrooms. In my own teaching and work with teachers, my colleagues and I have found that Boalian techniques also can help us re-enter classroom scenes that are still unsettling. Our peers can provide multiple possible ways of facing an impasse in our own classroom discourse (Rymes, Cahnmann-Taylor, & Souto-Manning, 2008). After discussion, we may be newly aware of the story a student never got to tell, of a question that might bring those stories back, or a new way to guide discussion after stories are over. But before we head back to the classroom, we can try to rehearse some of these options for action. Theater of the Oppressed, then, provides a means to practice acting on our reflections. Our methods, loosely adapted from Boal's teachings, are a way to step by step re-enact a classroom impasse, soliciting the possible solutions from your peers.

Spectacting a Transcript

If you are looking at a transcript from your classroom, pick a segment from that transcript that features an impasse between you and a student. Alternatively, focus on an interactional conundrum you have faced repeatedly, but in which you are unsure how to proceed. Then try to pinpoint a resource within that sequence that seems to be affecting the outcome. Is it the turn-taking? The narrative style? The institutional frame that the students are orienting to—and the language that institution frames as legitimate? Carefully analyze that segment to pinpoint features that are causing the interaction to be dysfunctional. Read through the transcript, acting it out as written. Then go back. Alter the resource that seemed troubling. Have a peer take over your role as teacher and try improvising an alternative way of turn taking, stance display, and narrative elicitation—whatever you think the source of the trouble is. After you redo the scene, ask the group whether that was a satisfying solution. Then have another spectactor step up and re-do the scene. And another. It is not important to arrive at the "correct" solution (there is no one correct solution). What matters is to present multiple possible ways of doing this classroom scene. As we return to the classroom, then, multiple possible ways of following an interactional thread are in our minds, pre-rehearsed, for any number of possible realities.

STEPS FOR SPECTACTING A TRANSCRIPT

1. Pick a sequence
2. Pick a resource (turn taking, contextualization, narrative, framing)
3. Do an analysis, pinpointing features that are troublesome
4. Act out the scene as written
5. Substitute a new spectactor as "teacher"
6. Repeat Steps 4–5.

Repeat many times—as long as new possibilities present themselves.

Spectacting With Students

The same spectacting steps described earlier also can be done with students. If you reach in impasse in a student discussion, for example, transcribe that interaction and take a particularly clear example of that sequence to the students for some spectacting.

The primary difference here is that students will replace themselves, not the teacher. When students are talking about a highly charged topic, they may stop listening to each other. Each side of an argument can be well articulated, but there may be no meeting of minds. Have students practice entering into this kind of talk more dialogically.

For example, in the following exchange, Mario, a former gang member, is trying to persuade Jorge and Luis, two active gang members, to give it up:

Mario: Friends aren't friends, homes. I'll tell you that.

Jorge: Yeah. Cuz you don't look at em as friends, that's why. You probably backstab em and shit that's why they ain't your friends anymore.

Mario: It ain't like that- I ain't considered them as my friends. I considering them as my <u>family</u>.
Where did your family get you, homes? ((*points his hand at Jorge and looks at Luis*))
Your friends, ése? ((*points at Jorge again and looks at Luis*))
He got you locked up, homes.

Luis: That's cuz I wanted to get locked up, homes.

Mario: You'd get locked up for a friend, homes? That's something <u>stup</u>id.

Luis: Fuck that, I don't get locked up for <u>all</u> my homeboys.

Mario: Well do your time while their ass is out here, you know getting smoked on and everything and what do you- what do you find out next time, homes?

Luis: I don't care.

Jorge: ((*to Mario*)) You ain't a true homeboy then. You ain't a true homeboy. You ain't a true homeboy.

Mario: That ain't family, getting f- getting locked up for a *vato*.

Luis: That's what we're trying to tell you though. The- that's my homeboy.

Mario: Homeboy, family, whatever, homes.
It ain't.
Well I'll tell you that much man.

Jorge: What happened to your homeboy?

Mario: He got shot, homes.
My best roll-dog, homes, my <u>chu</u>cho homes,
he got shot, ése. Fourteen bullets, homes.

Jorge: So that means that you just had a homeboy.

Mario: Where's he at now? That was my <u>roll</u>-dog ése. I had a *familia*. My homeboys were my *familia*, but that was my roll-dog. He got shot fourteen times homes. He was what, fifteen years old, ése. Where's he at now? Underground, homes.

Mario: You want your- you want your best dog underground, homes?

Jorge: Well don- don- don- come out with some stupid question like that man.

As I listened to this argument, marveling at the courage of Mario, age 17, to confront his teenage peers this way, I felt the pulse of the room change at "He got shot homes. . . . Fourteen bullets homes." Suddenly, the source of Mario's convictions was clear. Mario has the courage of someone who has seen the consequences of gang life. He has been heartbroken. His argument circulates largely around language: What is a true friend? What is family? Who's your roll-dog, your *familia*? But this language is powerful because it is defining how language is linked to reality—to who one is willing to *allow to die*. Mario is persuasive—to me at least. He thought he was a good friend to his roll-dog, but that friendship, that friend, is dead now. When a friend lets another friend do things that lead to death or jail, "Friends aren't friends." Even to the end, however, Jorge cannot compare Mario's relationship to his lost friend as equal to his own relationship with his friend Luis. Why not?

Later, when I talked to Mario in the ice cream shop where he worked afternoons, Mario said he doubted his talk affected Jorge and Luis much. In fact, he had thought they might jump him on the way to the bus.

Looking back at this talk, now, 10 years later, 3,000 miles away, I wonder how these students would have spectacted this transcript had I brought it to them the next day. How would they have redone this scene? I suspect this kind of spectacting could affect their relationships and lead them to continue thinking deeply about their commitments: How do they each define friendship, and what has led them to these definitions? What are the multiple possible ways of having this kind of argument? It is a discussion, I suspect, with which many Los Angeles kids are familiar. I have heard other former gang members make formal, institutionally sanctioned visits to schools to talk to kids about staying out of gangs, using the same language (homes, *ese, chucho, familia,* etc.) that marks gang affiliation. But why do these conversations repeat themselves again and again? What are new ways of having these kinds of talks?

I cannot predict what resources students would draw on as they revisited a scene like this. However, I can guarantee that spectacting this scene would be a powerful way to extend the dialogue. Redoing scenes like these is potentially as liberating for students as for teachers. After some practice enacting multiple possibilities, students, like teachers, may wake up the next morning able to try out new ways of talking, listening, and acting in class and in the world. Because after the redoing comes the revisiting.

Revisiting

Although Boalian redoings allow us to *rehearse* the classroom revolution, actually going back to the classroom and redoing routine interactions in new ways *is* the revolution. However, like "opening night," when no one can predict how a theater piece will come together, upon going back to the classroom, anything can happen. Boalian re-enactments help us understand those scenarios in an abstract sense. They draw our attention to the social norms that work against our own desires to understand our students or our students' desires to understand each other. But these rehearsals cannot account for the human intensity of a real interaction within a real classroom day, and the interactional contingencies that set us on edge or turn discourse in yet another unexpected direction. So we go back and look at the transcripts again and develop new analyses. Then, again, loaded with new resources, we try to redo the reality.

These recursive suggestions echo those more general guidelines from national organizations that emphasize the feedback loop in classroom teaching. The National Council for Teachers of English (NCTE), for example, calls this the "Responsive Teaching Cycle" and encourages observations of teaching practice to be reflected on, and for the meaning generated in this reflection and discussion to generate new plans. They represent this cycle in a reproducible format for teacher's use for record keeping:

OBSERVATION	MEANING	NEW PLANS

In a community of classroom discourse analysts, the first column in the NCTE chart, "Observation," includes recording talk, viewing that talk, and observing how language is used. "Meaning" is then developed by pinpointing relevant resources within the talk and analyzing how they are functioning in classroom interaction. In other words, meaning is developed through discourse analysis and discussion with peers and students. New possible meanings can also be developed through spectacting with peers. "New plans" are those strategies we bring back to the classroom after our analysis and possibly after our staged re-enactments of particular scenes. These new plans may focus on a change in turn taking, a new way of listening to narrative, a mitigated stance on "the truth." How our new plans work is unpredictable—how these resources function is both normative and interactionally contingent. But returning with a new way of doing things and new ears for listening to our students can be a powerful way to revisit those most vexing or perplexing classroom interactions while respecting the voices within them.

Each step of this cycle is part of the process of classroom discourse analysis, and each step fuels the others. As Phillips and Gallas (2004) write of the Brookline Teacher Research Group, "As we turned the spotlight on ourselves, we discovered the power of observation to change the nature of our interactions with children. . . . As time passed, we learned that the content of our meetings, individual members' stories, and the transcripts we deciphered with delight, came back with us into the classroom and played the role of observer as well" (pp. 4–5). These classroom researchers experienced a responsive teaching cycle generated through their collaborative classroom discourse analysis.

CONCLUSION

What is the difference between being a teacher and being a teacher who does classroom discourse analysis? Of course all teachers and all classroom discourse analysts are different, but the classroom discourse analyst has a new and powerful asset: a specially designed set of tools for exploring talk and learning in classrooms.

These tools can make a big difference in how classrooms run: We have tools helping us uncover the discourse that privileges some people and not others, the frames that legitimize an ideology that comforts some people and disadvantages others, the variations in narrative style, turn taking, or asking questions that distance us from different perspectives. These tools can help us recognize the possibility that language may mean differently for different people. Ultimately as discourse analysts, we hear new voices in our classrooms, and our own voice will begin to change. Once we analyze discourse, our talk will be finely tuned to the voices in our classrooms and not only to prepackaged discourse norms or interactional contingencies we cannot control.

Discourse is powerful. In this book, examples have touched on immigration, racism, ESOL minorities, poverty, prisons, and discrimination of countless kinds. There are so many inequities, and many times it can seem like the vastly ingrown institutional discourse norms of schooling will be difficult to penetrate, even with the best tools. But the rewards for even the tiniest change can be momentous. Even Wal-Mart, the largest corporation in the world and a proportionally massive force of global environmental damage, is able to create significant improvements in the environment, increases in the oil supply, reductions in deforestation, and so forth simply by slightly reducing the size of the packaging for one line of toys it carries. Similarly, the effects of mass schooling done wrong can do massive societal damage; however, a single shift in strategy can do massive societal good. What if we focus on one event? One feature of interaction? One child? What if? I am hoping classroom discourse analysis gives us the tools to try.

QUESTIONS AND ACTIVITIES

Critical Reflection

1. How flexible are the norms in your classroom? Which are school-wide norms? Which routines are built on your agenda for class? Which have developed from students' habits or language? Which would you rather not continue?
2. What tools of discourse analysis do you think you will be drawing on most in your analyses (e.g., turn-taking, contextualization, narrative, framing, spectacting . . .)? How and why?
3. How do you think re-enacting scenes can provoke more effective learning environments (and redefine learning) in your teaching context?
4. How does interaction in your classroom affect the futures of the children there?

Reflective Activities

1. Practice spectacting: With a group of peers, follow the spectacting instructions to act and re-enact this transcript (discussed in chap. 8):

   In a second-grade reading group in Georgia, a discussion prompted by a picture book is framed by ideas about what can and cannot be said (Rymes & Anderson, 2004):

Sally:	((*pointing to a picture in the* book)) They're white and everybody else is black.
Teacher:	Oh, so her friend is white and everybody else is black in the picture?
Danny:	Hey don't you be talking about that.
Teacher:	What is wrong with that?
Danny:	Nothing. ((Danny shakes his head))
Sally:	Nothing.
Teacher:	Is there anything wrong with that?
Students:	No. ((Sally shakes her head))
Teacher:	No, I didn't think so either,

2. Practice spectacting: With a group of peers, follow the spectacting instructions to act and re-enact a transcript of concern from your own classroom.
3. Practice spectacting with students: Take a sequence from your classroom in which you think students did not have voice. Have students act out the sequence as transcribed. Then have them follow the spectacting instructions to re-enact that scenario, replacing themselves as actors in the classroom, one at a time.

Suggestions for Further Reading

The Brookline Teacher Researcher Seminar is a group of teachers who record classroom talk and meet weekly to discuss talk in their classrooms and their teaching. Their discussions build on "turns" of teachers, who bring in transcripts to illustrate interactions within their classrooms that they want to understand more fully. If you are interested in work like this or would like to start a group of your own, their most recent publication, *Regarding Children's Words* (2004), is a compilation of their classroom research and includes a description of how their group works. For an introduction to the work of Augusto Boal (1979[1974]), his *Theatre of the*

Oppressed includes both a theoretical rationale for his work (rooted in Paulo Freire's pedagogy) and dozens of examples and exercises you may want to use as theater activities in your own teaching and classroom discourse work.

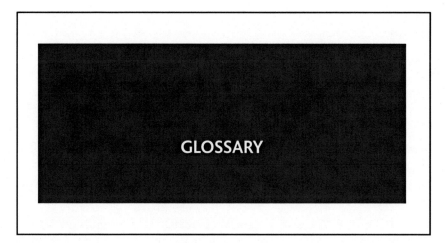

GLOSSARY

Adjacency pair A two-part interactional sequence in which the first part (e.g., a question) produces the expectation for the second part (e.g., an answer).

Animator (see Production format).

Anthropological perspective Viewing customary behaviors in a new light by not taking these common practices for granted and questioning the reasons we do these ordinary things.

Author (see Production format).

Communicative competence A term coined by Dell Hymes to describe the culturally specific communication tools needed to participate appropriately in culturally specific speech events.

Contextualization cues A term coined by the sociolinguist John Gumperz to describe the extralinguistic features we use as clues to understand how words are functioning. "Oh great," for example, spoken in a lowered tone and downward intonation might function as a sarcastic complaint. The same words spoken with rising intonation and volume might function differently—as a joyous exclamation!

Dialectic A term coined by Karl Marx to describe the powerful process of give and take between two social forces in which both forces influence the other and lead to reproduction and/or gradual change. Dialectics are frequently represented in diagrams using double arrows to indicate each side is influencing the other. For example, school ← → society.

Discourse Language in use. For example, from a discourse perspective, understanding what "I saw a tree" means involves understanding the speaker was *using* the word tree and her purpose for telling you she saw one. The capacity of language to do infinitely different things and mean differently *in use*, is the defining feature of discourse.

Discourse analysis The study of how language in use and context affect each other.

Establishing shots Recordings that capture the broader social context of an interaction.

Frames The interactional and social contexts that surround individual utterances. An individual's words are framed by larger social contexts and interactional norms that give meaning and functionality to those words.

Identity The kind of person someone is in a given situation. For example, the "problem child" kind of person may an "angel" in another class. As teachers, the language we choose, and the way we choose to understand the language used by our students, significantly shapes what "kinds of people" show up in our classroom.

Ideologies Unstated beliefs or assumptions held by the general public that guide our actions. Discourse frames construct and sanction those ideologies.

Indexing The work words do to make communication function in context. For example, the phrase "Go Dawgs!" in combination with a Georgia cheerleading outfit *indexes* the function of fan support. Indexing is always contextually contingent, however: That same combination, on Halloween, might *index* the function of trick-or-treating.

Individual agency in classroom discourse The influence an individual can have on how words are used and interpreted in a classroom interaction (e.g., When and why would an individual choose to use the term *dude*, and for what purpose? How much can an individual control its effects?).

Interactional context of classroom discourse The sequential or other patterns of talk within an interaction that influence what we can and cannot say, and how others interpret it within classroom discourse. (Contrast to "social context" of classroom discourse, which involves the context outside the immediate interaction.)

Interactional contingency The ever-present potential for interaction to change our intended or normatively expected meaning. How a word functions is always at least partially contingent on what happens subsequently in the interaction.

IRE sequence The Initiation, Response, and Evaluation pattern of classroom discourse, epitomized by this kind of sequence:

Initiation:	Teacher:	What time is it?
Response:	Jackson:	One Thirty.
Evaluation:	Teacher:	Very good, Jackson!

Known-answer question (also called a test, display, or convergent question). The prototypical IRE sequence initiator. The primary function of a known-answer question is to prompt students to display information already known to the asker. "What color is my shirt?" might test students' knowledge of color names that, presumably, the questioner already knows.

Learning An interactive process, through which learners gain the use of tools necessary to participate in their multiple social worlds. In classrooms, for example, students are not only learning new content, they are also necessarily and simultaneously learning new ways of speaking and participating.

Open-ended question (also called a genuine, information seeking, or divergent question). A question that does not imply a right answer. For example, the questioner may not have any predetermined answer in mind to questions like, "What's your favorite movie?" "Where are the crayons?" or "How are you going to continue this story?"

Overdetermination A term coined by Louis Althusser, a philosopher of language, for the effects of social histories on what words mean. Swearwords are prime examples of overdetermined words. Over its interactional history, a word like *shit* has been subject to the effect of other social structures and practices that change who can use it, what it will mean, and under what circumstances.

Participant structures defined by Susan Philips as "ways of arranging verbal interaction with students" (Philips, 1972, p. 377). For example, typical class agendas are often outlined in terms of these structures: (a) Group check-in; (b) Small groups, jigsaw; (c) Whole group discussion; (d) Individual quick writes; (e) Group sharing. Each of these kinds of configurations can lead to different interactional patterns and different kinds of language.

Principal (see Production format).

Procedural display A term coined by Shirley Brice Heath and elaborated by David Bloome and his colleagues to name the condition when teacher and students work collaboratively to appear successful, while minimal learning may be going on. The IRE sequence is an ideal vehicle for procedural display. Because, in many cases, students can participate superficially, this form or interaction can mask the lack of any deeper participation and understanding.

Production format A term coined by Irving Goffman (1981) to conceptualize the roles of speakers and listeners in any interaction. He named three distinct status roles for speakers: **animator** (the individual physically saying the word), **author** (the creator of the spoken words), and the **principal** (the institutional or individual whose beliefs are being represented—the party ultimately responsible) and two distinct roles for listeners: **ratified** participants (officially participating in the event) and **unratified** participants (overhearers or eavesdroppers).

Ratified participant (see Production format).

Register A way of speaking that varies according to activity. For example, most students will use a "casual" register (less concerned with standard grammar or pronunciation, sprinkled with youthful vocabulary and idioms) when talking with friends on the playground and a "formal" register (marked by standard grammar, pronunciation, and vocabulary) when greeting the principal or delivering a graduation speech. In any classroom, discourse analysis can reveal that varying registers will produce different effects.

Sequence The interaction that attends to an initiating first pair part—including the related side questions, the misunderstandings, and any other possibly related contributions.

Situated meaning A meaning of a word that varies according to the context in which it is used. All instances of language in use have unique, situated meanings. For example, "How are you?" means one thing in the counselor's office, something else in the hall, something else in the classroom.

Social context of classroom discourse The social factors *outside the immediate interaction* that influence how words function in that interaction (contrast to "interactional context" of classroom discourse, which involves sequential or other patterns of talk within an interaction).

Speech event Any typical classroom activity with discernable borders, and a normative set of social and interactional rules that, to varying degrees, guides how language can be used within that event. For example, in elementary classrooms, "Calendar Time" is a common speech event with its own set of conventions for participation.

Underlife The interaction that develops alongside more sanctioned institutional talk. For example, in a classroom, side conversations between students that are only obliquely related to the teacher's topic may emerge while a teacher is conducting a discussion. This term was initially coined by Irving Goffman (1961).

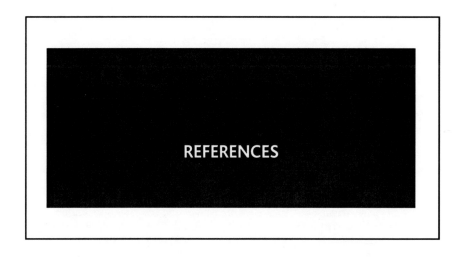

REFERENCES

Allington, R. L. (1980). Teacher interruption behaviors during primary grade oral reading. *Journal of Educational Psychology, 72*, 1–37.

Althusser, L. (1971). *Ideology and ideological state apparatuses.* In L. Althusser (Ed.), *Lenin and philosophy and other essays.* London: New Left Books.

Au, K. H. (1980). On participation structures in reading lessons. *Anthropology and Education Quarterly, 11*, 91–115.

Ballenger, C. (Ed.). (2004). *Regarding children's words: Teacher research on language and literacy.* New York: Teachers College Press.

Best, R. (1983). *We've all got scars: What boys and girls learn in elementary school.* Bloomington: Indiana University Press.

Blommaert, J. (2005). *Discourse: A critical introduction.* Cambridge, UK: Cambridge University Press.

Bloome, D., Carter, S. P., Christian, B., Otto, S., & Shuart–Faris, N. (2005). *Discourse analysis and the study of classroom language and literacy events: A microethnographic perspective.* Mahwah, NJ: Erlbaum.

Bloome, D., Puro, P., & Theodorou, E. (1989). Procedural display and classroom lessons. *Curriculum Inquiry, 19*(3), 265–291.

Boal, A. (1979[1974]). *Theater of the oppressed.* New York: Theater Communications Group.

Bruner, J. (1986). *Actual minds, possible worlds.* Cambridge, MA: Harvard University Press.

Bucholtz, M., & Hall, K. (2004). Language and identity. In S. Duranti (Ed.), *A companion to linguistic anthropology* (pp. 369–395). Maldon, MA: Blackwell.

Cazden, C. B. (1972). The situation: A neglected source of social class differences in language use. In J. B. Pride & J. Holmes (Eds.), *Sociolinguistics: Selected readings* (pp. 294–313). Harmondsworth: Penguin Books.

Cazden, C. B. (1981). Social context of learning to read. In J. Guthrie (Ed.), *Comprehension and teaching: Research reviews.* Newark, DE: International Reading Association.

Cazden, C. B. (2001). *Classroom discourse: The language of teaching and learning.* Portsmouth, NH: Heinemann.

Collins, J. (1996). Socialization to text: Structure and contradiction in schooled literacy. In M. Silverstein & G. Urban (Eds.), *Natural histories of discourse* (pp. 203–228). Chicago: University of Chicago Press.

Delpit, L. (1996). *Other people's children: Cultural conflict in the classroom.* New York: New Press.

Delpit, L., & Dowdy, J. K. (Eds.). (2002). *The skin that we speak: Thoughts on language and culture in the classroom.* New York: The New Press.

Duranti, S., & Ochs, E. (1988). Literacy instruction in a Samoan village. In *Culture and language development: Language acquisition and language socialization in a Samoan village* (pp. 189–209). Cambridge and New York: Cambridge University Press.

Eaton, W. O., & Enns, L. R. (1986). Sex differences in human motor activity level. *Psychological Bulletin, 100*(1), 19–28.

Elkind, D. (1991). *Backmatter from V.G. Paley, The boy who would be a helicopter: The uses of storytelling in the classroom.* Cambridge: Cambridge University Press.

Erickson, F. (1996). Going for the zone: The social and cognitive ecology of teacher-student interaction in classroom conversations. In D. Hicks (Ed.), *Discourse, learning, and schooling* (pp. 29–62). Cambridge: Cambridge University Press.

Fecho, B. (2000). Critical inquiries into language in an urban classroom. *Research in the Teaching of English, 34,* 368–395.

Ford, C. (1993). *Grammar in interaction: Adverbial clauses in American English conversations.* Cambridge and New York: Cambridge University Press.

Frank, C. (1999). *Ethnographic eyes: A teacher's guide to classroom observation.* Portsmouth, NH: Heinemann.

Freire, P. (1998). *Teachers as cultural workers: Letters to those who dare to teach.* Boulder, CO: Westview.

Fukunaga, N. (2006, November). "Those anime students": Foreign language literacy development through Japanese popular culture. *Journal of Adolescent & Adult Literacy, 50*(3), 206–222.

Gallas, K. (1994). *The languages of learning: How children talk, write, dance, draw, and sing their understanding of the world.* New York: Teachers College Press.

Gallas, K. (1995). *Talking their way into science: Hearing children's questions and theories, responding with curriculum.* New York: Teachers College Press.

Gallas, K. (1998). *"Sometimes I can be anything": Power, gender, and identity in a primary classroom.* New York: Teachers College Press.

Gallas, K. (2003). *Imagination and literacy: A teacher's search for the heart of learning.* New York: Teachers College Press.

Garfinkel, H. (1972). Remarks on ethnomethodology. In J. J. Gumperz & D. Hymes (Eds.), *Directions in sociolinguistics: The ethnography of communication* (pp. 301–324). New York: Holt, Rinehart, & Winston.

Gee, J. P. (2001). Identity as an analytic lens for research in education. *Review of Research in Education, 25,* 99–125.

Goffman, I. (1961). *Asylums: Essays on the social situation of mental patients and other inmates.* New York: Harper & Row.

Goffman, I. (1974). *Frame analysis: An essay on the organization of experience.* New York: Harper.

Goffman, I. (1981). *Forms of talk.* Philadelphia: University of Pennsylvania Press.

Goldhaber, D., & Anthony, E. (2004). Can teacher quality be effectively assessed? An on-line publication of the Urban Institute. Retrieved December 14, 2006, from http://www.urban.org/UploadedPDF/410958_NBPTSOutcomes.pdf.

Goodwin, M. H. (1990). *He-said-she-said: Talk as social organization among black children.* Bloomington: Indiana University Press.

Goodwin, M. H. (2002). Building power asymmetries in girls' interactions. *Discourse in Society, 13*(6), 715–730.

Green, L. (2002). *African American English: A linguistic introduction.* Cambridge and New York: Cambridge University Press.

Griffin, S. (2004). I need people: Story-telling in a second grade classroom. In C. Ballenger (Ed.), *Regarding children's words: Teacher research on language and literacy* (pp. 22–30). New York: Teachers College Press.

Gumperz, J. J. (1970). Crosstalk, the movie.

Gumperz, J. J. (1977). Sociocultural knowledge in conversational inference. In M. Saville-Troike (Ed.), *Linguistics and anthropology, Georgetown University round table on languages and linguistics 1977.* Washington, DC: Georgetown University Press.

Hankins, K. H. (2003). *Teaching through the storm: A journal of hope.* New York: Teachers College Press.

Heath, S. B. (1978). Teacher talk: Language in the classroom. *Language in Education: Theory and Practice, 1,* 1–30.

Heath, S. B. (1982). Questioning at home and at school: A comparative study. In G. Spindler (Ed.), *Doing the ethnography of schooling: Educational anthropology in action* (pp. 102–131). New York: Holt, Rinehart, & Winston.

Heath, S. B. (1983). *Ways with words: Language, life, and work in communities and classrooms.* Cambridge, UK: Cambridge University Press.

Honig, B. (1991). *The American Indian: Yesterday, today and tomorrow, A handbook for educators.* Sacramento, CA: California Department of Education.

Hymes, D. (1972). On communicative competence. In J. B. Pride & J. Holmes (Eds.), *Sociolinguistics* (pp. 269–293). Harmondsworth: Penguin.

Jefferson, G. (1984). Transcription notation. In P. Drew & J. Heritage (Eds.), *Structures of social action* (pp. ix–xvi). Cambridge: Cambridge University Press.

Johnson, K. (1995). *Understanding communication in second language classrooms.* Cambridge: Cambridge University Press.

Johnson, L. (2005). *Teaching outside the box: How to grab your students by their brains.* San Francisco, CA: Jossey-Bass.

Johnston, P. H. (2005). *Choice words: How our language affects students' learning.* Portland, ME: Stenhouse.

Johnstone, B. (2000). The individual voice in language. *Annual Review of Anthropology, 29,* 405–424.

Kulick, D., & Schieffelin, B. (2004). Language socialization. In A. Duranti (Ed.), *A companion to linguistic anthropology* (pp. 349–368). Malden, MA: Blackwell.

Ladson-Billings, G. (2001). *Crossing over to Canaan: The journey of new teachers in diverse classrooms.* San Francisco: Jossey-Bass.

Martin, R. P., Wisenbaker, J., Baker, J., & Huttunen, M.O. (1997). Gender differences in temperament at six months and five years. *Infant Behavior and Development, 20*(3), 339–347.

McGroarty, M. (1996). Language attitudes, motivation, and standards. In S. L. McKay & N. Hornberger (Eds.), *Sociolinguistics and language teaching* (pp. 3–46). New York: Cambridge University Press.

McLuhan, M. (1964). *Understanding media: The extensions of man.* New York: McGraw Hill.

Mehan, H.(1985). The structure of classroom discourse. *Handbook of discourse analysis, Vol. 3. Discourse and dialogue* (pp. 119–131). Malden, MA: Blackwell.

Michaels, S. (1981). Sharing time: Children's narrative styles and differential access to literacy. *Language in Society, 10,* 423–442.

Michaels, S., & Cazden, C. B. (1986). Teacher-child collaboration as oral preparation for literacy. In B. B. Schieffelin (Ed.), *The acquisition of literacy: Ethnographic perspectives* (pp. 132–154). Norwood, NJ: Ablex.

Möller, K. J., & Allen, J. (2000). Connecting, resisting and searching for safer places: Students respond to Mildred Taylor's *The Friendship. Journal of Literacy Research, 32,* 145–186.

Nystrand, M. (1997). *Opening up dialogue.* New York: Teachers College Press.

Ochs, E. (1979) Transcription as theory. In E. Ochs & B. B. Schieffelin (Eds.), *Developmental pragmatics* (pp. 43–72). New York: Academic.

Ochs, E. (1988). *Culture and language development: Language acquisition and language socialization in a Samoan village.* Cambridge and New York: Cambridge University Press.

Ochs, E. (1993). Constructing social identity: A language socialization perspective. *Research on Language and Social Interaction, 26*(3), 287–306.

Ochs, E., & Capps, L. (2003). *Living narrative.* Cambridge, MA: Harvard University Press.

Ochs, E., Gonzales, P., & Jacoby, S. (1996). When I come down I'm in the domain state: Grammar and graphic representation in the interpretive activity of physicists. In E. Ochs, E.A. Schegloff, & S.A. Thompson (Eds.), *Interaction and grammar* (pp. 328–369). Cambridge: Cambridge University Press.

Ochs, E., & Schieffelin, B.B. (1984). Language acquisition and socialization: Three developmental stories and their implications. In R.A. Shweder & R.A. LeVine (Eds.), *Culture theory: Essays on mind, self, and emotion* (pp. 276–320). Cambridge: Cambridge University Press.

Owocki, G., & Goodman, Y. (2002). *Kidwatching: Documenting children's literacy development.* Portsmouth, NH: Heinemann.

Paley, V. G. (1981). *Wally's stories: Conversations in the kindergarten.* Cambridge: Harvard University Press.

Paley, V. G. (1990). *The boy who would be a helicopter.* Cambridge: Harvard University Press.

Peterson, R., & Eeds, M. (1990). *Grand conversations: Literature groups in action.* New York: Scholastic.

Philips, S. U. (1972). Participant structures and communicative competence: Warm Springs children in community and classroom. In C. B. Cazden, V.P.

John, & D. Hymes (Eds.), *Functions of language in the classroom* (pp. 370–394). New York: Teachers College Press.

Philips, S. U. (1984). *The invisible culture.* New York: Longman.

Phillips, A., & Gallas, K. (2004). Introduction—Developing a community of inquiry: The values and practices of the Brookline Teacher Research Seminar. In C. Ballenger (Ed.), *Regarding children's words: Teacher research on language and literacy* (pp. 1–11). New York: Teachers College Press.

Postman, N., & Weingartner, C. (1969). *Teaching as a subversive activity.* New York: Delta.

Rampton, B. (1995). *Crossing: Language and ethnicity among adolescents.* London and New York: Longman.

Rampton, B. (2006). *Language in late modernity.* Cambridge and New York: Cambridge University Press.

Rex, L. (2006). Acting "cool" and "appropriate": Toward a framework for considering literacy classroom interactions when race is a factor. *Journal of Literacy Research, 38*(3), 275–325.

Rogers, R. (2004). *An introduction to critical discourse analysis in education.* Mahwah, NJ: Erlbaum.

Rowe, M. B. (1986). Wait time: Slowing down may be a way of speeding up! *Journal of Teacher Education, 37,* 43–50.

Rymes, B. (2001). *Conversational borderlands: Language and identity in an alternative urban high school.* New York: Teachers College Press.

Rymes, B. (2003a). Relating word to world: Indexicality during literacy events. In S. Wortham & B. Rymes (Eds.), *The linguistic anthropology of education.* Westport, CT: Greenwood.

Rymes, B. (2003b). Eliciting narratives, producing identities: Text-linked versus socially contingent processes for narrating the self. *Research in the Teaching of English, 37*(3).

Rymes, B. (2004). Contrasting zones of comfortable competence: Popular culture in a phonics lesson. *Linguistics & Education, 14,* 321–335.

Rymes, B., & Anderson, K. (2004). Second language acquisition for all: Understanding the interactional dynamics of classrooms in which Spanish and AAE are spoken. *Research in the Teaching of English, 29*(2), 107–135.

Rymes, B., & Pash, D. (2001). Questioning identity: The case of one second language learner. *Anthropology & Education Quarterly, 32*(3), 276–300.

Rymes, B., Cahnmann-Taylor, M., & Souto-Manning, M. (2008). Bilingual teachers' performances of power and conflict. *Teaching Education, 19*(2), 105–119.

Santa Ana, O. (1994). *Tongue tied: The lives of multilingual children in public education.* New York: Rowman & Littlefield.

Saville-Troike, M. (1996). The ethnography of communication. In S. L. McKay & N. Hornberger (Eds.), *Sociolinguistics and language teaching* (pp. 351–382). Cambridge and New York: Cambridge University Press.

Schieffelin, B. (1990). *The give and take of everyday life: Language socialization of Kaluli children.* Cambridge: Cambridge University Press.

Scollon, R., & Scollon, S. (1983). *Narrative, literacy, and face in interethnic communication.* Norwood, NJ: Ablex.

Silverstein, M. (2003). *Talking politics: The substance of style from Abe to "W."* Chicago: Prickly Paradigm Press.

Souto-Manning, M. (2008). Acting out and talking back: Negotiating discourses in American early educational settings. *Early Child Development and Care.*

Sterponi, L. (2007). Clandestine interactional reading: Intertextuality and double-voicing under the desk. *Linguistics and Education, 18*(1), 1–23.

Vasquez, V. (2004). *Negotiating critical literacies with young children.* Mahwah, NJ: Erlbaum.

Verplaetse, L. (2000) Mr. Wonderful: Portrait of a dialogic teacher. In J. Hall & L.S. Verplaetse (Eds.), *Second and foreign language learning through classroom interaction* (pp. 221–241). Mahwah, NJ: Erlbaum.

Wells, G. (1986). *The meaning makers: Children learning language and using language to learn.* Portsmouth, NH: Heinemann.

Young, J. P. (2004) Cultural models and discourses of masculinity. In R. Rogers (Ed.), *An introduction to critical discourse analysis in education* (pp. 147–171). Mahwah, NJ: Erlbaum.

Zentella, A. C. (1997). *Growing up bilingual: Puerto Rican children in New York.* Oxford: Blackwell.

AUTHOR INDEX

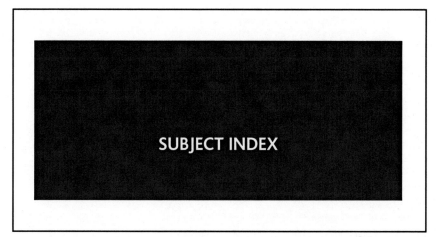

SUBJECT INDEX

Breinigsville, PA USA
19 December 2009
229487BV00001B/27/P